The Life and Actions of
Alexander the Great

The Life and Actions of
Alexander the Great

The Ancient Military Campaigns of the
Legendary King of Macedon

John Williams

LEONAUR

The Life and Actions of Alexander the Great
The Ancient Military Campaigns of the Legendary King of Macedon
by John Williams

FIRST EDITION IN THIS FORM

First published under the title
The Life and Actions of Alexander the Great

Leonaur is an imprint of Oakpast Ltd

ISBN: 978-1-915234-84-1 (hardcover)
ISBN: 978-1-915234-85-8 (softcover)

http://www.leonaur.com

Contents

Introduction

Greece, its islands, and the western part of Asia Minor, have, from the earliest ages, been the principal scene of the great struggle between the eastern and western worlds. Between the European and Asiatic, even under the same latitude, there exists a marked difference in feelings, manners and character. That this difference is independent of climate and of country, and attributable to long-established habits, and a system of education transmitted down from the remotest ages, is apparent from the well-known facts, that the Greek at Seleuceia on the Tigris, at Palmyra, Antioch, and the Egyptian Alexandreia, continued to be still a Greek; while the Arab in Andalusia and Grenada was still an Arab, and the Turk in Europe has retained all the feelings, manners and customs of his oriental ancestors. It is not wonderful therefore that two races, so inherently different from each other, should, where limitary, be engaged in perpetual warfare.

The great struggle has, in general, been in the vicinity of those narrow seas that separate Europe from Asia. It has now continued, with strange vicissitudes, for more than six-and-twenty centuries, and longer too, if we add well-founded traditions to historical records, and yet there appears no sign of an approaching termination. By a curious inversion of their relative positions, the Europeans are on the banks of the Ganges and on the shores of the Caspian, and the Asiatics on the banks of the Danube and the shores of the Adriatic. But my present object is, not to trace the result of the struggle down to our days, but to give a short sketch of its leading events previous to the invasion of Asia by Alexander.

I pass over the conquest of the Peloponnesus by the Phrygian Pelops, the establishment of a Phoenician colony in Boeotia, and of other oriental settlers in various parts of Greece. I dwell not on the Argonautic expedition, the conquest of Troy by Hercules, the seizure and occupation of Rhodes and its dependant islands by his immediate descendants, not from any doubt of the facts, but because they are not in the right line that conducts us down to the expedition of Alexander.

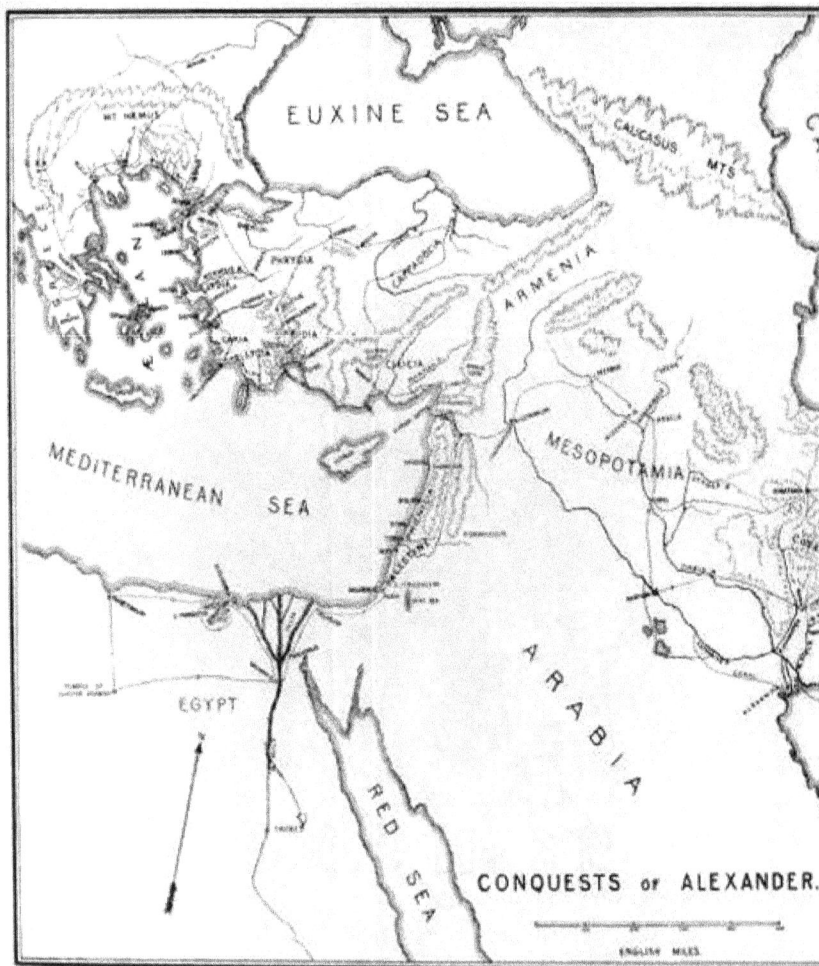

EUXINE SEA

CAUCASUS MTS

MEDITERRANEAN SEA

ARMENIA

MESOPOTAMIA

EGYPT

ARABIA

RED SEA

CONQUESTS OF ALEXANDER.

ENGLISH MILES

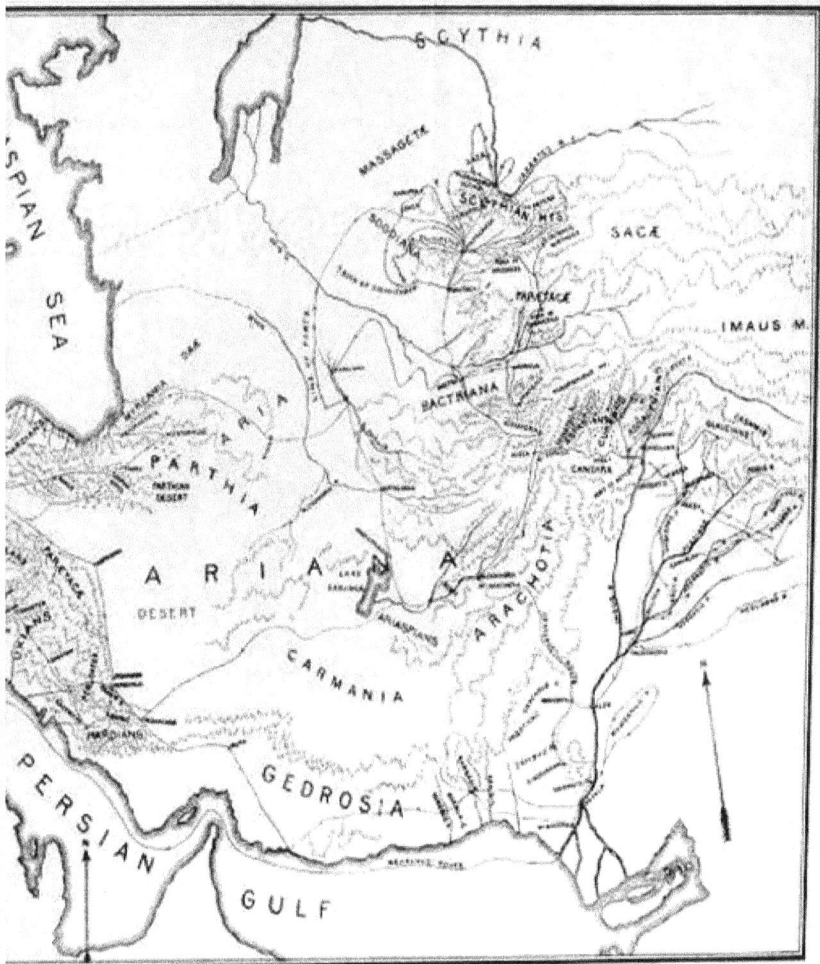

The result of the second Trojan War was far different, as the superiority attained by the Europeans in that contest enabled them to seize all the intervening islands, and to occupy the whole Asiatic coast, from Halicarnassus to Cyzicus, with their Dorian, Ionian and Æolian colonies. The first and last did not spread much, but the Ionians, the descendants of the civilized Achæans and Athenians, flourished greatly, covered the seas with their fleets, and studded the shores of the Euxine with wealthy and splendid cities. These colonists in Asia were the founders of Grecian literature.

From them sprung Homer and Hesiod, Alcæus and Sappho, Thales and Herodotus. And had they possessed a system of civil polity adapted for the purpose, they possessed strength, knowledge and energy sufficient to have conquered all Asia. But their circle of action was narrowed by their confined views of constitutional governments. Even Aristotle, superior as he was to his countrymen, wrote, in much later times, that a hundred thousand and five thousand citizens were numbers equally incompatible with the existence of a free state, as the greater number would render deliberation impossible, and the less be inadequate for the purposes of self-defence.

This limitation was grounded on the principle, that every Greek had an imprescriptible right to attend and vote in the great council of the nation, and to be eligible, in his turn, to the highest offices of the state. To fulfil these duties ably and with advantage to the commonwealth, the constitution supposed all free citizens to be gentlemen or wealthy yeomen, able to live upon their own means, without devoting themselves to any particular profession or pursuit. The number of such men, in comparison with the great mass of the population condemned to hopeless slavery was very limited.

Sparta, in the days of Aristotle, contained only nine thousand citizens. The loss of seven hundred warriors, at the Battle of Leuctra, had consequently proved fatal to her Grecian supremacy. The number of Athenian citizens varied from twenty to thirty thousand. When therefore one thousand, probably the prime and flower of the nation, had fallen at Chæroneia, the blow was regarded as irreparable, and all thoughts of further resistance abandoned.

Hence it is apparent that the erection of any powerful monarchy, in the vicinity of states constituted on this principle, must eventually prove fatal to their independence. Such was the fate of the Grecian colonies in Asia. Their neighbours, the Lydians, under the government of the Mermnadæ, a native dynasty, had become a powerful race; and the discovery of the gold excavated from Mount Tmolus, or sifted from the bed of the Pactolus, furnished them with the means of supporting a regular army. After a lengthened contest they therefore succeeded in reducing to subjection all the continental Greeks.

The conquered and the conquerors were united by Cyrus to his new empire, and became Persian subjects under Cambyses and Darius. The Ionians revolted from the latter, but were subdued after an unavailing struggle. At the commencement of the revolt, the Athenians sent a fleet to aid their colonists. The combined Athenian and Ionian forces marched to Sardes, and burnt the Lydian capital. This rash act drew on Athens and on Greece the whole vengeance of the Persian monarchs. After a long and deadly contest, the Greeks repelled the invaders, pursued them into Asia, and for a time liberated their Asiatic fellow-countrymen. But their own civil contests diverted their attention from foreign objects, and their splendid victories had no further result.

The same may be said of the two campaigns of Agesilaus in Asia, for the management of which Xenophon has praised him far beyond his merits. Then followed the disgraceful peace of Antalcidas, which once more consigned the Asiatic Greeks to the tender mercies of a Persian despot. From that period Persia changed her policy, and spared neither money nor intrigues in attempting to embroil the Grecian states with each other. For this conduct she had sufficient cause, for the expedition of the ten thousand had revealed to the hungry Greeks her weakness and their own strength. They had therefore, of late, been eager to free themselves from the harassing contests of the numerous aristocracies and democracies, and to unite, under one head, in a serious and combined attack upon the Persian monarchy.

Jason, the Thessalian, had nearly matured his plans, and had he not been suddenly arrested in his career, the Greeks would have probably invaded Asia under him as their captain-general: but his assassination only postponed the great event. Philip, the son of Amyntas, had followed the path marked out by Jason; and, by patience, prudence and vigour, succeeded in his great object. The Thebans and Athenians, who contested the Macedonian supremacy in the field, were defeated; and the Spartans, too proud to submit, too weak to resist, sullenly stood aloof from the general confederation, and withheld their vote from the Macedonian captain-general. But Persia was again saved from invasion by the death of Philip; and Alexander succeeded to his throne and pretensions, in the twentieth year of his age.

CHAPTER 1

Early Life of Alexander

Alexander, the third king of Macedonia of that name, and commonly surnamed the Great, was born at Pella three hundred and fifty-six years before Christ. His father Philip traced his origin through Temenus, the first Heracleid king of Argos, to Hercules and Perseus. The family of his mother Olympias was no less illustrious; for the royal race of Epirus claimed to be lineally descended from Neoptolemus, Achilles, and Peleus.

As he could thus refer his origin to Jupiter by the three different lines of Perseus, Hercules, and Peleus, it is impossible for us in the present day to calculate the impression made on his mind by so illustrious a descent. It is certain, however, that, from his earliest days, he proposed to himself to rival, and, if possible, surpass the renown of his ancestors.

Philip received the news of the birth of his son immediately after the capture of the city of Potidæa, the peninsular situation of which had enabled it long to resist the Macedonian arms. On the same day he received intelligence of a victory gained by Parmenio over the Illyrians, and of the success of his horses in bearing away the first prize at the Olympic games.

In after times the Asiatics remarked, with superstitious awe, that the magnificent temple of Diana at Ephesus had been destroyed by fire on the night of Alexander's birth, and that the general conflagration of Asia had been typified thus early by the destruction of its most splendid ornament.

Perhaps it ought to be remarked, as a proof of the eager and restless spirit of the times, that the incendiary, who ought to have remained nameless, was willing to purchase deathless notoriety at the expense of his life, and preferred an infamous death to an unrecorded life. Such a state of morbid feeling could be produced only in times of great and common excitement.

Nothing certain is known respecting the infancy and childhood of Alexander. The letter which Philip is supposed to have written to Aristotle on the birth of the prince, is, I fear, a forgery. For it is rather incompatible with the fact, that Aristotle did not take the immediate charge of his duties until his pupil had attained his fifteenth year. But as the philosopher's father had been the favourite physician in the Macedonian court, it is not unlikely that even the earlier years of the prince were under the superintendence of his great preceptor, and that his primary education was conducted according to his suggestions. If such was the case, we can easily deduce the principles on which both the earlier and more mature education of Alexander was conducted, from Aristotle's Treatise on Politics, where they are developed.

He divides a regular course of education into three parts. The first comprises the period from the birth to the completion of the seventh year. The second from the commencement of the eighth to the completion of the eighteenth year, and the third from the eighteenth to the twenty-first.

According to Aristotle, more care should be taken of the body than of the mind for the first seven years: strict attention to diet be enforced, and the infant from his infancy habituated to bear cold. This habit is attainable either by cold bathing or light clothing. The eye and ear of the child should be most watchfully and severely guarded against contamination of every kind, and unrestrained communication with servants be strictly prevented. Even his amusements should be under due regulation, and rendered as interesting and intellectual as possible.

It must always remain doubtful, how far Olympias would allow such excellent precepts to be put in execution. But it is recorded that Leonnatus, the governor of the young prince, was an austere man, of great severity of manner, and not likely to relax any adopted rules. He was also a relation of Olympias, and as such might doubtless enforce a system upon which no stranger would be allowed to act, strength, agility, and hardy habits of Alexander, are the best proofs that this part of his education was not neglected, and his lasting affection for his noble nurse Lannice, the daughter of Dropidas, proves also that it was conducted with gentleness and affection.

The intellectual education of Alexander would, on Aristotle's plan, commence with his eighth year. About this period of his life, Lysimachus, an Acarnanian, was appointed his preceptor.

The great Plutarch gives him an unfavourable character, and insinuates that he was more desirous to ingratiate himself with the royal family, than effectually to discharge the duties of his office. It was his delight to call Philip, Peleus; Alexander Achilles, and to claim for himself the honorary name of Phoenix. Early impressions are the strongest, and even the pedantic allusions of the Acarnanian might render the young prince more eager to imitate his Homeric model.

Aristotle mentions four principal branches of education as belonging to the first part of the middle period. These are literature, gymnastics, music, and painting, of which writing formed a subordinate branch. As the treatise on politics was left in an unfinished state, we have no means of defining what was comprehended under his general term literature, but commencing with reading and the principles of grammar, it apparently included composition in verse and prose, and the study of the historians and poets of Greece. During this period the lighter gymnastics alone were to be introduced, and especially such exercises as are best calculated to promote gracefulness of manner and personal activity.

Aristotle had strong objections to the more violent exertions of the gymnasium during early life, as he considered them injurious to the growth of the body, and to the future strength of the adult. In proof of this he adduces the conclusive fact that in the long list of Olympic victors only two, or at most, three instances had occurred in which the same person had proved victor in youth and in manhood. Premature training and over-exertion he, therefore, regarded as injurious to the constitution.

Not only the theory of painting, but also a certain skill in handling the pencil, was to be acquired. Aristotle regarded this elegant art as peculiarly conducing to create a habit of order and arrangement, and to impress the mind with a feeling of the beautiful.

Music both in theory and practice, vocal and instrumental, was considered by him as a necessary part of education, on account of the soothing and purifying effects of simple melodies, and because men, wearied with more serious pursuits, require an elegant and innocent recreation. By way of illustration, he adds that music is to the man what the rattle is to the child. Such were the studies that occupied the attention of the youthful Alexander between the seventh and fourteenth year of his age.

When he was in his eleventh year, Demosthenes, Æschines, and eight other leading Athenians, visited his father's court as ambassadors, and Philip was so proud of the proficiency of his son, that he ventured to exhibit him before these arbiters of taste. The young prince gave specimens of his skill in playing on the harp, in declamation, and in reciting a dramatic dialogue with one of his youthful companions. But if we can believe Æschines, Demosthenes was particularly severe on the false accents and Dorian intonations of the noble boy.

In his fifteenth year he was placed under the immediate tuition of the great philosopher, according to whose advice I have supposed his earlier education to have been conducted. In the year B.C. 342, Aristotle joined his illustrious pupil, and did not finally quit him until he passed over into Asia.

The master was worthy of his pupil, and the pupil of his master. The mental stores of Aristotle were vast, and all arranged with admirable accuracy and judgement. His style of speaking and writing pure, clear, and precise; and his industry in accumulating particular facts, only equalled by his sagacity in drawing general inferences. Alexander was gifted with great quickness of apprehension, an insatiable desire of knowledge, and an ambition not to be satisfied with the second place in any pursuit.

Such a pupil under such a master must soon have acquired a sufficient knowledge of those branches described before, as occupying the middle period of education. He would then enter on the final course intended for the completion of his literary studies. This comprehended what Aristotle calls Matheses, and included the branches of human learning arranged at present under the general term mathematics. To these, as far as they could be scientifically treated, were added moral philosophy, logic, rhetoric, the art of poetry, the theory of political government, and the more evident principles of natural philosophy. On these subjects we still possess treatises written by Aristotle, in the first place most probably for the use of his pupil, and afterwards published for the public benefit.

We learn also from a letter of Alexander, preserved by Plutarch, that Aristotle had initiated his pupil in those deep and mysterious speculations of Grecian philosophy, which treated of the nature of the Deity, of the human soul, of the eternity and other qualities of matter, and of other topics which prudential reasons prevented the philosopher from publicly explaining, As the letter gives a lively idea of the exclusive ambition of Alexander, I here insert it. It was occasioned by the publication of Aristotle's treatise on that branch of knowledge, called from that very book *Metaphysics*.

Alexander to Aristotle,
Health.

You did wrong in publishing those branches of science hitherto not to be acquired except from oral instruction. In what shall I excel others if the more profound knowledge I gained from you be communicated to all. For my part I had rather surpass the majority of mankind in the sublimer branches of learning than in extent of power and dominion.—Farewell!

But the great object of Aristotle was to render his pupil an accomplished statesman, and to qualify him to govern with wisdom, firmness, and justice, the great empire destined to be inherited and acquired by him. It was his province to impress deeply upon his mind the truths of moral philosophy, to habituate him to practise its precepts, to store his mind with historical facts, to teach him how to draw useful inferences from them, and to explain the means best calculated to promote the improvement and increase the stability of empires.

It is difficult to say what were the religious opinions inculcated by Aristotle on his pupil's mind. In their effects they were decided and tolerant. We may therefore conclude that they were the same as are expressed by Aristotle, who maintained the universality of the Deity, and the manifestation of his power and will under various forms in various countries.

As in modern, so in ancient times, great differences of opinion prevailed on the subject of education. Some directed their attention principally to the conduct of the intellect, others to the formation of moral feelings and habits, and a third party appeared more anxious to improve the carriage and strengthen the body by healthful exercise than to enlighten the mind. Aristotle's plan was to unite the three systems, and to make them co-operate in the formation of the perfect character, called in Greek, the καλος και αγαθος.

In truth, no talents can compensate for the want of moral worth; and good intentions, separated from talents, often inflict the deepest injuries, while their possessor wishes to confer the greatest benefits on mankind. Nor can it be doubted, that a sound constitution, elegance of manner, and gracefulness of person, are most useful auxiliaries in carrying into effect measures emanating from virtuous principles, and conducted by superior talents.

It is not to be supposed that Aristotle wished to instruct his pupil deeply in all the above-mentioned branches of education. He expressly states that the liberally educated man, or the perfect gentleman, should not be profoundly scientific, because a course of general knowledge, and what we call polite literature, is more beneficial to the mind than a complete proficiency in one or more sciences; a proficiency not to be acquired without a disproportionate sacrifice of time and labour.

It was also one of Aristotle's maxims that the education should vary according to the destination of the pupil in future life; that is, supposing him to be a gentleman, whether he was to devote himself to a life of action, or of contemplation. Whether he was to engage in the busy scenes of the world, and plunge amidst the contentions and struggles of political warfare, or to live apart from active life in philosophic enjoyments and contemplative retirement. Although the philosopher gave the preference to the latter mode living, he well knew that his pupil must be prepared for the former; for the throne of Macedonia could not be retained by a monarch devoted to elegant ease, literary pursuits, and refined enjoyments. The successor of Philip ought to possess the power of reasoning accurately, acting decisively, and expressing his ideas with perspicuity, elegance, and energy.

I have mentioned these particulars because it would be difficult to form just conceptions of the character of Alexander without taking into consideration, not only the great advantages enjoyed by him in early youth, but also the recorded fact that he availed himself of these advantages to the utmost. Amidst his various studies, however, Homer was the god of his idolatry; the Iliad, the object of his enthusiastic admiration. The poet, as Aristotle emphatically names him, was his inseparable companion: from him he drew his maxims; from him he borrowed his models. The preceptor partook in this point of the enthusiasm of his pupil, and the most accurate copy of the great poem was prepared by Aristotle, and placed by Alexander in the most precious casket which he found among the spoils of Darius.

Eager as Alexander was in the pursuit of knowledge, it must not be supposed that Philip would allow his successor to form the habits of a recluse; on the contrary, he early initiated him in the duties of his high station. At the age of sixteen he was appointed Regent of Macedonia, while his father was detained at the siege of Byzantium, and on a prior occasion astonished some Persian deputies by the pertinency of his questions, and the acuteness of his intellect, His studies were diversified even by the toils of war, and in his eighteenth year he commanded the left wing of the army at the celebrated Battle of Chæroneia, and defeated the Thebans before Philip had been equally successful against the Athenians.

In the following year Philip destroyed the peace of his family by marrying Cleopatra, the niece of Attalus, one of his generals, and by disgracing, if not divorcing, Olympias. Philip had married many wives, but they were the sisters or daughters of Thracian, Illyrian, and Thessalian chiefs, and probably not entitled to the honours of sovereignty. But his marriage with a Macedonian lady of high rank and powerful connections could only tend to a formal rupture with Olympias. To widen the breach, Philip changed his bride's name from Cleopatra to Eurydicè, his mother's name.

That this was done by way of declaring her the legitimate queen, may be inferred from the fact, that when a princess called Adea married Aridæus, Alexander's successor, her name also was changed into Eurydicè. The natural consequence was, that Alexander became suspicious of his father's intention about the succession, and a misunderstanding took place, which ended in the flight or banishment of several of the prince's most intimate friends, and in his own retirement with his mother into her native country: Subsequently a reconciliation took place, and Olympias and the prince returned into Macedonia. Alexander, the reigning king of Epirus, and the brother of Olympias, accompanied them, and the re-union was celebrated by his marriage with Cleopatra, the daughter of Philip.

During the festivities attendant on the nuptials, Philip was assassinated by Pausanias, one of the great officers of his guards. As this event led some writers to question the fair fame of Alexander, it will be necessary, in order perfectly to understand the subject, briefly to glance at the previous history of the Macedonian monarchy.

CHAPTER 2

Of the Macedonian Monarchy

In the earliest ages of Greece, Macedonia was inhabited by various tribes of barbarians, described by Homer as bearing arms in defence of Priam, at the siege of Troy. About the year B.C. 700, and probably at the period when the Argives changed their form of government from a monarchy into a republic, three Heracleid princes were banished from Argos, and took refuge first on the Illyrian coast; thence they marched inland, and finally fixed their seat at Ægæ or Edessa. Here Perdiccas, the youngest of the princes, became the founder of the Macedonian dynasty. The name Macedonia is evidently taken from the Macednian tribe which Herodotus places in the vicinity of the original Dorian settlements of the Heracleids.

In this neighbourhood, as well as in Asia, were found Phrygians, or Bryges; and the gardens of Midas, and the fountain where that monarch was said to have caught the satyr, were shown in the vicinity of Ægæ, and at the foot of Mount Bermius, Herodotus writes, that even in his time, wild roses of surpassing beauty, size, and fragrance, marked the spot.

Extending their conquests from this centre, the Argive colonists gradually dispossessed the native tribes of their territories, and became masters of all the country between the Strymon and the Peneius. On the west their territories were bounded by the great ridge of mountains that separates the waters that flow into the Ægean from those that flow into the Adriatic. But in the struggle, they appear to have lost a part of their southern civilization, and the Greeks so far lost sight of them, as to render it necessary for Alexander, their seventh king, to prove his Argive origin before he was allowed to compete with his fellow Greeks at the Olympic games.

Time and mutual intercourse had, in a considerable degree, assimilated them to the various tribes of Illyrians and Thracians, with whom they alternately warred and intermarried. Before the year B.C. 413, when Archelaus, the ninth king, commenced his reign, the Macedonian cities were few; those on the sea coast were mostly in the possession of the Southern Greeks, who regarded the Macedonian kings as barbarous chiefs, on whose territories they might legitimately encroach, provided they had the necessary power.

Archelaus did more for the civilization of Macedonia than his eight predecessors. He formed roads, built cities, disciplined the irregular cavalry, and clothed the infantry with heavy armour. He was also a patron of Greek learning, and his court was the favourite residence of the poet Euripides. He was assassinated by his favourite, Craterus, who caused himself to be proclaimed king, but he and his fellow conspirators were destroyed on the fourth day, and Orestes, the infant son of Archelaus, placed on the throne. Aeropus, being appointed regent, abused his trust, slew his ward, and usurped the sovereignty. After a short reign of two years, he died also, and was succeeded by his son Pausanias.

The direct line of the royal family had ended in Orestes. The right of Pausanias was, therefore, disputed by Amyntas, who claimed the crown as the lineal descendant of Alexander the First. He dethroned Pausanias, and assumed the sovereign power. His reign commenced B.C. 394, and ended B.C. 370. During the greatest part of it, Macedonia was torn to pieces by intestine factions and foreign invaders. All the advantages derived from the improvements of Archelaus were lost, and the kingdom more than once ceased to have an independent existence. There can be no doubt that his title was defective. Some historians write that a competitor, named Argæus, reigned for two years, while Amyntas was in banishment.

He was succeeded by his eldest son, Perdiccas, who, in less than two years was assassinated by Ptolemy Alorites. The condition of the royal family, at this time, is thus described by Æschines:

"Amyntas and Alexander, the eldest brother, had perished not long before. Perdiccas and Philip were yet children. Eurydicè was betrayed by those who pretended to be her friends, and the banished Pausanias had now recovered his strength, and was returning to take possession of the throne."

This Pausanias was apparently the son of Aeropus, whom Amyntas had only expelled, and not killed, as asserted by Diodorus. Eurydicè, in her distress, placed herself and children under the protection of Iphicrates, the Athenian general, who drove out Pausanias, and restored the supreme power to Eurydice and her friends. Ptolemy Alorites was appointed Regent, but at the end of three years was slain by the young king Perdiccas, who thus avenged the death of his eldest brother.

Perdiccas was, at the end of five years, defeated in a great battle by the Illyrians, and fell on the field. He was succeeded by the youngest brother, Philip, who reigned for twenty-four years.

The Macedonian throne was, to a certain extent, elective, and it was election alone that could give Philip a title to it; for his brother Perdiccas had left a son, by name Amyntas, whose hereditary right on modern principles was clear, but in ancient times, the brother's claim was in case of the infancy or boyhood of the sons of the last sovereign often preferred. But these, when grown up, invariably proved dangerous competitors to their uncles. Justin, who can scarcely be supposed to have invented the case, writes, that Philip for a considerable period acted only as Regent for his nephew, and that the crown was forced upon him by the urgent entreaties of his countrymen.

Macedonia, at this period, contained several principalities, the chiefs of which, independent in other respects, owed a species of feudal homage to the king. The two principal dynasties were the Orestian and Lyncestian. Their dominions were situated in the mountains to the west of Macedonia, where they rebelled, revolted, and proclaimed their own independence whenever they could do so with any prospect of safety and advantage. The Orestian princes claimed their descent from an Orestes, a supposed son of the Argive Orestes. The princes of Lyncestis were descended from the Bacchiadæ, the princely merchant family of Corinth. Both these families used to intermarry with the royal house of Macedonia, and these intermarriages were likely to give their chiefs a chance of succeeding to the throne.

Aeropus, whose son Pausanias was dethroned by Amyntas, the father of Philip, was probably a Lyncestian; as, according to Plutarch, all Macedonia, at Philip's death, regarded Alexander, the son of Aeropus, the Lyncestian, as the rightful heir to the throne.

But Philip, confiding in his great success and popularity, made light of the superior claims of the Lyncestian house, and of his nephew, Amyntas, the son of Perdiccas. The Lyncestian princes held high offices about his person, and he made his nephew his son-in-law by giving him his daughter Cyna in marriage. These princes had probably viewed the dissensions between the father and son with pleasure, and the reconciliation must have been regarded with very different feelings. It is curious that we have no account of the conspiracy against Philip's life from any author of credit. The authorities followed by Plutarch, Diodorus, and Justin, were evidently some low writers of Southern Greece, totally ignorant of the very constitution of the Macedonian court. According to them the death of Philip was an act of private vengeance, perpetrated by the youthful Pausanias, whom a denial of justice, under the most atrocious injuries, had driven to the act of assassination.

But luckily for the truth of history, and for the character of Alexander, Arrian in his first book, and twenty fifth chapter, has left on record that Heromenes and Arrhabæus, two Lyncestian princes, and the brothers of Alexander, the son of Aeropus, had been active accomplices in the murder of Philip. The leading assassin was Pausanias, an Orestian prince, who filled the important office of *somatophulax*, or commander of the body guard, the highest honour, (as we shall hereafter see,) in the Macedonian court.

No young man in Philip's veteran army could have by any possibility been raised to an office of so great responsibility and honour. Philip was slain late in the autumn of the year B.C. 336. He had succeeded in all his projects, and intended with the spring to lead the combined forces of Greece into Asia.

He was celebrating the nuptials of his daughter Cleopatra with Alexander, King of Epirus, with great pomp and magnificence. The religious sacrifices, the processions, the theatrical representations, and the attendant festivities, were on the most splendid scale, and testified to the world the joy of Philip in being reconciled to his son and the royal family of Epirus.

On one of these public days, Pausanias, whose office furnished him with ample opportunities, stabbed his sovereign to the heart as he was entering the theatre. He was immediately cut to pieces by the guards, who were too much attached to Philip to hesitate under such circumstances.

This event appears to have paralyzed the conspirators, who apparently were ill prepared for such a result. In the confusion Alexander, the son of Aeropus, was the first to buckle on his armour, to seek the prince, and escort him to the palace. The, troops and the leading Macedonians were summoned to a tumultuary assembly, and Alexander was declared king by general acclamation. He returned thanks in an energetic speech; and expressed his hopes that his conduct would soon cause them to say, that nothing but the name of their king had been changed.

Even Justin allows that his first care was to put his father's assassins to death. Pausanias had already expiated his guilt with his life. The three leading men that suffered on the occasion, were Heromenes, Arrhabæus, and Amyntas, the son of Perdiccas. Alexander, the son of Aeropus, was also accused of having participated in the plot, nor was there much doubt of his guilt. His conduct after the assassination ensured his safety, although it did not prove his innocence. Amyntas, the son of Antiochus, another prince of the blood royal, either from fear, conscious guilt, or treasonable intentions, escaped into Asia. He was received with open arms by the Persian court, and at a later period entrusted with the command of the Greek mercenaries in the service of Darius.

It is more than probable that the conspirators were in correspondence with the Persian court, and that ample promises of protection and support were given to men undertaking to deliver the empire from the impending invasion of the Captain General of Greece. Alexander, in his answer to the first proposals of Darius, openly charges the Persians with having been the instigators of his father's murder; and the transactions connected with Amyntas, the son of Antiochus, and Alexander the Lyncestian, hereafter to be noticed, show that the Persian court of that day was as little scrupulous about the means of destroying a formidable enemy as it had been in the days of Clearchus.

Demosthenes was then the principal agent of Persia in Greece, and Charidemus, one of his great friends and supporters, was at Ægæ when Philip's death occurred. The event was public, and could not be concealed. The deputies of all Greece were assembled there; and no private messenger from Charidemus to Demosthenes could have outstripped the speed with which the news of such an event passes from mouth to mouth in a populous country; not to mention that Charidemus would not have been the only deputy likely to dispatch a messenger on such an occasion.

Yet Demosthenes announced the death of Philip to the Athenian assembly long before the news reached Athens from any other quarter. He confirmed the truth of his assertion with an oath, and ascribed his knowledge of the event to an immediate revelation from Jupiter and Minerva. The accuracy of his information and the falsehood respecting the alleged sources of his intelligence, almost indisputably prove that he was an accessary before the fact, and that he had previous notification of the very day on which the conspirators were to act.

CHAPTER 3

Transactions in Europe Previous to the Invasion of Asia

Alexander had scarcely completed his twentieth year when he was thus suddenly called to fill his father's place. His difficulties were great, and enemies were rising on every side. The federal empire established by Philip was threatened with instant dissolution. The Barbarians on the west, north, and east of Macedonia were preparing to renounce their subjection, and resume their hostile and predatory habits. In southern Greece Sparta, standing aloof from the general confederacy, claimed the supremacy as due to her, and presented a rallying point for the disaffected.

Athens, smarting under her humiliation, and eager for novelty, was ready to renounce her forced acquiescence in the terms of the union, and renew her engagements with Persia. But Alexander was equal to the crisis. After punishing the murderers of his father, and arranging the internal affairs of Macedonia, he marched to the south at the head of a chosen body of troops.

The Thessalians had been for many years the firm friends and supporters of the Macedonian kings. They had restored Amyntas to his throne; and Philip, in conjunction with the noble family of the Aleuadæ, had rescued them from the domination of tyrants. The Thessalians, in return, elected him as the national chief, and under his patronage enjoyed peace and tranquillity, to which they had long been strangers. But as in all Grecian states there existed violent factions, perhaps we ought to give credit to those historians who write that an attempt was made to occupy the pass of Tempè, and prevent Alexander from entering Thessaly.

If such were the case, it proved unavailing, and the king reached Larissa without any serious resistance. The General Assembly of Thessaly was called together, and by a unanimous vote decreed the same authority and honours to the son as had been enjoyed by the father. His Thessalian friends escorted him to Thermopylæ, where the Amphictionic Council had been summoned to meet him. The assembled deputies recognised him as one of their number, and as the successor of his father in the important office, to which the execution of the decrees of the council belonged.

Hence, he hastened to Corinth, where a PanHellenic Council met, in which he was appointed Captain-General of the Greek confederacy, and empowered to make war on the Persians, their common enemies. The Lacedæmonians again dissented, and proudly alleged that it had been always their practice to lead, and not to follow. The Athenians, whose conduct could not bear strict investigation, were more lavish of their honours to Alexander, than they had been to Philip.

It is impossible to account for his great success in these delicate negotiations without confessing that all his proceedings must have been guided by the most consummate wisdom. But Alexander had made no change among his father's ministers; the spirit of Philip still presided in the council-room, and the interpreters of his opinions predominated there. Antipater and Parmenio are repeatedly mentioned by the Athenian orators as the two great ministers of Philip. To the former he trusted in civil, to the latter in military affairs. Two anecdotes, recorded by Plutarch, are well adapted to throw light upon the supposed characters of the two men. Their truth, in such a case, is of little importance.

Philip at times loved to drink deeply. On one occasion, when he observed his party rather reluctant to steep their senses in forgetfulness, "Drink," said he, "drink; all is safe, for Antipater is awake."

In allusion to the numerous generals whom the jealousy of the Athenian democracy united in the command of their armies, and whom its impatience often replaced by an equal number, Philip said, "Fortunate Athenians, in possessing so many generals, while I have never seen one but Parmenio."

Greater credit is due to Alexander in this respect, as these two great men naturally adhered to Philip in the misunderstanding that took place between him and his son; and the youthful monarch had personal friends, of distinguished merit, who at his father's death were exiles on his account. These were Harpalus, Ptolemy the son of Lagus, Nearchus, Erygius, and his brother Laomedon. They were of course recalled from exile, but their promotion to high offices was slow, though certain. Their names will often recur during the following life.

Diogenes, commonly called by the Greeks ο σκύλος, or the dog, and from whom the Cynic philosophers were named, resided then at Corinth. His contempt for all the decencies and proprieties of civilized life, joined to great rudeness of manner and readiness in sharp and pithy replies, had procured him great notoriety. His usual residence was a tub, placed under the walls of the Corinthian gymnasium. From this he declaimed to all willing listeners against the habits of civilized life, and upon the great superiority of savage existence. Alexander was tempted to visit him; and after questioning him respecting his doctrines, requested to know if he could be of any service. "Be so good" (said the basking philosopher, true to his principles) "as to stand from between me and the sun."

The king was so much struck with the independent spirit manifested in this reply, that he said to his officers, "Were I not Alexander, I should wish to be Diogenes." The king was young, the philosopher far advanced in years, yet their death occurred about the same period. Diogenes was one morning found dead in his tub, with his face enveloped in his cloak. His friends and disciples, for he had many, could not decide whether his death had been caused by a voluntary suppression of breath, or by indigestion. More probably from the latter cause, as his last meal had been the raw leg of an ox: at least so says his biographer and namesake, Diogenes Laertius.

After having thus successfully arranged the affairs of Southern Greece, and succeeded in all his projects, Alexander returned to spend the winter in Macedonia, and to prepare for an early expedition against his more turbulent northern and western neighbours. With the spring he marched against the Thracians of Mount Hæmus and its vicinity.

The army set out from Pella, reached Amphipolis, crossed first the Strymon, then the Nestus, and in ten marches from the banks of the latter river arrived at the southern foot of Mount Hæmus, the modern Balkan. He found the defiles in possession of the mountaineers and other independent Thracian tribes. They had occupied the summit of a mountain that completely commanded the pass, and rendered advance impossible. Alexander carefully examined the mountain range, but failed to discover any other practicable defile. He determined therefore to storm the enemy's position, and thus force his way.

The mountain's brow was crowned with a line of waggons, intended not only to serve as a rampart, but to be rolled down precipitously upon the ascending *phalanx*. In order to meet this danger, Alexander ordered the soldiers to open their ranks where the ground would allow it, and permit the waggons to pass through the intervals; where that was impossible, to throw themselves on the ground, lock their shields together in that position, and allow the waggons to roll over them. The shields of the Macedonian *phalanx* could be interlinked in cases of necessity. This enabled them to disperse the pressure of the wheels among many bucklers. And when the first shock had been withstood, the waggons glided lightly over the brazen pavement and quitted it with a bound.

A few were injured by the crush, but not a man was killed. Encouraged by the success of their new manoeuvre, they rose, charged up the hill, gained the summit, and the victory was won; for the half-armed barbarians could not withstand the charge of the serried line of pikes, and fled over the hills in every direction.

The pass by which Alexander crossed Mount Hæmus continues to be the main road between the plains of Hadrianople and the vale of the Danube. It follows the course of the Adra, one of the tributaries of the Hebrus or Marizza; it then crosses the main ridge, and descends along the Iatrus, still called the Iantra, into the vast plain between the northern foot of Hæmus and the Danube. This plain, at the period of Alexander's invasion, was possessed by the Triballi, a warlike Thracian tribe, against which Philip had often warred with varying success. They had not long been masters of the country, because in the time of Herodotus it formed the principal seat of the Getæ, whom the Triballi drove beyond the Danube.

The modern maps of this country, except on the line of the great roads, are not to be trusted. Even Macedonia is, to a great extent, unexplored by modern travellers, and the site of its ancient cities is only matter of conjecture. Syrmus, the Triballian chief, did not wait to be attacked, but retired with his court and family into a large island in the Danube. The Greeks named it Peucè, probably from the number of its pine-trees. Strabo places it twelve miles from the sea, and adds that Darius bridged the Danube either at its lower or upper end. But his Byzantine epitomist, who was perfectly acquainted with the coast, describes it as a triangle, enclosed between the two main branches of the Danube and the sea.

The latter description is still applicable, and the name Piczina is easily identified with Peucè or Peucinè.

Nor ought it to be regarded as wonderful that a river of the size and rapidity of the Danube has effected so slight a change during twenty centuries. For although it cannot be denied, mathematically speaking, that the annual tribute of soil carried by rivers to the sea must, in the countless lapse of ages, wear down the mountains and fill the seas, yet, as far as I have been enabled to form a judgment, the actual changes within the last two thousand years have been very trifling. Polybius, in his second book, writes that the Palus Mæotis was in his days all but filled, yet his description is as applicable to it now as in former ages.

Azov, the ancient Tanais, is still the great emporium where the merchants of Europe and Asiatic Tartary meet and exchange productions. Even that sluggish lake, between the isthmus of Perekop and the Mæotis, still retains its ancient name, the Putrid Sea, and remains apparently in the same state as when described by Strabo. Pliny writes that the Tauric Chersonese was once an island; and no doubt it was easy to infer that such might have been the case: the isthmus, however, has not been sensibly enlarged since the period of Greek colonisation. What is still more extraordinary, that long and narrow neck of land, that juts to the south between the Liman of the Borysthenes and the sea, is accurately described by various ancient authors, as existing in their days, a thousand *stadia* in length, and four in average breadth.

Even the Nile, with all the operative power ascribed to it by Herodotus, has not advanced perceptibly since he wrote. The ruins of Canopus are even covered by the sea. Nor does the land in general bulge more to the south than it did in the time of Ptolemy. For that great geographer places Alexandreia in latitude 31°, and the Phatnitic mouth or the embouchure of the Damietta branch in latitude 31° 10'. The Bolbitine or Rosetta branch, which in Ptolemy's time was in latitude 31° 5', has apparently advanced, but in its present unsupported state is liable to be cut short by any coincidence of a furious sea and a powerful land flood.

If, therefore, the operations of the Nile, when even concentrated in two main channels, instead of being dispersed as in former days over the whole Delta, have proved so very trifling, there is no reason to suppose that the encroachments of the Danube upon the Euxine have been greater.

Within three days' march of the Danube Alexander crossed a stream called by Arrian, Lyginus. The name is not found in other authors, and was probably given upon the spot to one of the slow streams that meander through the plain. In English its name is equivalent to the willow-river. Alexander was marching upon Peucè when he received information that the great body of the Triballi had taken a circuit, passed to his rear, and posted themselves on the banks of the Lyginus. This movement must have intercepted all communication between him and Macedonia. He immediately turned round, marched his army back, and found the Triballi drawn up in the wood that lined the banks of the stream.

A sharp engagement took place, in which the Triballi were not inferior as long as it continued a contest of missiles, but when the cavalry supported by the *phalanx* had reached their main body, the charge was irresistible, and they were driven first into the ravine and then into the river. Three thousand Triballi were slain; the prisoners were few, as the enemy could not be safely pursued through the thickets that covered the banks of the Lyginus.

Alexander then resumed his march in the direction of the island, and in three days arrived at the point where the Danube divided round it. Here he found his fleet that had sailed from Byzantium for the purpose of co-operating with the land army. He embarked a few troops on board the ships, which were not numerous, and attempted to make a descent upon the upper angle of the island. The ships descended the main stream, but the troops failed to make their landing good at the point, and if they swerved either to the right or to the left, the current, always strong below the point of division, hurried them down. To these difficulties was added the resistance of the enemy, who crowded to the banks and fought bravely in defence of their last refuge. The attempt, therefore, failed, and the ships were withdrawn.

The invader of such a country cannot retreat with impunity. The first news of a serious repulse followed by a movement to the rear, converts every barbarian into an eager, resolute, and persevering assailant. The Getæ, the ancient enemies of Philip, were collecting in crowds on the opposite bank. Alexander finding the island impregnable, determined to cross the main stream and attack the Getæ. He ordered rafts on inflated skins to be constructed, and collected the numerous canoes used by the natives both for fishing and piratical purposes. In these and on board his own fleet he threw across in the course of one night, a thousand cavalry and four thousand infantry.

The troops landed in a plain waving deeply with standing corn.

The *phalanx* marched first, and grasping their long pikes in the middle, levelled the opposing grain and formed a wide road for the cavalry. On reaching the open ground they discovered the Getic forces. But these, alarmed the unexpected boldness of the movement, and astonished at Alexander's success in crossing the Danube in one night and without constructing a bridge, waited not to be attacked, but fled to their city. There they hastily placed their wives, families, and more portable valuables upon their numerous horses and retired into the desert. Their town was captured, and the booty considerable; for the demands of the Greek market had thus early converted these Scythians into an agricultural and commercial people.

While the soldiers were employed in conveying the plunder to the right bank, Alexander offered sacrifices on the left to Jupiter the Preserver, to Hercules, the supposed ancestor of the Scythian nations, and to the river god who had permitted him to cross his mighty stream in safety. The same day witnessed the commencement and the termination of the expedition, for before night had closed upon them all the troops had regained their former camp.

The Getæ at this period were in a depressed state, otherwise Alexander might have had cause to repent this act of aggression. As it was, the result was fortunate, for all the neighbouring tribes sent deputies requesting peace and alliance. Even Syrmus, dazzled by the brilliancy of the exploit, renewed the treaty which had existed between him and Philip. The barbarians on both sides of the Danube had been engaged in long and bloody wars with Philip. Strabo even hints that in his war with Ateas, King of the Getæ, Philip had penetrated to the vicinity of the Borysthenes. All, therefore, had been taught by experience to acknowledge the superiority of the Macedonian arms and discipline, and were now unwilling to renew the contest with their former conquerors, who, as was proved by the skill and vigour of their youthful king, had lost no advantage by the death of his father.

Among other ambassadors came deputies from the Celtæ, who lived to the north-east of the Adriatic gulf. These were probably Scordisci, a Celtic tribe of great power and name, who had seized the country immediately to the west of the Thracian Triballi. Alexander, whose whole heart was fixed upon the Persian expedition, spared no means likely to conciliate his turbulent visitors. The deputies were feasted with all the magnificence which camp accommodations would allow. The wine circulated freely, and in the moment of exhilaration, Alexander asked whom or what they most dreaded? Perhaps the king expected a passing compliment to Macedonian valour and his own rising reputation.

But the Celts were not inclined to gratify his vanity at the expense of their own self-importance, and proudly answered, "our only fear is lest the sky should fall on us." From some acquaintance with Celtic dialects and their figurative mode of expression, I venture to interpret the above answer as equivalent to the English expression, "we fear no enemies but the gods." A bold answer never displeased Alexander: he declared the Celtæ his friends, and formed an alliance with them. He added, however, that the Celts were great boasters; a character which, from the Scordisci down to the Gascons and the modern Celts of Ireland, they most undoubtedly have deserved.

As Alexander was marching back from the Danube, intelligence met him that two Illyrian chiefs, Cleitus the son of Bardylis, and Glaucias, Prince of the Taulantii, were in arms and preparing to assert their independence. He had now reached Pæonia, situated between the rivers Nestus and Strymon. It had formerly been independent, but Philip had annexed it to Macedonia. We are informed by Hippocrates, that the Pæonians were once a more civilized race than the Macedonians. Asteropæus, their chief in the Trojan War, is described by Homer as possessing singular dexterity in the use of arms.

He engaged Achilles in single combat, and is the only warrior to whom Homer ascribes the honour of wounding that redoubtable hero. According to their own account, recorded by Herodotus, they were a Teucrian colony. The interesting description given of them in his Fifth Book, represents them as a fine race of people, distinguished for their ingenuity and industrious habits. It is to the age their supremacy that Thracian civilization and Linus, Orpheus, and Musæus should be referred. The nation was divided into several tribes or clans, of whom the Agrians, occupying the upper vale of the Strymon and the vicinity of Mount Pangæus, were at this period the most predominant.

Langarus, the Agrian chief, had been the youthful companion of Alexander, and their intimacy had ripened into friendship. He now came to receive the commands of his sovereign, and to communicate all the information which he had gathered respecting the enemies' motions. Cleitus and Glaucias had summoned other Illyrian tribes to their assistance, and among them had engaged the Autariatæ to invade Macedonia from the north, while they entered it from the west. It is a curious instance of the migratory habits of these tribes, that Alexander had to ask Langarus who these Autariatæ were who threatened to attack his flank. The Agrian replied that they were the weakest and most insignificant of the Illyrian nations, and that he would engage to invade their territories, and find ample work for them in their own country.

But in Strabo's time the Autariatæ were the most powerful tribe in Illyricum, and occupied the whole country between the Agrian borders and the Danube. Alexander proposed to cement the friendship existing between him and the Pæonian chief by giving him his sister Cyna in marriage. But the premature death of Langarus at the close of the campaign, prevented the accomplishment of his wishes. The fact, however, is important, as it proves that Cyna was already a widow, and that consequently, Amyntas the son of Perdiccas, had been put to death immediately after the assassination of Philip.

The operations of Langarus enabled Alexander to direct all his efforts against the western Illyrians. Cleitus, his present opponent, was the son of the famous bandit Bardylis, who, through the various trades of charcoal-burner, robber, warrior, and conqueror, had become a powerful prince. He fell in a great battle when ninety years old, after witnessing the total defeat of his troops by Philip. This success enabled the latter to make the lake Lychnidus or Ochrida, the boundary between him and his restless neighbours. Alexander marched up the River Erigon, entered Illyricum, and found Cleitus posted advantageously on the hills above the city of Pellium.

Alexander encamped on the banks of the river, and prepared to attack the town. The Illyrian troops, anxious to save their city, partially descended from their commanding position, and drew the king's attack upon themselves. He routed them, and gained the post occupied shortly before by Cleitus and his chiefs. A shocking spectacle here awaited the victor's eyes.

Three young maidens, three youths, and three black rams, had been immolated to the god of war. Their gloomy superstition taught them to believe that the united blood of the thrice three victims would form a potent charm of victory, or at least secure the lives of the leading chiefs.

The majority of the enemy had taken refuge in Pellium, round which Alexander was preparing to draw lines of circumvallation, when the arrival of Glaucias, chief of the Taulantii, at the head of a numerous army, compelled him to desist. The Macedonians were thus placed in a critical situation, as the enemy were far superior in cavalry and light troops, and the narrow and rugged ravine in which they were engaged did not allow the *phalanx* to act with effect. Their forag-

31

ing parties were intercepted, and as provisions could not be procured, a retreat became necessary. The Illyrians had already occupied the hills in the rear, and regarded their success as certain.

It was not without great difficulty that Alexander extricated his troops from their dangerous situation. He formed his *phalanx* into a deep column where the pass required it, he gradually extended it into line where the valley became wider. He protected the flanks as well as he could by his light troops, and ordered the *phalanx* when threatened with a serious attack from either side, to bring their spears laterally to the charge, instead of projecting them to the front. By retiring cautiously in this manner, he gained the brow of a hill, whence, if he could in safety cross the river that flowed at its foot, his army would be comparatively secure.

The descent was considerable, and the enemy on both flanks and in the rear were ready to fall on the troops while descending and in the act of fording the river. To obviate the danger, Alexander himself, with the engines attached to the army, first crossed and disposed them in the most commanding positions on the opposite bank. The *phalanx* was then ordered to descend from the hill and ford the river with the greatest rapidity, consistent with the preservation of order. The enemy pursued, but the discharge of missiles from the engines checked their advance, and enabled the Macedonians to pass over in safety.

Here Alexander halted for two nights, and refreshed his troops after their fatigues. The Illyrians, with the usual confidence of barbarians, did not pursue their advantage, but gave themselves up to exultation and festivities. Their whole army encamped loosely on the heights, no regular watches were established, no ramparts thrown up, nor fears entertained that the fugitives might become assailants. Alexander observed their negligence, and, as the dangers of his position would not allow him to be magnanimous, determined to steal a victory.

In the silence of the third night, he formed his troops into columns, re-passed the river, surprised the Illyrians in their tents, routed them in all directions, slew the greater part, and pursued the remainder to the borders of the Taulantii. Those who did escape threw away their arms, and thus incapacitated themselves for future operations. The blow was so severe that the Illyrians gave no further molestation to Macedonia during Alexander's reign. Cleitus took refuge first in Pellium, but set it on fire in despair, and retired into the territories of his ally.

This victory was very seasonable, as important tidings from the south rendered Alexander's presence in that quarter indispensable. Philip, after the battle of Chæroneia, had banished the leaders of the democracy, and placed a garrison in the Cadmeia, the citadel of Thebes. The exiles availing themselves of Alexander's absence, returned suddenly, entered Thebes by night, surprised Amyntas and Timolaus the Macedonian governors, and put them to death. These officers suspecting no danger had quitted the Cadmeia and resided in the city. With the dawn the exiles, supported by their accomplices, summoned the Thebans to an assembly. Under the specious names of liberty, independence, and deliverance from the Macedonian yoke, they exhorted them to revolt. They scrupled not to assert that the king had fallen in the Illyrian campaign; and their assertions received the more credit, because the partial success of the enemy had intercepted all communications between Alexander and Greece.

In an evil hour the assembly listened to the agitators, and Thebes revolted. The Macedonian garrison was still in the Cadmeia. It was, therefore, encircled with a double line of circumvallation, for the sake both of repressing its sallies and starving it into submission. The work had scarcely been completed, when Antipater at the head of the troops of the confederacy arrived in the neighbourhood.

In the meantime, the revolt of Thebes threw all Greece into a state of excitement. Demosthenes, according to his own confession, had been mainly instrumental in encouraging the exiles to make the attempt. He now exerted all his eloquence to induce the Athenians to follow their example. Even when the assembly had prudently decreed to wait for further information respecting the reported death of Alexander, the orator ceased not to intrigue with the neighbouring states and to aid the Thebans from his own private resources. The Lacedæmonians not included in the confederacy, were known to be anxious for the formation of a powerful anti-Macedonian league.

The court of Persia had already placed large sums of money at the disposal of its Grecian agents, and active exertions would ensure an ample supply of the sinews of war from the treasures of the Great King. Still, if we can believe Æschines, the Persian agents behaved most culpably on the occasion, as the garrison of the Cadmeia, composed of mercenaries, offered to deliver the citadel to the Thebans for the paltry sum of five *talents*, which, nevertheless, Demosthenes refused to advance.

Alexander saw that the long-continued labours of his father and his own fair prospects of a glorious career were likely to prove vain, and that another desperate struggle against Persian gold and Grecian valour awaited the Macedonian arms. His deep conviction of the importance of the crisis may be inferred from the rapidity of his movements. In seven days, he passed from the scene of warfare along a rugged and mountainous road to Pellenè or Pellinæum on the banks of the Peneius. In six more days, he reached the gates of Thermopylæ, and soon after encamped at Onchestus, a small town crowning the summit of a hill between Thebes and the lake Copais.

The deluded Thebans could not believe that the king himself had thus suddenly arrived from the mountains of Illyricum. It was only a body of troops sent from Macedonia to reinforce Antipater! Even when the truth could no longer be concealed, and Alexander was known to be their commander, the ringleaders boldly affirmed, that it could not be Alexander the King, but the son of Aeropus the Lyncestian.

Their doubts were not destined to continue long; for the king, the next day after joining Antipater, approached the city, and encamped near the consecrated grove of Iolaus, the friend and companion of Hercules. He hoped the Thebans would repent, and acknowledge their error. But so far from doing this, they sallied forth in considerable numbers, and slew a few Macedonians. Alexander contented himself with repulsing the attack. Next day he marched round the city, and encamped on the road leading to Athens. In this position he intercepted all communication with their well-wishers in the south, and was near his own troops in the Cadmeia, from the foot of which nothing separated him but the circumvallation constructed by the Thebans. His wishes and interest were to recover Thebes by gentle means.

On this day the assembly met within the city, and the Macedonian party proposed to send a deputation in order to see what grace they could obtain from the king. But the ringleaders, who, without a doubt, must have suffered the same fate which they had inflicted on Amyntas and Timolaus, persuaded the majority of the citizens that their cause was common, and that there was no safety except in arms.

It should also be remembered, that Grecian cities had not in previous wars been liable to immediate capture by force of arms. Starvation or treachery were the only means of gaining possession of fortified towns. All the forces of the Peloponnesians and their Allies had failed to capture the small city of Platæa by open force. They had rolled down the forests of Mount Cithæron, piled them in huge heaps, and set them on fire, in hopes of burning out the brave little garrison; but all their efforts failed, and it required a blockade of three years before they could gain possession of the place. The interval between the siege of Tyre by Alexander and the surrender of Platæa does not amount to a century, while a thousand years, in the gradual progress of human invention, are scarcely sufficient to account for the difference between the science and enterprise of the two besieging parties.

Even the Athenians, supposed to be more advanced in the art called wall-fighting by the Spartans, were ruined, because they could not destroy the paltry fort of Deceleia, within half a day's march of the Parthenon. Nor were the Macedonians distinguished for their greater success in this species of warfare, as Perinthus and Byzantium long withstood the utmost efforts of Philip. The Thebans, therefore, had no cause to expect the terrible fate that so suddenly overtook them.

According to Ptolemy, the son of Lagus, the fatal assault was commenced more from accident than design. Perdiccas being placed with his brigade of the *phalanx* near the circumvallation, perceived as he thought a favourable opportunity, and, without waiting for orders, made a furious attack on the outer line, tore down the defences, and broke into the enclosed space. Amyntas, the son of Andromenes, followed his example, and the king seeing his troops thus far engaged, ordered the light-armed to enter the breach, while he brought his guards and the flower of the *phalanx* to the entrance. Perdiccas, in the meantime, had broken through the inner line of the circumvallation, and reached the open space between it and the citadel. But in the attack, he received a severe wound, was carried out fainting, and narrowly escaped with life.

Within the last-described space stood a temple of Hercules, with a hollow road leading to it. The brigade of the wounded general, supported by the light troops, drove the Thebans before them as far as this temple. Here the latter rallied, raised the Theban war-cry, charged the pursuers, slew Eurybates the commander of the Cretan archers, and drove the assailants back into the breach. Alexander allowed his broken troops to disengage themselves, and then, with his men in close order, attacked their pursuers, carried all before him, passed the temple of Hercules, and reached the city gates together with the retreating Thebans.

The crush was so great, that the Macedonians made their ground good on the inside before the gates could be closed. Others entered the Cadmeia, and being joined by the garrison, descended into the city by the temple of Amphion. This appears to have been situated at the end of the street leading from the citadel to the town. It was occupied by Thebans, who defended the post for some time. But when the division with Alexander, and others who had scaled the walls in various parts, had reached the market-place, the Thebans gave up the contest in despair. The cavalry galloped through the opposite gates, and reached Athens in safety. The infantry dispersed and saved themselves as they could.

But it is not probable that many of them escaped. In the Army of the Confederates there were Phocians, Platæans, Thespians, and Orchomenians—men whose injuries had been great, and whose vengeance was dreadful. No mercy was shown to age or infancy; the distinctions of sex were disregarded. The virgin at the foot of the altar met with the same fate as the warrior who refused quarter, and struck at the enemy while life remained. The Macedonians at last succeeded in staying the butchery, and saving the surviving inhabitants.

The ultimate fate of Thebes was then submitted to the decision of the Assembly of the Confederates. According to the terms of their decree, the Cadmeia was occupied by a garrison; the city was levelled with the ground; the territory, with the exception of lands consecrated to religious purposes, was confiscated, and the captured Thebans, with their wives and families, were condemned to be sold by public auction. All priests and priestesses, all the friends of Philip and Alexander, all families publicly connected with the Macedonians, were exempted from the consequences of this decree.

The exceptions are comprehensive enough to embrace every family, a single member of which had made the slightest opposition to the late revolt. Alexander personally interfered in behalf of the descendants of the great lyric poet of Thebes: these remained uninjured, both in person and fortune. The very house which he had hallowed by his: residence was left standing among the ruins. The greatest of modern poets has amply repaid the honours conferred on his brother bard:

Lift not thy spear against the muse's bower.
The great Emathian conqueror bad spare
The house of Pindarus when temple and tower
Went to the ground.

We involuntarily invest a nation with a species of existence independent of the ever-shifting individuals that compose it. This abstraction is in ordinary thought and language imagined to exist for centuries, deserving gratitude in age for the good deeds of youth, and obnoxious in decrepitude and feebleness for the crimes of its earlier existence. Thus, the accumulated guilt of centuries becomes concentrated in one unhappy generation; and the penalties due to the numerous offences of their forefathers, are exacted with interest from the individuals then happening to exist.

This is an instinctive feeling, never to be eradicated by philosophical reasoning, and has been implanted for wise purposes in the human breast. For a community, abstraction as it is, possesses public feelings, a sense of right, and a respect for justice and mercy, that can never be violated without the most destructive reaction upon itself. And a nation that has lost its character, loses self-respect, and becomes as reckless in its future conduct as the malefactor whom public justice has degraded from his place in society.

Arrian truly states that he could not see how the conflagration of the Persepolitan palace by Alexander was any retaliation upon Xerxes and his army; yet there was a moral lesson conveyed in it that ought deeply to impress the powerful, that any tyrannical deed on their part may be severely visited on themselves, or their descendants. And although the disciples of Epicurus may say with the heartless Frenchman, "after me, the deluge,"—yet the great majority of mankind will always feel a strong interest in the stability of their works, and the welfare of their posterity,

The idea of national retribution may be carried so far as to become ridiculous, as when the French republicans pretended to exact vengeance from the helpless successor of St. Peter, for the injuries inflicted on Vercingetorix by the first Cæsar.

The case of Thebes was far different, their misdeeds had been of late occurrence, their memory was still fresh, and the Thebans of that day were profiting by the iniquity of their fathers. They had willingly and actively aided Xerxes and Mardonius in the attempt to enslave Greece. They had compelled the Lacedæmonians to pass the merciless decree, according to which the captured Platæans were butchered in cold blood, their city razed to the ground, and their territory rendered desolate. Their vote had consigned Athens to a similar fate, when the Lacedæmonian conquerors refused to put out one of the eyes of Greece.

In the period of their supremacy, they had attacked their neighbours, the Orchomenians, once equal to themselves in wealth and renown; stormed their city, put all the men to the sword, and sold the women and children into captivity. They could not, therefore, complain if their own city at last received the same measure which they had meted to others. Alexander is said to have regretted in after-life his

37

severity against Thebes. But of this we have no proof beyond the assertion of Plutarch. Alexander never concealed his feelings, and had they been those of deep regret on this occasion, he would have naturally relieved their bitterness by ordering the restoration of the ruined city.

The suddenness of the blow, and the severity with which it was followed up, struck terror into the boldest leaders of the Anti-Macedonian party. The Arcadians were already on the road to Thebes when its fate was announced. It is difficult to account for the real cause of their conduct; some impute it to the gift of ten *talents* which Antipater, previous to Alexander's arrival, had sent to them; others impute it to the terror caused by the fall of Thebes. The result is not disputed; the troops, as in many other similar cases, brought their leaders to trial, and put them to death.

The Athenians being more deeply implicated in the intrigue, felt proportional alarm. The presence of the Theban fugitives announced the ruin of Thebes to the citizens, then engaged in celebrating the Eleusinian mysteries. The holy rites were intermitted; Eleusis, its temple, and goddesses forsaken, and all the inhabitants, with their more valuable effects, took refuge within the walls of Athens. Nor was the alarm causeless, for the Thessalians of the confederacy had already decreed to march into Attica, and Alexander himself was known to be exasperated against the Athenian leaders.

Demosthenes, a great statesman and matchless orator, was not a good man. His failings, perhaps his vices, were notorious. But his devotion to the cause of Athenian supremacy was boundless. His zeal, his activity, and, at times, his success in that cause, had distinguished him as the champion of the Greeks against the encroachments of Philip. When the Battle of Chæroneia had raised the Macedonians to the supremacy, successively possessed by Lacedæmonians, Athenians, and Thebans, Philip had laid aside all animosity, and permitted Athens to enjoy an unqualified independence. But in the mind of Demosthenes the defeat of his measures deeply rankled, and he welcomed the tidings of Philip's murder with unmanly exultation.

He advised the Athenians to offer the same sacrifices on the occasion as were customary when intelligence of a victory arrived. He went further, he proposed to deify the assassin, and erect a temple to his memory. He had loaded the youthful king with the most opprobrious epithets, and pronounced him a new Margeitis. The name was well known in Greece; for Margeitis was the hero of a mock-heroic poem, attributed to Homer: the interest of which depended on the ludicrous situations in which the vanity, folly, and cowardice of the hero were perpetually involving him. Demosthenes and his party had, therefore, much to fear, and little to hope from Alexander. Short time, however, was left for deliberation when the assembly met and decreed that ten citizens should wait on the young king, and congratulate him on his safe return from Thrace and Illyricum, and on the suppression of the Theban revolt. Demosthenes was appointed one of this deputation, but his heart failed him, and he returned from the centre of Mount Cithæron. This fact, mentioned by Æschines, proves the truth of Plutarch's assertion, that the first deputation consisted of the Anti-Macedonian party, and that Alexander refused to admit them to an audience.

The assembly, therefore, met a second time, and Demades, Phocion, Æschines, with several others, known friends to the Macedonian interests, were deputed to the king. These were received with affability and kindness, and were, perhaps, the advisers of the letter which they brought from Alexander. In this he required the Athenians to surrender eight orators, of whom the principal were Demosthenes and Hypereides, and two oratorical generals, Chares and Charidemus. He proposed to bring them to trial before the deputies of the Grecian confederacy. He accused them of being the common disturbers of Grecian tranquillity, of having caused the Chæroneian war, and its calamities, of being the authors of the gross insults offered to his father's memory, and to himself. He added that he knew them to be as guilty of the Theban revolt as the actual agents.

Demosthenes had no courtesy to expect from the Macedonian; and, even if the natural magnanimity of the king should induce him to overlook the insults offered to himself, yet filial piety might compel him to take vengeance for the indecent outrages offered to his father's memory. The orator, therefore, exerted all his eloquence to dissuade the assembly from complying with the king's demand. He described himself and fellow demagogues as the watchful dogs, Alexander as the wolf, and the Athenians as the simple sheep of the fable. His eloquence prevailed, and a third deputation was sent, beseeching the king to remit his anger against the accused, for the sake of his Athenian friends.

Alexander, after the destruction of Thebes, could afford to be merciful, and withdrew his demand. Charidemus alone was excepted, and compelled to retire from Greece. It is impossible to account for the king's inflexibility in his case, without inferring that he had discovered proofs of his connexion with his father's assassins. The banished general withdrew to the Persian court.

Alexander returned to Macedonia after a campaign hitherto unrivalled in Grecian history, and which alone was sufficient to prove that no equal military genius had yet appeared among men. The invasion of Thrace, the passage of Mount Hæmus, the defeat of the Triballi, the passage of the Danube, the victory over the Getæ, the march into Illyricum, the defeat first of Cleitus, then of the united troops of Cleitus and Glaucias, the rapid descent into Boeotia, the more rapid conquest of Thebes, and the settlement of all the excited nations of Southern Greece, were all crowded into one spring, summer and autumn. The winter was spent at Ægæ, the primitive capital of Macedonia. There, with due pomp and magnificence, he offered sacrifices to the Olympian Jove, and diversified the festivities of the court with gymnastic contests and theatrical representations.

Not far from the city of Dium, and at the eastern foot of Mount Olympus, a monument and statue had been erected in memory of the Thracian Orpheus. The country was the ancient Pieria, and the natives referred to their own Pimpleian spring as the original and favourite resort of the muses. They observed with awe that the statue of the father of song continued for many days during this winter to be bedewed with apparent perspiration.

The prodigy was duly reported, the diviners consulted, and an answer received from the most sagacious of their number, pronouncing the omen propitious, and auguring brilliant success to Alexander, and proportionate labours to the poets. The interpretation perhaps would have been more germane had the cold sweat of the tuneful bard been attributed to an overwhelming anticipation of the frigid conceits of Choerilus, and the other poetasters of Alexander's court.

The omen and its explanation were, however, hailed with delight, and sacrifices, with due honours, offered to the muses. But they are capricious in their favours, and never smiled on the efforts of the versifiers of Alexander's great actions.

CHAPTER 4

Period of Alexander's Invasion of Asia

To speculate on the condition of the rest of the known world at this period would be worse than idle, for we know nothing of it. I shall, therefore, confine myself to the consideration of the state of the three great powers which then predominated on the shores of the Mediterranean. These were the Persian, Carthaginian, and Grecian nations.

The Persian dynasty, after a continued series of able and magnificent monarchs, had been threatened with destruction during the long and feeble reign of Artaxerxes Mnemon. In the north the Cadusians had renounced their allegiance, and baffled the king's personal attempt to reduce them to subjection. In the south, Egypt had recovered and asserted in arms her ancient independence. In the west, the great *satraps* of Asia Minor had openly revolted, and withheld the usual tribute from their great sovereign. Artaxerxes Ochus, who succeeded to his father's throne, had been signally defeated in his attempt to recover Egypt, and his misfortunes led to the immediate revolt of Phoenicia, Cyprus, and the other maritime powers.

But the empire had been saved from impending dissolution, by the vigour of the *eunuch* Bagoas, the chief minister of Ochus, and by the military talents of his associate, Mentor, a Rhodian soldier of fortune. Phoenicia and Egypt had been reconquered, and the western provinces reunited to the empire. These were placed under the unlimited control of Mentor, while Bagoas superintended the internal government. During the short reign of Arses, the successor of Ochus, these ministers, freed from domestic troubles, had been enabled to direct their attention to Greece.

And we have the testimony of Demosthenes, that Philip's operations against Perinthus and Byzantium had been baffled by the mercenary troops of Persia. The lineal descendants of Darius Nothus ended with Arses, and Codomannus, said to have been the surviving representative of Achæmenes by a collateral branch, was raised to the throne by Bagoas, and assumed the name of Dariús. The whole empire acknowledged his authority, and the personal courage which he had displayed in early youth, induced his subjects to expect a vigorous administration from his mature years.

His resources were ample; his treasures full, and, if he distrusted the valour of his own people, he could command the services of the most valiant and skilful warriors then existing. But the death of Philip had freed the Persian court from immediate terror, and little danger was anticipated from the efforts of the boy Alexander.

The Carthaginian Empire had been gradually rising in importance; Northern Africa and Southern Spain might be regarded as component parts of it. The western islands in the Mediterranean had been subdued, and the Carthaginians were pressing hard on the Sicilian Greeks. But they were not likely to interfere in the present contest,

41

except as the Allies of their mother city Tyre.

The Greeks in Italy were rapidly losing their military superiority, and the Lucanians and Samnites, exercised in continual wars with Rome, as yet unknown in the history of the world, were threatening the degenerate colonists with subjugation. The Greeks in Asia and the Asiatic islands had long been familiarised with Persian despotism, and nothing but decided success on the part of their liberators was likely to make them active partisans of a cause to which they had so often proved victims.

Within Greece itself there existed a warlike population, ill adapted, from want of concert and pecuniary resources, for a combined and continued exertion; yet fully able to resist all foreign aggression, or active interference with their liberties. Justin calculates, and apparently without exaggeration, that the states to the south of Macedonia could, at this period, bring two hundred thousand men to the field.

The Macedonian supremacy depended upon opinion and the good will of the majority of the confederates. Without this it was a mere name. Gently and generously as it was used, the Spartans under Agis nearly suceeeded in overthrowing it, even while Alexander's conquest of the Persian empire appeared almost certain. And the Athenians, after his death, fairly drove Antipater from the field, and blockaded him within the walls of Lamia. The seasonable arrival of the great general Craterus, with the Macedonian veterans, gave the victory at the end of the second campaign to Antipater; yet both these generals failed to subdue the more warlike and resolute Ætolians. Without taking these facts into consideration, it is impossible fairly to estimate the difficulties encountered and surmounted by Alexander.

The Macedonian had no resources for the maintenance of the future war except in his own great mind. The orators of Southern Greece were loud in their assertions, that Philip owed all his success to his unsparing profusion of money. With this he burst asunder the gates of hostile cities; with this he purchased the services of party leaders. If it were so, their virtue must have been cheaply estimated, for Philip could not have purchased it at a dear rate. He was poor at the commencement of his reign, and poorer at his death. Alexander at his accession found sixty *talents* in his treasury, and a few gold and silver cups in the palace. But the debts amounted to five hundred *talents*, and before he could move from Macedonia, he had to mortgage the royal domains for eight hundred more.

Nearly two hundred years had elapsed since the commencement

of the wars between Greece and Persia; it would, therefore, be folly to say that they were ignorant of each other's mode of warfare, or that one party enjoyed any advantage over the other with respect to arms and discipline. The Persians could command the services of the best tacticians, armourers, engineers, and soldiers of Greece; and it is a curious fact that Alexander had to combat full fifty thousand Greeks, before he entered Syria.

The infantry of the invading army, according to the best authorities, consisted of twelve thousand Macedonians, seven thousand confederates, five thousand mercenary Greeks, the same number of Thracians, Triballians, and Illyrians, and one thousand Agrians. The cavalry amounted to fifteen hundred Macedonians, fifteen hundred Thessalians, nine hundred Thracians and Pæonians, and six hundred confederates. The whole force, therefore, was thirty thousand infantry, and four thousand five hundred cavalry.

CHAPTER 5

First Campaign in Asia

In the spring of the year B.C. 334, Alexander placed himself at the head of his assembled forces, and marched to Amphipolis. Passing by the cities Abdera and Maroneia, he crossed, first, the Hebrus, and then the Melas. On arriving at Sestus he found his fleet, consisting of one hundred and sixty *triremes*, already assembled. Parmenio was ordered to superintend the passage of the troops, while Alexander indulged his youthful feelings of enthusiasm and poetry in performing pilgrimages to the shrines consecrated by the genius of Homer. At the southern point of the Thracian Chersonese was raised the tomb of Protesilaus. There Alexander sacrificed to the manes of the hero who had first set his foot on the hostile shore of Asia, and besought his influence to save him whose intentions were the same from a similar fate.

He then embarked, and steered for the Achæan harbour. On gaining the middle of the Hellespont, a bull, the Homeric sacrifice to Neptune, was offered to the Deities of the sea, and due libations made from golden cups.

With his own hand he steered the vessel, and when it neared the shore, was the first to spring on Asiatic ground. He was in complete armour, and brandished his spear, but there was no Hector to encounter the new Protesilaus, nor a Laodameia to lament him had he fallen. The inhabitants of the Troas were peaceful Æolians, more inclined to remain neutral spectators of the contest, than to side actively with either party.

If Achilles had his Patroclus, Alexander had his Hephæstion, a young nobleman of Pella; an early partiality for whom had ripened into a steady friendship, equally honourable to both parties. The tumuli of the two Homeric friends were still conspicuous; while, therefore, Alexander duly honoured the monumental pillar of Achilles, Hephæstion offered garlands and sacrifices at that of Patroclus.

Thence Alexander ascended to the sacred and storm-exposed city of Priam, worshipped in the temple of the Ilian Minerva, and hung his own arms as a votive offering on the walls. In exchange he took down a suit of armour said to have been worn by one of the Homeric heroes. The shield, of great size and strength, might have graced the left arm of the Telamonian Ajax, and in all his after fields was borne before Alexander by one of his armour-bearers.

The venerable Priam was not forgotten, and the descendant of Pyrrhus sought by sacrifices to avert the anger of the royal shade. Would that he had also honoured the tomb of the amiable and patriotic Hector! But the representative of Achilles had no sympathy to spare for the slayer of Patroclus.

He turned with scorn from the lyre of Paris, accustomed to guide the voices of feeble women, but eagerly demanded a sight of the harp with which Achilles had soothed his soul and sung the glorious deeds of heroes. I quote a very interesting passage from Arrian:

> It is also said that he pronounced Achilles happy in having Homer to herald forth his praise. And in truth Achilles could, in this light, be justly pronounced happy by Alexander, as he himself did not experience his general good fortune in this respect, nor have his deeds been worthily blazoned among men, either in prose or heroic verse. Nor has he been sung in lyric strains, like Gelo, Theron, Hiero, and others, not to be compared to Alexander. Thus, his exploits are far less known than the most trifling ancient deeds.
>
> Even the ascent of the ten thousand that aided Cyrus against King Artaxerxes, and the sufferings of Clearchus and of the generals captured with him, and the retreat under Xenophon's command, are, through Xenophon's own writings, far more renowned among men, than Alexander and his achievements; although he was not the auxiliary of a foreign potentate, nor in

his flight from the great king overcame those who attempted to prevent his retreat to the sea-coast, but stands unrivalled among Greeks and barbarians, both for the multitude and magnitude of his splendid actions. This was the reason that induced me to undertake this history, as I do not regard myself unworthy to spread among men the renown of Alexander's deeds.

Arrian succeeded partly, but not to the extent of his anticipations, nor will the life of Alexander be ever worthily written, before the eastern be as well-known as the western world.

According to the accurate Strabo, the king was deceived in believing the Ilium of his day to have been the city of Priam. Yet a mistake scarcely seems possible; for the Æolian colony was not later than sixty years after the capture of Troy, and no event from that period occurred to destroy the pure vehicle of tradition. Herodotus, a better authority than Strabo on this head, writes that Xerxes ascended to the Pergamus of Priam, and offered sacrifices to the Ilian Minerva, and duly honoured the memory of the heroes.

It is, therefore, to be hoped, that the enthusiasm of Alexander was not expended upon a spurious object. If, however, the Pergamus was further inland, the Simois, the Scamander, the broad Hellespont, and the summits of Ida, were points which could not be mistaken, and it remained for modern travellers, labouring under the most inconceivable ignorance, to confound the streams, and metamorphose the Scamander into some obscure puddle, far removed from the scenes of the Iliad.

The Troad is almost a peninsula, placed between the Gulf of Adramyttium, on the south, and the Gulf of Cyzicus, on the north. In the intermediate space rises Mount Ida, stretching westward to Cape Lectus or Baba, and eastward as far as the vale of the Rhyndacus. The common road, leading from the Troad to the south-eastern provinces, crossed the western extremity of Mount Ida, and passed through Antandrus and Adramyttium. But Alexander was not allowed to choose his road.

The Persian *satraps* had been evidently taken by surprise by the rapid movements of the invader. They had thus, without making a single attempt to molest the passage, allowed him with a far inferior fleet to convey his troops into Asia. Receiving intelligence that they were rapidly collecting their forces at Zeleia, on the Propontis, he determined to march in that direction.

The army under the command of Parmenio had advanced from Abydos to Arisba, where the king joined it. Next day he advanced to Percotè, and the day after, leaving Lampsacus on the left, encamped on the banks of the Practius. This river, flowing down from Mount Ida, enters the northern part of the Hellespont. It bears no name on modern maps, but Percotè and Lampsacus still exist as Bergasè and Lamsaki. Colonæ and Hermotus, the next stations, are both obscure. The first was inland from Lampsacus, and was, perhaps, connected with the tomb of Memnon, mentioned by Strabo.

During this advance the Persian camp became the scene of much discussion. The death or removal of Mentor had left the *satraps* without a commander in chief. His brother Memnon was present, but merely as an auxiliary, not entrusted with the command even of the Greek mercenaries. Spithridates, the *satrap* of Lydia and Ionia, was the highest officer, but does not appear to have possessed more authority than Arsites, the governor of the Hellespontian Phrygia, the scene of action. Four other Persians, Arsames, Rheomithres, Petenes, and Niphates, are mentioned by Arrian as equal in authority to Spithridates and Arsites.

À council of war was held, to which Memnon was admitted. His advice was to burn and lay waste the country, to avoid a battle, and in the words of a modern Persian, "to encircle the enemy with a desert." But Arsites declared that he would not permit a single habitation entrusted to his care to be wilfully destroyed. As Alexander's advance left no alternative between risking a battle and leaving Ionia and Lydia open to an invader, the spirited resolution of Arsites was more in accordance with the feelings of the *satraps* than the cautious advice of Memnon.

They, therefore, determined to advance and contest the passage of the Granicus. Strabo writes that the Granicus, the Æsepus, and the Scamander rise from the same part of Mount Ida, and that a circle of twenty *stadia* would enclose the three sources. The Granicus must, therefore, from the length of its course, be a considerable river, and in spring, when increased by the melting snows of Mount Ida, present a formidable appearance. Behind this natural barrier the Persians drew up their forces.

On advancing from Hermotus, Alexander had received the submission of the city of Priapus, thus named from the worship of the Hellespontian God. The army was preceded by strong reconnoitring parties, composed of the Prodromi, employed to examine the roads and report obstacles. The main body was not far from the Granicus, when the scouts returned and announced the position of the enemy on the opposite bank. Alexander began immediately to form his line and prepare for battle, when Parmenio, whose great reputation in war gave him weight and influence, attempted to check the eagerness of his youthful sovereign by the following observations:

It appears advisable to encamp for the present on the river's side as we are. For the enemy, far inferior in infantry, will not in my opinion dare to spend the night in our vicinity; so that we may cross with ease in the morning, before their troops can be formed and brought to oppose us. But the attempt at present appears dangerous, because we cannot lead our army in line through the river, as many parts of it are evidently deep, and the banks are, as you see, very high, and in some places precipitous. When, therefore, our men reach the opposite bank in disorder and in separate columns, they will be exposed to the attacks of the enemy's cavalry drawn up in line. Should this our first attempt prove a failure, the immediate consequences must prove disastrous, and the final issue of the contest be seriously affected.

Alexander replied:—

I am aware of all this, Parmenio, but feel ashamed, after crossing the Hellespont without difficulty; to allow this petty stream to prevent us from fording it as we are. I regard such conduct as inconsistent with the glory of the Macedonians, and my own eagerness to encounter dangers. I feel also, that the Persians, if they do not instantly suffer evils correspondent to their fears, will recover their courage, as being able to face the Macedonians on the field of battle.

Had the passage of the Granicus been the sole object, the veteran general's proposition was no doubt the safest. For we know, from the writings of Xenophon, that a Persian Army, consisting principally of cavalry, could not safely encamp near an enemy superior in infantry. But Alexander felt the necessity of making a strong impression, and refused to steal an advantage, as much from a chivalrous impulse, as from a well-grounded belief that one field fairly and openly won is, in its ultimate effects, worth ten advantages attained by stealth, stratagem, or treachery.

Immediately above the right bank of the Granicus there was a step, or narrow strip of level ground, extending from the river to the foot of a long line of low hills, running parallel with the stream. The Persian cavalry, 20,000 in number, were drawn up in line on this step. The hills in their rear were crowned by an equal number of Greek mercenaries under the command of Omares, a Persian.

The Macedonian *phalanx* was composed of eight brigades, containing 2,000 men each, and commanded by eight generals of equal rank. These could act separately or conjointly, as every brigade was complete in itself. It was divided into regiments of 1,000 each, commanded by their own colonels. Each regiment was composed of two battalions of 500 each, officered in the same manner. Each battalion was subdivided into eight companies, led by their own captains. For the purpose of command, the Macedonian Army was divided into two wings. Alexander always commanded the extreme right, and the most confidential officer the extreme left. The brigades of the *phalanx* were attached arbitrarily either to the right or the left wing.

On the present occasion, the right wing consisted of the Companion cavalry, the Agrian infantry, and the archers under Philotas, the heavy lancers, and the Pæonians under Amyntas, the son of Arrhabæus, and the royal foot guards, also honoured with the title of Companions, under Nicanor, the son of Parmenio. Next to him were drawn up five brigades of the *phalanx* commanded successively by Perdiccas, Coenus, Craterus, Amyntas, the son of Andromenes, and Philip, the son of Amyntas. All were under the immediate command of Alexander.

On the extreme left were posted the Thessalian cavalry, commanded by Calas, the son of Harpalus, the confederate cavalry under Philip, the son of Menelaus, and the Thracians under Agathon. Next to him were the three remaining brigades of the *phalanx* commanded in the order of their names, by another Craterus, Meleager, and a third Philip, whose brigade touched that of his namesake the son of Amyntas. All these were under Parmenio's orders.

As soon as the Persians perceived that Alexander had placed himself at the head of the Companion cavalry, on the extreme right, they strengthened their own left with denser masses of horse. The king was easily recognised by the splendour of his arms, the white plume in his helmet, his gorgeous shield and polished *cuirass*, and by the magnificent and dazzling equipments of his immediate retinue. Both armies halted on the very brink of the river, and surveyed each other for some time. A deep silence prevailed during this moment of hesitation and doubt.

Then Alexander mounted the gallant charger destined to carry him triumphant over so many fields, and briefly exhorted his immediate companions to follow him and prove themselves good warriors.

Ptolemy, the son of Philip, whose right it was on that day to lead the attack, first entered the river. He was supported by Amyntas, the son of Arrhabæus, and Socrates, who led forward the heavy lancers, the Pæonians, the Prodromi, and one brigade of infantry. Then the whole right wing was led by Alexander into the current amidst the sound of trumpets and the loud *pæans* of the troops.

Amyntas, Ptolemy, and Socrates, soon reached the opposite bank, but struggled in vain to make their landing good, as the Persians, not content with showering their missiles from the upper ground, rode down and combated the Macedonians in the water. As Memnon and his sons, together with the flower of the Persian cavalry, were engaged in this quarter, they succeeded either in cutting down this vanguard or driving it back on Alexander, who was now advancing. He, himself, with the Companion cavalry, charged where he saw the densest mass and the greatest number of Persian chiefs assembled. The battle was more of a personal struggle between individuals than regular charges of cavalry.

In the shock Alexander shivered his lance to pieces, and called upon Aretas, his chief groom, to furnish him with another. The same misfortune had happened to him, although he continued fighting bravely with the broken stump. Holding this up, he desired his sovereign to ask someone else. Demaratus, the Corinthian, one of the Companions, then lent him his. The superior strength and skill of the Macedonians were now manifest, and the Persian javelins and scimitars were found ineffectual against the Macedonian lance, the shaft of which was made of tough cornel wood. The efforts of the cavalry drove the Persians from the bank, and Alexander, with the head of the column, gained the level step between the river and the mountains.

There he was instantly marked out by Mithridates, the son-in-law of Darius, who dashed at him at the head of a troop of horse drawn up in the form of a wedge, with a very obtuse angle. As Mithridates was in front, Alexander did not wait the attack, but spurred his horse forwards, and directing his lance against the face of his antagonist, slew him on the spot. While he was disengaging his weapon, Rhoesaces, another Persian nobleman, rode up, and with his sword struck off a part of the king's plume and helmet: Alexander pierced his breast through the corslet, and brought him also to the ground.

But this could hardly have been done without wheeling round and recharging. While he was engaged in this second single combat, Spithridates, the Ionian *satrap*, came behind him and had raised his scimitar to strike a blow, when his purpose was anticipated by Cleitus, the son of Dropidas, who, with one tremendous stroke, severed the Persian's shoulder from his body.

Cleitus was the brother of Larnicè, the nurse of Alexander, and was captain of the royal troop of the Companion cavalry, to which in an especial manner the safety of the king's person was entrusted. On this occasion he was at his post and did his duty. We have no reason to suppose that the light scimitar of Spithridates would have made a greater impression on the proof armour of Alexander than a similar weapon in the hand of Rhoesaces. But what would have been thought of the royal guards, had they allowed their sovereign, after bringing down the two foremost champions of the enemy, to be slain by the third?

On equal ground the Persians failed to withstand the charge of the Macedonian lances, and their line, gave way, first at the point where Alexander himself was engaged, finally in all directions. For Parmenio and the Thessalian and confederate cavalry had completely defeated the Persian right wing. The rout was therefore general, but the actual loss of the Persians was not great, as there was no pursuit. Among the thousand horsemen, who fell on the field, were, in addition to the chiefs before mentioned, Niphates, Petenes, Mithrobarzanes, governor of Cappadocia, Arbupales, son of Darius Artaxerxes, and Pharnaces, the brother of the queen.

The surviving leaders, among whom was Memnon, fled disgracefully, and left the Grecian mercenaries to their fate. These had remained in their position, idle spectators of the short but desperate contest which in a few minutes had dispelled the delusion that Greece could never furnish a cavalry equal to the Persian. The *phalanx* was not engaged; and the defeat of 20,000 Persian horse was achieved by the light troops and cavalry alone.

But as the mercenaries under Omares still kept their ground, the *phalanx* was brought up to attack them in front, while Alexander and Parmenio with their cavalry assailed them on both flanks. Omares fell at his post, and the whole body, with the exception of 2,000 prisoners, was cut to pieces. These saved their lives by throwing themselves on the ground and permitting the terrible *phalanx* to march over their bodies. Their lives were spared, but they were loaded with chains, and sent to till the ground in Macedonia. It is difficult to sympathise with men who for daily pay could be thus brought to array themselves against their fellow countrymen, and to fight the battles of barbarians against the captain-general of Greece.

Of the Macedonians, there fell twenty-five of the Companion cavalry, sixty other horsemen, and thirty foot soldiers. It must not be imagined that no more fell, but it is clear that the generals who wrote the account of Alexander's campaigns, mentioned the loss of only the native born Macedonians. The fallen were all buried on the field of battle, clad in their armour, the noblest shroud, according to Xenophon, for a slain warrior. The twenty-five Companions were honoured with monumental statues of bronze, the workmanship of Lysippus, the favourite sculptor of Alexander. They were erected at Dium, in Macedonia, where they remained until the rapacious Romans carried them away to Italy.

The Persian leaders were also buried with due honours, as well as the mercenary Greeks who had fallen in a bad cause.

The king was particular in his attentions to the wounded; he visited every individual, examined his wounds, and by asking how, and in what service he had received them, gave every man an opportunity of recounting and perhaps of exaggerating his deeds.

Alexander selected 300 *panoplies* as an offering for the Athenian Minerva. They were sent to Athens, and suspended in the Parthenon, with the following inscription:

Alexander, the son of Philip, and the Greeks, except the Lacedæmonians, these, from the barbarians inhabiting Asia.

This is generally regarded as a compliment to the Athenians:—if so, it was intended for the Athenians of former days, not for the contemporaries of Demosthenes; for no distinction was made between the Athenians captured in the enemy's ranks and the prisoners belonging to other states.

From the very beginning Alexander regarded Asia as his own, and the Asiatics as his subjects, His first admonition to his soldiers was, to spare their own. There occur no instances of plunder, no system of devastation, similar to that practised by Agesilaus and described by Xenophon. The only change was to substitute a Macedonian instead of a Persian *satrap*. Acting on this principle, he appointed Calas, the son of Harpalus, governor of the Hellespontian Phrygia, and ordered him to exact no more from the provincials than the regular revenue payable to Darius.

The chief city of the *satrapy* was Dascylium, situated on the Propontis, to the east of the Rhyndacus. Parmenio was sent forward, and took possession of it without resistance. Alexander himself visited Zeleia, a Homeric city on the banks of the "dark flowing waters" of the Æsepus. The river is now called Biga, and the town of the same name cannot be far from the site of the ancient Zeleia.

Alexander might have marched up the vale of the Rhyndacus, surmounted the pass called by the Turks, *the Iron Gate*, and descended into the plain of the Caicus. But he returned to Iium, as distinctly mentioned by Strabo, and marched into Southern Asia by the more frequented road through Antandrus, Adramyttium, Pergamus, and Thyateira.

The intervening towns offered no resistance, and when within eight miles of Sardes, he was met by a deputation, headed by the principal citizens and accompanied by Mithrenes, the Persian governor of the citadel. The Lydians, once a warlike and powerful nation, had, since their subjugation by Cyrus the Elder, been Persian tributaries for nearly 200 years. The yoke was, perhaps, not burdensome, but still their happiness must have depended on the character of their *satrap*, at whose mercy the policy of the Persian Government completely placed them.

But their recollections of ancient glory and independence still remained. Men in their situation seldom have an opportunity of testifying their love of the latter except by changing their masters. And such a change, if unattended with danger, is always welcomed. The deputation presented the keys of the Lydian capital to the descendant of Hercules, and had they known the weak side of their new master, would have expressed their joy at returning under the Heracleid dominion, after the long-continued usurpation of the Mermnadæ and Achæmenidæ.

Mithrenes, who came to surrender the citadel and the treasures entrusted to his care, was a traitor—perhaps a weak man, paralyzed by the defeat and death of Spithridates, his superior, and overcome by the prayers of the Sardians. But treason had been busy in the western provinces, and it appears unaccountable that so many of the connections of Darius should have been without command in the Persian camp, except we suppose that the *satraps* had disowned their authority, and fought the Battle of the Granicus in defence of their own governments, and not of the empire.

Whatever were the motives of Mithrenes, his act was base and fatal to his country. The citadel of Sardes was the most important fortress in Western Asia, and the surrender of it at this critical period furnished Alexander with money, of which he was greatly in need, and enabled him to pursue Memnon, the only antagonist in Asia Minor from whom he had anything to dread.

Alexander encamped on the banks of the Hermus, whence he issued a decree, by which all their laws, rights, and privileges, as existing before the Persian conquest, were restored to the Lydians. Their nominal independence was also proclaimed, and hailed with as much applause as if it had been real. He then ascended to the Sardian citadel, impregnable from its natural position. A lofty mountain, triangular in figure, rises abruptly from the plain of the Hermus. A deep ravine, rendering the southern side a perpendicular precipice, separates it from the frowning masses of Mount Tmolus. The summit of this isolated rock was crowned by the towers and palace of the Lydian monarchs.

According to a long-cherished tradition, an oracle had forewarned an ancient king of Lydia, that if he carried his son Leon, or as some translate it, the Lion, his son, round the citadel, it would always remain impregnable. He obeyed partially, but thought it useless to go round the precipitous side, which nature itself had apparently rendered impregnable. Alexander was struck with the boldness of the situation and extent of view from the summit. He proposed to occupy the site of the Lydian palace with a splendid temple of the Olympian Jupiter—but did not live to execute his plan. The Argives of the army, apparently in compliment to the Heracleid connection, were left to garrison the citadel.

From Sardes Alexander marched to Ephesus. Here he came first in contact with the aristocratic and democratic factions, which for the two preceding centuries had destroyed the happiness and tranquillity of every Grecian city of consequence. The aristocratic party had always been patronized by Persia, and Memnon had lately overthrown the existing democracy at Ephesus, and committed the powers of government to the opposite party. But the news of the victory at the Granicus, followed by the rumoured approach of Alexander, caused the Persians to retire to Miletus. With them also retired Amyntas, the son of Antiochus, and other Macedonian exiles, who had made Ephesus their city of refuge.

This flight restored the supremacy to the democratic faction, which proceeded with more violence than justice to take vengeance on its opponents. Some of the aristocratic leaders were immediately stoned to death, and a general massacre was threatened, when Alexander arrived and compelled his friends to be satisfied with a bloodless supremacy. Arrian writes, that this active interference of the king in defence of the adverse party, gave him more immediate renown than any other of his deeds in Asia Minor. The conduct of the Lacedæmonians and Athenians, the two great patrons of the opposite factions, had been so different on similar occasions, that we need not be surprised at the natural effect of Alexander's more merciful and judicious conduct.

The temple of Ephesus, destroyed by fire on the night of his birth, was in the act of being rebuilt. He assigned the revenues, paid by the city to the great king, to the promotion of the work. In after-times he offered to bear the whole expense, great as it must have been, on condition of having his name alone inscribed on the building. The Ephesians prettily evaded the offer, by saying "that it did not become one god to dedicate a temple to another."

Alexander paid due honours to the great Diana of the Ephesians. The misshapen statue, the heaven-fallen idol was carried in procession, while he, at the head of his troops, formed a part of the pageantry. The disciple of Aristotle was a Polytheist in the most extensive sense of the word, and, could bow his head with equal reverence in Grecian, Tyrian, Ægyptian, and Assyrian temples.

From Ephesus Alexander marched to Miletus, the Ionian capital, celebrated for its wealth, naval power, and colonies. The governor had promised to give up the city without resistance, but the arrival of the Persian fleet, far superior to the Macedonian, had induced him to retract his word.

Miletus was situated at the mouth of the Mæander, which then emptied its waters into the upper end of a considerable creek. This is now filled up, and the fair harbour of Miletus converted into a fertile plain. This is a well-known fact, and often paralleled, for the undisturbed water of a long creek acted upon by an operative river, will necessarily become firm land. Nor does this admission contradict the observations formerly made on this subject, as they referred more to the action of rivers, the mouths of which have reached the open sea.

The entrance to the Milesian harbour was narrow, but the Macedonian fleet had occupied it previous to the arrival of the Persians. The Milesians, thus blockaded by sea and land, intimated to Alexander their wish to be neutral, and their willingness to receive the Persian as well as the Macedonian fleet into the harbour. As they had not the power to enforce their proposed system of neutrality, their offer could be regarded only as an insult. As such Alexander viewed it, and told the deputy to depart instantly and warn his fellow citizens to prepare for an assault. The deed followed the word, and Miletus was carried by storm. Three hundred Greek mercenaries, partly by swimming, partly by floating on their broad shields, reached a small island in the harbour. Alexander admiring their gallantry, spared their lives, and incorporated them with his own troops.

Although the Macedonian fleet had prevented the Persians from entering the harbour, it was not strong enough to face the enemy on the open sea. Hence its future motions became a subject of grave deliberation. Parmenio proposed the embarkation of a chosen body of the land forces, and a sudden attack on the enemy's fleet. But Alexander, whose exhausted exchequer severely felt the naval expenses, was for immediately dismantling it. He refused to risk his gallant soldiers in a contest on the unsteady and tottering waves, where the superior skill of the Phoenician and Cyprian sailors might render bravery and military discipline unavailing.

Much might be said in favour of both propositions, and the arguments of the veteran general and of the monarch are equally weighty. But it may surprise a modern reader to find that, either from policy or faith, the question mainly turned on the right interpretation of an omen. An eagle had by chance perched on a Macedonian vessel, which had been drawn ashore. Parmenio argued that as the bird's face was directed seaward, a naval victory was clearly indicated. Alexander, on the contrary, contended that as the ship on which the eagle had perched was on shore, the fair inference was that they were to obtain the victory by watching the enemy's motions from the shore, and preventing them from landing in any spot. His reasoning prevailed in the council, and the fleet was laid up in the harbour of Miletus. Parmenio was sent, at the head of a strong force, to receive the submission of the great cities Magnesia and Tralles, in the vale of the Meander; and Alexander himself marched along the coast to Halicarnassus.

Darius, on receiving intelligence of the defeat at the Granicus, and of the death of so many *satraps*, appointed Memnon his lieutenant-general, with unlimited power of action in Lower Asia and its maritime dependencies. Memnon had collected a fleet of four hundred *triremes*, with which he prepared to counteract the projects of Alexander. The rapidity of the latter's movements had wrested Ionia from the empire; but every effort was made for the preservation of Caria. Halicarnassus, its capital, situated on the south-western shore of the Ceramic gulf, was carefully fortified and provisioned. It was guarded by two citadels, one called by Strabo the island-fort, and the other Salmacis, celebrated for the supposed effeminating qualities of its fountain.

The island fortress is now united to the continent, and continues, under the name of Boodroom, to be the strongest place on that coast. The city itself was protected on the land side by an immense ditch, thirty cubits wide and fifteen deep. The besiegers had to fill this, before they could bring their battering engines to bear on the wall. Memnon had abundance of troops, of all denominations and races.

Numerous sallies took place, in one of which Neoptolemus, the son of Arrhabæus, a Macedonian exile of high rank, fell, while bearing arms against his country. In another skirmish the Persians had become masters of the bodies of some Macedonian soldiers, which, according to the laws of Grecian warfare, Alexander demanded by herald, for the purpose of burial. Diodorus writes that Memnon complied with the request, in opposition to the advice of two Athenian leaders, Ephialtes and Thrasybulus. Mitford from this draws an inference to prove the inhuman ferocity of the Demosthenean party: but this, like many other of his deductions, is unfair.

Among the southern Greeks no skirmish, however trifling, took place that was not followed by the erection of a trophy. As both parties were bound to bury their dead, the inability to do this without requesting the leave of the opposite party, was the test of defeat, and a trophy erected under such circumstances was regarded legitimate, and consequently sacred. But the Macedonians had long ceased to raise trophies, and scrupled not to destroy them if erected. The fair inference therefore from the above-mentioned fact is, that the Athenian generals were unwilling to restore the bodies unless Alexander would allow them to raise a trophy—a circumstance which, as he did not understand trifling in war, he was not likely to approve of.

As the works of the besiegers were advancing, the Athenian, Ephialtes, at the head of a chosen body of troops, and supported by Memnon, made a bold attempt to burn the works and the engines. A regular battle took place, in which the assailants were, not without difficulty, driven back. The Macedonians lost nearly as many men as at the battle of the Granicus. Among others fell Ptolemy, a general of the body guard; Clearchus, commander of the archers; and Addæus, a chiliarch or colonel of a regiment. The Persians, regarding the city as no longer tenable, set it on fire, and retired to the citadels. As these appeared impregnable, a body of troops was left to observe and blockade them.

The city was the capital of a race of princes, who, in subjection to Persia, had long governed Caria. Hecatomnus, in the preceding generation, had left three sons and two daughters. According to a practice common among the royal families in Asia, Mausolus, the eldest brother, had married Artemisia, the elder sister, who, by a law peculiar to Caria, was entitled to the throne if she survived her husband. She became a widow, and testified her respect for his memory by the erection of the splendid and tasteful monument that has given the name of Mausoleium to all similar structures. Grief soon destroyed her, and she was succeeded by the second brother, Hidrieus, who had married the younger sister, Ada. She survived him, but had been dethroned by the youngest brother, Pexodarus. Orontobates, a Persian nobleman, had married his daughter, and the Persian court had thus been induced to connive at the usurper's injustice. The deposed queen still retained the fortress of Alinda, where she was visited by Alexander, and restored to the Carian throne. She adopted her benefactor as her son; nor did he disdain to call her mother.

This princess, accustomed to the refinements and delicacies of an oriental court, was shocked at the plain fare and simple habits of the Macedonian soldier. During his stay at Alinda, she regularly supplied his table from her own kitchen, and when he was departing presented him with some of her best cooks and confectioners; but he refused to accept them, saying, "he had been supplied with better cooks by his governor, Leonnatus-a march, before day, to season his dinner, and a light dinner to prepare his supper." On this occasion he added, that Leonnatus used to examine the chests and wardrobes in which his bedding and cloaks were put, lest something of luxury or superfluity should be introduced by Olympias.

The summer was now drawing to a close, and Alexander rendered it memorable by an act of kindness, which has been oftener praised than imitated. He granted permission to all his soldiers, who had lately married, to return and spend the winter with their brides. No distinction was made between officers and privates; and the whole body marched homewards under the command of three bridegroom generals, Ptolemy, the son of Seleticus, Coenus and Meleager.

Should we view this as an act of policy, and not as emanating from the kind feelings of a warm heart, the success would be the same. Young warriors, with their laurels still green, returning to their homes and their youthful partners, and spreading over all Greece their partial accounts of the valour, generosity and kind feelings of their victorious captain-general, would be the most influential agents that ever roused eager spirits to take up arms and rush to war.

Parmenio conducted the Thessalians, the Greeks of the Confederacy, and the baggage and artillery, to Sardes, into winter quarters. But winter could not arrest Alexander's own exertions. Advancing into Lycia and Pamphylia, he proceeded to wrest the whole line of sea-coast from the enemies, and thus paralyse the operations of their superior fleet. On entering Lycia, Telmissus, a city on the banks of the Calbis, and celebrated for its race of diviners, opened its gates. He then crossed the River Xanthus, and received the submission of the cities Patara, Xanthus and Pinara. These were the seats of the Homeric heroes, Glaucus and Sarpedon, whose amiable and warlike character belonged to the Lycians in general.

The contrast between their conduct and the villainies and everlasting robberies of all the other inhabitants of the recesses of Mount Taurus, may induce the reader to dwell a moment on their character. It is delightful to feel that a free and civilized people should for so many ages have dwelt in peace and happiness, under a long succession of foreign masters. It is Strabo who gives the account:.

> While the pirates of Pamphylia and Cilicia were in their greatest state of prosperity, and masters of the sea as far as Italy, the Lycians continued their constitutional and temperate mode of life. They were not excited by any desire of dishonest gains, and adhered steadfastly to the constitution of the Lycian confederacy as established by their ancestors. Twenty-three cities are entitled to vote. Deputies from each state meet in a common council, assembled in the city previously fixed upon. The most powerful cities possess three votes each, the next in rank two, the rest one. Their contributions and liability to public offices and burdens follow the same proportion.
>
> The six most powerful, according to Artemidorus, are Xanthus, Patara, Pinara, Olympus, Myra, and Tlos. In the common council first the Lyciarch is chosen, then the other officers of the confederacy. Courts of justice, with general jurisdiction, are appointed. Formerly they deliberated concerning war, peace, and foreign alliances: but this power is now necessarily vested in the Romans; nor are they allowed to entertain such topics, except with the permission of the Romans or for their advantage. Judges and archons are, however, still elected according to

the majority of state votes. Being thus under the government of good laws, well administered, they, under the Romans, still retain their freedom, and cultivate their inherited patrimonies, and have witnessed the total extermination of the pirates.

But these quiet and good men, when incensed by wrong, used to exhibit desperate valour. Twice has Xanthus, their capital city, been distinguished in history for resisting to death and extermination, first, Harpagus, the general of Cyrus the Great, and secondly, the Roman Brutus, whose treatment of these free and brave men was singularly wicked and atrocious.

It is much to the credit of Alexander's character and policy that not a sword was drawn to oppose his progress. He, according to his general principles, would respect their franchises and privileges; and they, Cretans by descent, and living apparently under the institutions of Minos, would naturally not be averse to a Greek connection.

Alexander, continuing his march up the Xanthus, arrived in that part of Lycia called, from its original inhabitants, Milyas. There he was overtaken by deputies from the important city of Phaselis, bringing a crown of gold and offers of submission.

In descending from Milyas to Phaselis, he had to cross a mountainous ridge, the pass over which was commanded by the Pisidian town Termessus. This he took by storm, and thus conferred a signal favour on the peaceful occupiers of the lowlands, who had long been harassed by its bandit possessors.

It was now mid-winter; and the rich and luxurious city of Phaselis enabled Alexander to recruit the strength of his troops, and to enjoy a short repose himself. But this was disagreeably interrupted by a communication from Parmenio, announcing a traitorous correspondence between Alexander, the son of Aeropus, and the Persian court. We have before seen that he was almost known to have participated in the conspiracy to which Philip fell a victim, and that nothing but his apparent exertions in favour of Alexander, at a very critical period, had saved him from the fate of the other traitors. He was now the first prince of the blood, in high favour with Alexander, who had lately appointed him commander-in-chief of the Thessalian cavalry.

The purport of Parmenio's communication was, that he had arrested a suspicious-looking stranger, by name Asisines, who, when questioned, had confessed himself to be a Persian emissary: that Amyntas, the son of Antiochus, on deserting, had carried some written proposals from the son of Aeropus to Darius; that he, the emissary, had been commissioned to confer with the Lyncestian, to offer him the Macedonian throne and a thousand *talents*, provided Alexander the kings were put out of the way. The Persian was sent in chains to be interrogated by the king and council.

The king immediately placed the information before his friends, who unanimously accused him of rashness, in bestowing the most important command in the army on a man whose past conduct had rendered him justly liable to suspicion. They advised therefore his instant removal, before he could ingratiate himself with the Thessalians, and be thus enabled to do mischief.

But the management of the affair required considerable delicacy. Parmenio had only one company of Macedonians: even the Sardian garrison was Argive, and the remainder of the force under his command consisted of the Thessalians and other Greek confederates. It appeared therefore probable, that if the Lyncestian obtained the slightest hint of the discovery of the plot, he might excite some serious disturbance, or at least carry a part of the troops over to the enemy. No written orders were therefore judged prudent, but Amphoterus, an officer of high rank, was dispatched with a verbal message to Parmenio. Disguised in the native dress, and guided by Pisidians, he arrived safely at Sardes, and delivered his orders, according to which the Lyncestian was instantly taken into custody.

Phaselis was situated at the foot of that part of Mount Taurus which terminates opposite the Chelidonian islands. The highest point of the range, immediately overlooking the sea, was anciently called Solyma, from the warlike Solymi of Homer. A little to the south of this was the mountain Chimæra, with its Bellerophontic fables. It is curious that a strong flame, called by the Turks *yanar,* still burns there unconsumed, and proves to this day the connection between the fabulous poetry of the Greeks and natural *phænomena.* Mount Solyma itself is 7,800 feet high, and some of its eastern ridges, under the name of Climax, or the Ladder, descend almost abruptly to the western shore of the gulf of Attalia. Alexander therefore, in advancing from Phaselis to Perga, had either to cross the almost precipitous ridge of Mount Climax, or to march along the sea shore, at the foot of the cliffs. He preferred the latter; and as Strabo's account of this renowned adventure is particularly clear, I introduce it:

Mount Climax overhangs the Pamphylian sea, but leaves a narrow road upon the beach. This, in calm weather, is dry, and passable by travellers; but when the sea flows, the road, to a great extent, is covered by the waves. The passage over the hills is circuitous and difficult: consequently, in fine weather, the shore road is used. But Alexander, although the weather was boisterous, trusting principally to chance, set out before the swell had ceased, and the soldiers had to march during the whole day up to their middle in water.

It was a rash adventure, and attended with danger; for had a strong south wind arisen, the whole army would have been dashed against the rocks. As, on the contrary, a smart north wind had succeeded violent storms from the south, ample occasion was given to the royal sycophants to proclaim aloud, that the sea had acknowledged the sovereignty of Alexander, and obsequiously retired before its lord and master. Alexander himself made no miracle of the event: in his letters, as quoted by Plutarch, he simply wrote—

I marched from Phaselis by the way called Climax.

I quote from Langhorn's *Plutarch* in his pleasant way, refers to this pretended miracle in one of his comedies:

Menander,
How like great Alexander! Do I seek
A friend? Spontaneous he presents himself.
Have I to march where seas indignant roll?
The sea retires, and there I march.

This is in far better taste than the attempt of Josephus to illustrate the miraculous passage of the Red Sea, by a reference to this adventure.

Thence he visited in succession Perga, Aspendus, Sidè, and Sillium. At the last place his further progress eastward was arrested by hearing that the Aspendians, who had agreed to pay fifty *talents* and deliver up the horses which they were breeding for the Persian Government, were inclined to evade both conditions, and preparing to withstand a siege. He instantly retraced his steps; and, arriving sooner than these men expected, made himself master of the lower town, on the banks of the Eurymedon, and confined the Aspendians within their mountain citadel. Overawed by this activity, they submitted to harder terms than they had before refused to execute.

Thence he returned to Perga, and marched up the narrow vale of the Cestrus, with the intention of crossing Mount Taurus and entering the greater Phrygia. During this route he had to pass through the territories of the Pisidæ-Mountaineers, who retained a wild independence amidst their hill fortresses, and whose hand was always raised to smite their more civilized neighbours. A strong pass in the main ridge of Taurus, and probably in the ravine of the Cestrus, was commanded by the inhabitants of a second Telmissus. Alexander forced his way through the defile, but despaired of capturing the city without his battering train. He therefore continued his march up the Cestrus.

The Sagalassians, a powerful Pisidian tribe, possessed the upper part of the vale. These were joined by the Telmissians, who by mountain roads outstripped the Macedonian Army. The united tribes fought a gallant battle in front of Sagalassus, but were defeated, and the city was taken. The Selgæ, who dwelt in the upper vales of the Eurymedon and its tributary streams, entered into alliance with Alexander, who then brought the whole of Pisidia to acknowledge his sovereignty. This winter campaign among the snows, torrents and precipices of Mount Taurus, is one of Alexander's greatest achievements. Apparently, he was the first foreigner that ever conquered the Pisidians.

A march of five days brought him to Celænæ, the capital of the greater Phrygia. Its situation, at the sources of the Marsyas and of the Mæander, has been elegantly described by Xenophon. The town submitted without resistance; but its citadel, crowning the summit of a dark frowning rock, equally high and precipitous, was impregnable if honestly defended. The garrison however, consisting of mercenary Greeks and Carians, engaged to surrender if not relieved by a certain day. Alexander agreed to their proposal, and left fifteen hundred men to watch the fortress, and receive its submission at the appointed period. Antigonus, the son of Philip, who had married Stratonicè, either the daughter or sister of the late king, was declared *satrap* of the greater Phrygia. After the king's death he became one of his most distinguished successors. He had hitherto been the commander of the Greeks of the Confederacy.

From Celænæ Alexander sent orders to Parmenio, to join the headquarters at Gordium, whither he was himself marching. Here the whole army reunited; for the bridegrooms from Macedonia, attended by a strong body of recruits, arrived there also. At the same time came an Athenian embassy, to request Alexander to liberate the Athenians captured at the Granicus. Their request was refused, as it was judged impolitic to lead others to regard the bearing arms against united

Greece, in behalf of barbarians, as a light offence. They were, however, told to renew their petition at a more favourable season.

Gordium, in the time of Phrygian independence, was the capital of a powerful kingdom, and could boast a long line of resident monarchs. It was situated on the left bank of the River Sangarius, and as late as Livy's age, was a commercial mart of some importance. Within the citadel were built the palaces of Gordius and Midas. Thither Alexander ascended in order to examine the famous Gordian knot, the solution of which was to indicate the future sovereign of Asia. The tradition of the Phrygians respecting it is highly interesting, as presenting a vivid picture of the ancient Asiatics.

Gordius, according to the tale, was a husbandman, possessing a small plot of ground and two yokes of oxen, one for his plough and another for his cart. As he was ploughing his field an eagle perched upon the yoke, and remained till the termination of the day's labour. Anxious to obtain an explanation of the singular omen, he set out to consult the diviners of Telmissus. As he was approaching one of their villages, he saw a young maiden who had come forth to draw water: to her he opened his case. She was of the gifted race, and advised him to return home and sacrifice to Jupiter the King.

Gordius persuaded his fair adviser to accompany him, and teach him how to perform the ceremony duly and rightly. She consented, the sacrifice was completed, and the grateful husbandman married the maiden. Midas was their only son, and grew up a handsome and spirited man. In the meantime, the Phrygians had suffered severely from civil dissentions.

In their distress they consulted the gods, who answered, "that a cart should bring them a king who would terminate their internal broils." As the whole assembly was deliberating on the meaning of this oracular promise, Midas drove up his father and mother in their rustic vehicle, to the outer circle, and was immediately recognised as the sovereign promised by the oracle. In memory of the event, he consecrated the cart to Jupiter the King, and placed it in the citadel, to which he gave his father's name. The yoke was tied to the pole by a band formed of the bark of the cornel tree, and the knot on this was the celebrated test of future eminence.

In this account we see manifest traces of the existence of a republic of husbandmen in Phrygia, who, unable to free themselves from the evils of faction in any other manner, chose, like the Israelites, a king. Long before Homer's age the Phrygians had been subjected to monarchal rule, as he makes even the aged Priam refer to his youthful campaigns on the banks of the Sangarius, when he bore arms in aid of the Phrygian kings Otreus and Mygdon, against the invading Amazons, who most probably were the loose-robed Assyrians.

Various accounts were spread of the mode in which Alexander solved the difficulty. The most prevalent is, that baffled by the complicated nature of the knot, he drew his sword and cut it asunder.

This, as being supposed most accordant with his character, has obtained universal belief. But Aristobulus, who was probably present, wrote, that he took out the pin that traversed the pole, and was thus enabled to detect the clews before invisible. At all events he did not descend from the citadel without satisfying the public that he had fulfilled the tradition, and was thenceforward to be regarded as the lord of Asia.

CHAPTER 6

The Second Campaign in Asia

Alexander's object in concentrating his forces at Gordium, was the conquest of the two powerful provinces of Paphlagonia and Cappadocia. With the spring, therefore, he marched from Gordium to Ancyra, the modern Angora. Here a deputation from the Paphlagonian chiefs waited on him, professing their submission, but requesting as a favour not to be visited by an armed force. Such messages in aftertimes met with little favour from Alexander. But the period was critical, and he knew from Xenophon, that the Paphlagonian sovereign of his day could bring 100,000 horsemen into the field. Their submission was, therefore, received, and they were ordered to place themselves under the government of Calas, the *satrap* of the Hellespontian Phrygia.

He then advanced into Cappadocia, and subdued the whole country within the Halys, and a considerable part of that beyond it. The whole of Cappadocia was entrusted to the care of a *satrap* called Abistamenes by Curtius, Sabictas by Arrian. Thence he marched southward into Cilicia. The south-eastern part of Cappadocia is an elevated step, whence the waters that do not flow into the Halys, have fall sufficient to burst through the barriers of Mount Taurus in their course to the Cilician Sea. The ravines are, consequently, very narrow, and of great depth, and form defiles "where one man is better to prevent than ten to make way."

The main pass is situated between Tyana and Tarsus, and has often been celebrated in ancient histories. But its value as a military post has been much exaggerated by historians. Of this the best proof is, that no successful defence of it is recorded in history. The main ridge of Mount Taurus is intersected in this vicinity by so many streams, that great advantages are placed at the command of the assailant, and enable him to choose his point of attack.

One day's march to the north of the main pass was a fortified camp, attributed by Arrian to the Younger, by Curtius to the Elder Cyrus, who, in the campaign against Croesus, fortified it as a stationary position. As Alexander came from the Ancyra road, he did not follow the steps of the Younger Cyrus, who, we know from Xenophon, formed no stationary camp there. We may be, therefore, certain, that Curtius on this occasion followed the better authority. Parmenio, with the main body, was ordered to halt in this camp, while Alexander, with his own guards, the archers, and his favourite Agrians, entered the mountain passes by night, and turned the enemy's position.

On discovering this, the defenders of the pass fled, and left the road to the plain open. Next day the whole army surmounted the main defile and commenced the descent into Cilicia. Here information reached Alexander that Tarsus was threatened with conflagration by its *satrap* Arsames, who, according to Memnon's plan, had already laid waste a great part of the province. Alexander, with his cavalry, reached Tarsus with extraordinary speed, and saved it from destruction. But overpowered with heat and covered with dust, and seduced by the limpid appearance of the waters of the Cydnus, he imprudently bathed. Although it was summer in the plain, the stream partook more of the temperature of the melting snows of Taurus than of the circumambient atmosphere. The consequence was a violent reaction, and a fever that nearly proved fatal.

Even without the intervention of the cold waters of the Cydnus, it is almost impossible to conceive how a prince of Alexander's early age and unseasoned habits, could have borne up under the numerous mental anxieties, and the unceasing bodily labours endured by him since his accession to the throne. If we except the short repose at Dium, it had been one uninterrupted scene of violent exertion. We ought not, therefore, to wonder that nature should at last vindicate her rights, and compel a short cessation from fatigue.

Philip, an Acarnanian, was the physician on whom, at this critical period, devolved the responsibility of attending the royal patient. The fate of the two continents depended upon the result, and the Macedonians, to whom, at that moment, their king's life was literally the breath of their nostrils, were not likely to discriminate nicely between the inevitable decree of nature and the work of treason. Therefore, it may truly be said, that the lives of both physician and patient trembled in the same balance.

At the very turn of the disease, when the king was preparing to take a powerful medicine, he received a letter from Parmenio, announcing a strong suspicion that the Acarnanian had been bribed by Darius, and that his prescriptions were to be avoided. Alexander, like Julius Cæsar, and some other noble spirits, would probably have preferred being poisoned or stabbed a thousand times, rather than prolong a wretched life under the conviction that no friends, no dependants were to be trusted. While, therefore, with one hand he presented Parmenio's letter to Philip, with the other he steadily carried the medicated potion to his lips, and drank it with unhesitating confidence.

I have read, that the king before he swallowed the draught must have seen the innocence of the physician in the expression of his countenance, on which conscious truth and virtuous indignation would alone be impressed. It might have been so, but the natural effect of so serious an accusation from so high a quarter, joined with the known uncertainty of all remedies, would be an overpowering feeling of anxiety, easily to be confounded with the indications of a guilty conscience. Arrian writes:

I praise Alexander, for the confidence he placed in his friend, and for his contempt of death.

His noble conduct met with its reward. The remedy succeeded, youth prevailed, and the soldiers had soon the happiness to see their king and captain once more at their head.

Then Parmenio was sent with a strong force to occupy the passes between Cilicia and Syria. He himself, with the rest of the army, marched to the sea-coast and visited the ruins of Anchialus. These, according to Aristobulus and Ptolemy, bore witness to the former existence of a mighty city. Among other remains they saw the statue of Sardanapalus, the last monarch of Upper Assyria. It crowned the summit of a monument dedicated to his memory.

The hands of the statue had one palm across the other, as in the act of clapping. The inscription was characteristic of the man.

Sardanapalus, the son of Anacyndaraxes, built Anchialus and Tarsus in one day. But do you, O stranger, eat, drink, and be merry, as all other human pursuits are not worth this; (alluding to the clapping of his hands.)

But the Macedonian strangers were not inclined to take advice from the Assyrian debauchee, whom, on the strength of the above inscription, Mitford has attempted to raise to the character of a moral philosopher. The Assyrians, in the time of their prosperity, had penetrated into those regions, and made important settlements. Since, all the inhabitants of Cappadocia, taken in its largest acceptation, were Syrians or Assyrians. These were zealous practisers of the precepts of Sardanapalus, and consequently, the most degraded and vilest of mankind. In proof of this assertion, I refer to the account given by Strabo, of the abominations carried on under the cloak of religion, in the two great Comana temples of Cappadocia.

From Anchialus he moved westward to Soli. Thence he made an incursion into the rugged Cilicia, and connected the line of his maritime communications with the point where the revolt of Aspendus had stayed his further progress. On returning to Soli, he received dispatches from Ptolemy, the governor of Caria, and Asandrus, his *satrap* of Lydia, announcing a complete victory over Orontobates, who had been appointed the successor of Pexodarus by Darius. The victory was followed by the capture of the fortresses which had hitherto held out, and the accession of the island of Cos. Thus, the whole of Asia Minor had been subdued in the month of September, B. C, 333,

This important victory, and his own recovery, were celebrated with public games, theatrical representations, and the festivities that usually accompanied the performance of a great sacrifice. The whole army attended the image of Æsculapius, in solemn procession, and the amusing spectacle of the lamp race was exhibited at night.

Memnon had commenced naval operations with the spring. From Samos he had sailed to Chios, which was betrayed into his hands. Thence he sailed to Lesbos, and soon induced four out of the five cities of the island to renounce the Macedonian alliance, and to submit to the terms imposed on the Greeks by the peace of Antalcidas. But Mytilenè, the chief city, withstood a siege. As Memnon was eagerly pressing this forwards, he fell ill and died. This, according to Arrian, was the severest blow that could befall Darius. Memnon's plans were to reduce the islands, occupy the Hellespont, invade Macedonia, and subsidise the Southern Greeks.

How far he was capable of carrying them into effect must now remain unknown. His plans procured him a great name, but his actions are not worthy of being recorded. He was a Rhodian, whose sister, a lady of great personal beauty, had married Artabazus, the Persian *satrap* of the Hellespontian Phrygia. Hence, he became early involved in the intrigues of the Persian court. Artabazus was one of the rebellious *satraps*, and although supported by Memnon, had been compelled with him and his family to take refuge in the Macedonian court, where Philip had given them a hospitable reception. The high appointment of Mentor must have introduced Memnon again upon the stage of Asiatic politics; yet, at the commencement of the war, his situation in the Persian camp appears to have been very subordinate.

At the battle on the Granicus, he fought bravely, but, as a general, displayed no more self-possession and talent than his companions. A brave man would have taken his station with the Greek mercenaries; an able man, from a fugitive cavalry 19,000 in number, and not pursued, would have rallied some, at least, and brought them back to support the retreat of the infantry. At Ephesus his plans were counteracted; at Miletus he was too late; and at Halicarnassus he lost the strongest maritime fortress in Asia, although he was master of the sea and of 400 *triremes*, and had unlimited resources in men and money at his command. If we judge of him by his actions, we must infer that party spirit invested him with talents that did not belong to him.

Pharnabazes, his sister's son, was appointed his successor. He, in conjunction with Autophradates, the admiral, forced Mytilenè to subjection, and separated Tenedos from the confederacy. Here their enterprise and success ceased. Thymodes, the son of Mentor, arrived with a commission to convey all the Greek mercenaries to Syria. The fleet was thus left comparatively helpless.

But the hopes of the anti-Macedonian party in Greece, were great during the whole of this summer. The Persian fleet commanded the Ægean, and all the information that reached Greece was from the partisans of Persia. The Battle of Issus was not fought till October: not a single military exploit of consequence had marked the progress of the great army during the previous summer. Darius was known to have passed the Great Desert, and his camp was thronged with republican Greeks, offering and pressing their military services; and eager to reassert the supremacy of the Southern Greeks on the plains of Syria. The translation of the following passage from the famous speech of Æschines, will illustrate this assertion. He is addressing Demosthenes:

But when Darius had arrived on the sea-coast with all his forces, and Alexander, in Cilicia, was cut off from all his communications, and in want of all things, as you said, and was on the point, as you expressed it, of being trodden under foot, together with his troops, by the Persian cavalry; when the city could not bear your insolence, as you went round with your dispatches hanging from every finger, and pointed me out as melancholy in countenance and downcast in spirits, adding, that my horns were already gilt for the impending sacrifice, and that I should be crowned with the garlands as soon as any misfortune befell Alexander, yet even then you did nothing, but deferred acting till a better opportunity.

Demosthenes was content with speaking, but Agis, the king of Sparta, was more active: he sailed in a *trireme*, and had an interview with Pharnabazus at the small island of Syphnus, where they conferred on the best manner of forming an anti-Macedonian party in Greece. But the arrival of the information of the defeat at Issus, put a sudden end to their deliberations.

Darius had encamped in the great plain between the Syrian Gates and the modern Aleppo. There he prepared to wait the attack of his antagonist. But the long delay caused by the illness of Alexander, by the expedition into Western Cilicia, and by the apparent necessity of waiting the result of the operations in Caria, induced Darius to imagine that his opponent had no intention to give him battle.

The Persian king was not without Greek advisers; among others was Charidemus, the Athenian exile. This democrat, having sought the court of a despot as a refuge, was not forgetful of his liberty of speech; but having overstepped those limits of decorum, of which the Medes and Persians were immutably jealous, was put to death. Amyntas, the son of Antiochus, besought Darius to remain in his camp, and assured him, from his knowledge of Alexander's character, that he would be certain to seek his enemy wherever he was to be found. But Darius was confident of success, and hostile to delay; the principal part of the equipage and court was, therefore, sent to Damascus, and the army began to march into Cilicia.

From Soli, Philotas with the cavalry crossed the great alluvial flat formed by the depositions of the Cydnus and the Sarus, and called the Aleian plain by the ancients, while Alexander conducted the infantry along the sea-coast, and visited, first, a temple of Minerva, built on a rising mound called Magarsus, and then Mallus. To this city, an Argive colony, he remitted all the public taxes, and sacrificed to their supposed founder, Amphilochus, with all the honours due to a demi-god. The Persians had, of late years, behaved tyrannically to most of their subjects in Western Asia. Caria, as we have already seen, had been deprived of its native princes: so, had Paphlagonia and Cilicia: for the Syenesis, (long the name of the independent kings of the latter province,) had been replaced by a *satrap*. The natives had, consequently, all welcomed with pleasure their change of masters.

At Mallus, Alexander received information of the advance of the Persian Army to a place called Sochi, within two days march of the Syrian Gates. On this he summoned a council of war, and consulted it as to ulterior measures. The council unanimously advised him to advance and give the enemy battle. In accordance with this resolution, the army moved forwards, and in two days arrived at Castabala. There Parmenio met the king. He had forced his way over the western ridge of Mount Amanus, through the pass called the lower Amanian gates, had captured Issus, and occupied the more eastern passes into Syria. In two days more the army surmounted the Xenophonteian gates of Cilicia and Syria, and encamped at Myriandrus. A heavy storm of wind and rain confined the Macedonians within their camp during the ensuing night. Next day Alexander was surprised by the intelligence that Darius was in his rear.

The Persians had marched through the upper Amanian gates into the plain of Issus, captured that town, and put the Macedonian invalids to a cruel death. Thence Darius advanced to the Pinarus, a river that flows through the plain of Issus into the western side of the head of the gulf.

Alexander could not at first believe that Darius was in his rear; he therefore ordered a few of the Companions to embark in a thirty-oared galley, to sail up the gulf, and bring back accurate intelligence. Nothing can be a stronger proof either of the overweening confidence or of the extraordinary imbecility of the Persian leaders, than that, with the full command of the sea, with innumerable ships, and with time sufficient to have concentrated their whole naval force, they had not apparently a single vessel in the Issic gulf, or on the Cilician coast. The Companions on board the galley executed their orders, and reported that the curve of the bay had enabled them to see the whole country, to the west of the gates, covered with the enemy's troops. Upon this Alexander summoned the generals, the chief officers of the cavalry, and the leaders of the confederates, and addressed them in a speech, of which Arrian has enumerated the principal topics.

When he had finished speaking, the veteran officers crowded round their young captain, embraced his hands, cheered his hopes by their confident speeches, and desired him to lead them to the field without delay. The day was now drawing to a close, the men took their evening meal, and the whole army, preceded by a strong reconnoitring party, retraced its steps towards the gates. At midnight it reoccupied the defile. Strong watches were stationed on the surrounding heights, whilst the rest were indulged with a short repose. The king ascended a mountain, whence he could see the whole plain blazing with the camp fires of the Persian host. There he erected an altar, and with his usual attention to religious duties, sacrificed by torch-light to the patron gods of the place.

With the dawn the army moved down the road, in single column as long as the pass was narrow; but as it opened, the column was regularly formed into line, with the mountain on the right and the sea on the left hand. Alexander, as usual, commanded the right and Parmenio the left wing. Craterus under Parmenio, and Nicanor under Alexander, commanded the wings of the *phalanx*.

Darius, whose movements were embarrassed by the multitude of his forces, ordered his 30,000 cavalry and 20,000 light troops to cross the Pinarus, that he might have more room to form his lines. In the centre he stationed his heavy armed Greek mercenaries, 30,000 in number, the largest Greek force of that denomination mentioned in history. On each side he distributed 60,000 Persians, armed in a similar manner.

These troops were called Cardaces, all natives of Persis, or Persia Proper, and trained to arms from their youth. To the extreme left of these were posted 20,000 light troops, on the side of a hill, and threatening the rear of Alexander's right wing. To understand this, it must be supposed, that the mountain at the western foot of which the Pinarus flows, curves to the east with an inclination to the south. Alexander's troops, who occupied a much shorter portion of the course of the Pinarus, were thus not only outflanked, but had their right wing completely turned.

While Darius was thus forming his line, Alexander brought up his cavalry, and sending the Peloponnesians and other confederates to the left wing, retained the Companions and the Thessalians. His orders to Parmenio were to keep close to the sea and avoid being turned.

But when Darius had recalled his cavalry and posted it between the Cardaces of the right wing and the sea, Alexander, alarmed for the safety of his own left, weak in horse, dispatched the Thessalians by the rear to the support of Parmenio. In front of the Companions were the Prodromi and Pæonians. The Agrians, supported by a body of archers and cavalry, were so drawn up as to face the enemy posted on the hill commanding the rear.

Alexander had determined to make the main attack with his right wing, he made a trial of the gallantry of these troops on the enemy's left, and ordered the Agrians, the archers, and the before-mentioned cavalry, to charge them. But instead of waiting to receive the attack, the cowards, numerous as they were, retired from the side to the summit of the hill. Satisfied, therefore, that he had nothing to dread from that quarter, Alexander incorporated the Agrians and archers with the right wing, and left the 300 cavalry to keep their opponents in check.

The infantry with which he proposed to support the charge of the Companion cavalry were the guards and the Agema, composed of the picked men of the *phalanx*. The *phalanx* itself, consisting on the present occasion of only five brigades, was drawn up to face the Greeks. The two lines were now in sight of each other, and the Persians remained motionless on the high banks of the Pinarus. The Greek tacticians had imputed the defeat on the Granicus to the false position of the cavalry, and the want of a sufficient number of Greek infantry.

Here both mistakes were avoided, and a Grecian force, which even Charidemus had judged sufficient, brought into the field. They were also admirably posted, as the banks of the Pinarus were in general precipitous, and intrenchments had been thrown up where access appeared most easy. No doubt can be entertained of the very critical situation in which Alexander was placed;—all his communications with his late conquests were cut off, and he had no alternative between victory and starvation: but he could rely upon his troops.

As the Macedonians were advancing slowly and in excellent order, the king rode down the lines, exhorting them all to be brave men, and addressing by name, not only the generals but the captains of horse and foot, and every man, Macedonian, confederate, or mercenary, distinguished either for rank or merit. His presence and short addresses were hailed with universal acclamations, and urgent requests not to lose time but to lead forwards.

As soon, therefore, as the line was within reach of the Persian missiles, Alexander and the right wing charged rapidly, crossed the Pinarus, and engaged the enemy hand to hand. The clouds of missiles did not interrupt their progress for a moment. The Cardaces, panic-struck by the suddenness and energy of the charge, fled almost without a blow; but Darius, who with the Kinsmen and the Immortals were stationed behind them, must have presented a vigorous resistance, for a considerable time elapsed before Alexander could turn his attention to the operations of his centre and left.

In the meantime, the *phalanx* had not been so successful. The broken ground, the river and its precipitous banks, ill adapted for its operations, had been ably turned to advantage by the Greeks. Yet the contest had been desperate; on one side the Macedonians exerted every nerve to support the reputation of the *phalanx*, as being hitherto invincible, and the Greeks, from a long existing spirit of jealousy, were as anxious to break the charm; but the victory indisputably had inclined in favour of the Greeks. They had penetrated the *phalanx* in various parts, and had slain Ptolemy, a general of brigade, with 120 Macedonians of rank, when Alexander, now completely victorious, attacked the Greeks in flank, and instantly changed the face of affairs. The *phalanx*, thus relieved from the immediate pressure, finally contributed to the utter defeat of their opponents.

We hear nothing of the behaviour of the Cardaces in the right wing, probably their conduct was equally disgraceful with that of their countrymen on the right. The behaviour of the Persian cavalry was totally different. They did not even wait to be attacked on the right bank of the Pinarus, but crossed it and engaged the Thessalian and confederate horse with spirit and success. Parmenio, with all his skill, supported by the acknowledged gallantry of the Thessalian cavalry, had with difficulty maintained his position, when the decisive information reached the Persians that the king had fled. Then they also, acting on a well-known Asiatic principle, joined him in his flight.

They were closely pursued by the Thessalians, who overtook many, as the Persian horses were unable to move rapidly after the fatigues of the day, under the heavy weight of their steel-clad riders. Ten thousand Persian horsemen and 100,000 infantry are said to have fallen in this battle. Perhaps the statement is not exaggerated, for as the only mode of regaining Syria was by the vale of the Pinarus, thousands of the Persian infantry must have been crushed beneath the horses' hoofs of their own cavalry, which was the last body to quit the field.

Alexander did not pursue until he witnessed the repulse, or more properly speaking, the retreat of the Persian cavalry. Then he attempted to overtake Darius, who had fled in his chariot as long as the ground would permit him; on reaching rougher roads he mounted a horse, and left his chariot, shield, bow, and royal robe behind him, nor did he cease his flight till he had placed the Euphrates between him and the victor. We must charitably hope that he did not finally despair of winning the field before it was too late to attempt to save his wife, son, and daughters. The battle lasted long, for the Macedonians marched from the gates at break of day, and night overtook Alexander after a short pursuit, when he returned and took possession of the Persian camp.

Thus terminated this great battle, contrary to the expectation of all nations, who had universally regarded the contest as certain of terminating in the destruction of the invader. The same feeling had partially pervaded the Macedonian camp. Harpalus, Alexander's youthful friend, whom as his constitution rendered him incapable of military duties, he had appointed his treasurer, fled into Greece a few days before the battle, and carried with him the military chest and its contents; and many of the confederates, among whom Aristodemus the Pheræan and Brianor the Acarnanian are mentioned by Arrian, deserted to the Persians. Men could hardly be brought to imagine that a force like that conducted by Darius could possibly experience a defeat.

It is needless to mention nations and multitudes, perhaps of no great service in the day of battle, but there were five bodies of men in the Persian Army, which alone formed as formidable an army as ever was brought to meet an enemy. These were:

The heavy armed Greeks	30,000
The Persian cavalry	30,000
The Immortals	10,000
The troops called the Royal Kinsmen	15,000
The Cardaces	60,000

Hence it is manifest, that the Macedonians on this day conquered not the Persians alone, but the united efforts of Southern Greece and Persia. It is this galling truth that, among other causes, rendered the republican Greeks so hostile to Alexander. All the active partisans of that faction were at Issus, nor were the survivors dispirited by their defeat. Agis, King of Sparta, gathered 8,000 who had returned to Greece by various ways, and fought with them a bloody battle against Antipater, who with difficulty defeated them, the Spartans and their Allies. Without taking these facts into consideration, it is impossible duly to estimate the difficulties surmounted by Alexander.

According to Plutarch, the Macedonians had reserved for the king the tent of Darius, with all its Persian officers, furniture, and ornaments. As soon as he had laid aside his armour, he said to his friends, "Let us refresh ourselves after the fatigues of the day in the bath of Darius."

"Say rather," said one of his friends, "in the bath of Alexander, for the property of the vanquished is and should be called the victor's."

When he viewed the vials, ewers, caskets, and other vases, curiously wrought in gold, inhaled the fragrant perfumes, and saw the splendid furniture of the spacious apartments, he turned to his friends and said: "This, then, it seems, it was to be a king." While seated at table, he was struck with the loud wailings of women in his immediate vicinity. On inquiring into the cause, he was informed that the mother, queen, and daughters of Darius had recognised the royal chariot, shield, and robe, and were lamenting his supposed death. Alexander immediately commissioned Leonnatus to inform the mourners that Darius had escaped in safety; and to add, that they were to retain their royal state, ornaments, and titles, that Alexander had no personal animosity against Darius, and was only engaged in a legitimate struggle for the empire of Asia.

I quote Arrian's words:

> The above account is given by Aristobulus and Ptolemy. A report also prevails, that Alexander, accompanied by no one but Hephæstion, visited the princesses on the following day, and that the queen-mother, not knowing which was the king, as the dress and arms of the two were the same, prostrated herself before Hephæstion, as he was the taller. But when Hephæstion had drawn back, and one of the attendants had pointed to Alexander, as being the king, and the queen, confused by her mistake; was retiring, Alexander told her there had been no mistake, for his friend was also Alexander. I have written this report not as true, nor yet as altogether to be disbelieved. But if it be true, I praise Alexander for his compassionate kindness to the princesses, and the affection and respect shown by him to his friend; and if it be not true, I praise him for his general character, which made writers conclude, that such actions and speeches would, if ascribed to Alexander, appear probable.

In the present case we must be content with the latter clause of the eulogy, for long after this, Alexander, in a letter quoted by Plutarch, writes:

> For my part, I have neither seen nor desired to see the wife of Darius; so far from that, I have not suffered any man to speak of her beauty before me.

On the following day, although he had received a sword wound in the thigh, he visited the wounded, and buried the dead with great magnificence. He himself spoke their funeral oration. The soldiers and officers who had principally distinguished themselves were publicly praised, and received honours and rewards according to their rank. Among the Persians slain were Arsames, Rheomithres, Atizyes, and Sabaces, the *satraps* respectively of Cilicia, the Greater Phrygia, Paphlagonia, and Egypt. These, and others of high rank, were buried according to the orders of Sysigambis, the mother of Darius.

Of the Greek mercenaries who fought in the battle, 4,000 accompanied Darius in his march to the Upper Provinces, 8,000 under Amyntas, the son of Antiochus, reached Tripolis in Phoenicia. There they embarked on board the fleet which had conveyed many of them from the Ægean. Amyntas then persuaded them to sail into Egypt and seize upon it, vacant by the death of the *satrap*. On landing, Amyntas first gave out that he came as the legitimate successor of Sabaces, but unable to restrain his troops from plundering and maltreating the natives, he was soon discovered to be an impostor. A war then took place, in which, after some successes, Amyntas fell. Thus perished a Macedonian prince of considerable talents, and who had distinguished himself by inveterate enmity against Alexander.

From Cilicia, Parmenio, at the head of the Thessalian cavalry, was sent to seize the treasures, equipage, and court of Darius at Damascus. This easy service, accompanied with the probability of great booty, was assigned to the Thessalians as a reward for their exertions and sufferings in the late battle. Alexander himself marched southward along the coast. The island Aradus, with its dependencies on the continent, was the first Phoenician state that submitted. The king was with the Persian fleet, but the prince presented Alexander with a crown of gold, and surrendered his father's possessions.

Aradus was then a maritime power of some consequence. The city covered with its buildings the modern island of Rouad. It possessed another town on the continent, by name Marathus. Here ambassadors from Darius overtook Alexander, and as their proposals and the answer of Alexander are highly interesting, and illustrative both of the manners and diplomacy of the age, I introduce the whole from Arrian. Darius wrote:

> That between Philip and Artaxerxes there had existed a treaty of friendship and alliance; that Philip, without provocation, had attacked Arses; that since the accession of Darius, Alexander had sent no one to confirm the ancient treaty of friendship and alliance, but had crossed over into Asia, and most seriously injured the Persians; that he had, therefore, descended to the sea-coast to defend his territories and recover his inherited empire; that the will of some deity had decided the fate of the battle; that he, a king, requested a king to restore his captured mother, wife, and children; that it was his wish to form a treaty of friendship and alliance with Alexander, and therefore desired him to send back Meniscus and Arsimas, his ambassadors, accompanied by persons commissioned to treat on the subject, and give and receive the necessary pledges.

Alexander returned an answer by Thersippus, his own messenger, whose orders were merely to deliver the letter into the hands of Darius, and not to enter into any oral communications. This is the letter:

> Your ancestors, without any provocation, invaded Macedonia and the rest of Greece, and inflicted serious injuries on us. I, being elected Captain-General of the Greeks, passed over into Asia, in order to take vengeance on the Persians. It was you commenced the war, for you aided the Perinthians, who had aggrieved my father, and Ochus sent a military force into Thrace, a part of our empire. In your own public letters, you boasted to all the world that you had suborned the assassins of my father. You, with your accomplice Bagoas, slew Arses, and seized the government, contrary to justice, contrary to the Persian law, and in violation of the rights of the Persian nation.
>
> You also, in a spirit of hostility to me, wrote letters inciting the Greeks to war against me, and offered money to the Lacedæmonians and other states, which the Lacedæmonians accepted, but all the other states refused. You bribed my friends to betray my interests; you attempted to destroy the peace established by me in Greece. I therefore warred on you, as you had evidently been the first to commence hostilities. Since I conquered first your generals and *satraps*, and lately yourself and army, and by the gift

of the gods possess the country, I treat with particular attention those of your soldiers who fell not on the field of battle, but took refuge with me; and so far from their continuance with me being compulsory, they are willing to serve under my banners. As I therefore am now master of all Asia, come in person to me. any fears for your personal safety, send some friends to receive my pledged faith. On coming to me, ask for your mother, wife and children, and whatever else you may wish, and receive them; for every reasonable request shall be granted. Henceforth, if you have any communication to make, address me as the King of Asia; and pretend not to treat with me on equal terms, but petition me as the master of your fate: if not, I shall regard it as an insult, and take measures accordingly. If, however, you still propose to dispute the sovereignty with me, do not fly, but stand your ground, as I will march and attack you wherever you may be.

This certainly is not worded in the style of modern dispatches: but were it made a model for drawing up such papers, the art of diplomacy might be reduced to very simple principles. There is no attempt to delude, no wish to overreach, no desire to lull his antagonist into a fatal security: but the final object in view, and the resolution to attain it, are distinctly mentioned, and the sword made the only arbiter of the dispute.

The Persian court, with the treasures and the families of the principal Persians, and the foreign ambassadors, had been captured by Parmenio. The whole body had moved eastward, but had been overtaken through the activity of the Thessalians, or the treachery of their own guides. The Thessalians reaped a rich harvest of booty upon the occasion. Alexander ordered Parmenio to conduct the whole convoy back to Damascus, and to send the foreign ambassadors to headquarters. Among these were Theban, Athenian, and Lacedæmonian envoys.

Alexander ordered the Thebans to be immediately set at liberty, as he felt conscious that they were justified in having recourse to any power likely to restore their country. The Lacedæmonians, with whom he was virtually at war, were thrown into prison, but released after the Battle of Arbela. According to the law of Greece the Athenian ambassadors were traitors; and it is difficult to say in what capacity they could appear at the Persian court, with which, in their confederate character, they were at open war. They, however, were immediately set at large, principally, as Alexander himself alleged, for the sake of their chief, Iphicrates, the son of the protector of Eurydicè and her infant princes.

From Marathus Alexander marched to Byblus, an ancient town celebrated for the worship of Adonis. The king was with the Persian fleet, but the inhabitants, like the Aradians, submitted.

The Sidonians did not wait to be summoned, but eagerly availed themselves of the opportunity of shaking off the Persian yoke. Twenty years had not elapsed since Sidon had been captured by Ochus, and burnt by the inhabitants in a fit of phrenzy and despair. Forty thousand Sidonians are stated to have perished in the conflagration. If we can believe Diodorus, the conduct of Mentor the Rhodian, on the occasion, was most execrable. He commanded the auxiliaries in the Sidonian service, and betrayed his employers into the hands of their tyrants.

Alexander was now in the centre of Phoenicia, the cradle of Greek literature, and intimately connected with the remote traditions of the earliest colonization of Greece. With Phoenicia are connected the names of Europa, Minos, and Rhadamanthus, of Cadmus, Semele, and Dionysus; and not even Egypt had left a deeper impress of her intellect and arts on the plastic mind of Greece. But events unhappily occurred which prevented Alexander from hailing her as the mother of letters, commerce and civilization, and caused the siege of Tyre to be the most mournful page in his history. While he still remained at Sidon, a Tyrian deputation waited upon him, presented him with the customary crown of gold, and expressed the wish of the Tyrians to acknowledge his authority and execute his commands.

He dismissed the deputies with honour, and announced to them his intention to visit Tyre, and to offer sacrifices in the temple of Hercules; "not the Grecian hero, his ancestor," says Arrian, "but another Hercules, worshipped many ages before him in a temple the oldest known on earth." Selden, in his treatise concerning the Syrian gods, has identified this Hercules with the Scripture Moloch, on whose altars the Tyrians and their Carthaginian colonists used, on extraordinary occasions, to offer human victims. It was consequently in the temple of Moloch, "horrid king," that Alexander wished to sacrifice, but certainly not with the impious rites, of his oriental worshippers.

The Tyrians, imagining it more easy to exclude than to expel their royal visitor, refused Alexander admission within their walls; and, according to Curtius, informed him that the original temple was still standing in Old Tyre, where the god might be duly honoured.

On receiving this refusal, Alexander summoned a general council of officers, and thus spoke:

Friends and Allies! In my opinion we cannot march safely into Egypt while the Persians are, masters of the sea; nor pursue Darius while, in our rear, Tyre remains undecided in her policy, and Cyprus and Egypt are in the power of the Persians. The latter alternative is peculiarly hazardous, both for other reasons and on account of the state of Greece: for should we pursue Darius and march to Babylon, I fear the Persians, taking advantage of our absence, might re-capture the maritime cities, gather a powerful force, and transfer the war to Greece. The Lacedæmonians are already our open enemies; and the Athenians are restrained more by their fears of our arms than affection to our cause.

But if we capture Tyre, and thus take possession of all Phoenicia, the Phoenician fleet, the most numerous and efficient part of the Persian Navy, will most probably come over to us: for when they hear that we are in possession of their homes and families, the seamen and naval combatants will not be likely to endure the hardships of sea and war in behalf of strangers. Should this be the result, Cyprus must either willingly follow, or be invaded, and easily subdued. When we sweep the seas with the united navies of Phoenicia, Macedonia and Cyprus, our maritime superiority will be undisputed, and the expedition to Egypt facilitated.

Finally, by the conquest of Egypt, all future alarms for the safety of Greece and Macedonia will be removed, and we shall commence our march to Babylon with a conscious feeling of the security of our homes, and with additional fame, from having deprived the Persians of all communication with the sea, and of the provinces to the west of the Euphrates.

These arguments easily induced the Macedonians and their Allies to commence the siege of Tyre.

The Tyrians, although not so early celebrated either in sacred or profane histories, had yet attained greater renown than their Sidonian kinsmen. It is useless to conjecture at what period or under what circumstances these eastern colonists had quitted the shores of the Persian Gulf, and fixed their seats on the narrow belt between the mountains of Lebanon and the sea. Probably at first, they were only factories, established for connecting the trade between the eastern and western world. If so, their origin must be sought among the natives to the east of the Assyrians, as that race of industrious cultivators possessed no shipping, and was hostile to commerce.

The colonists took root on this shore, became prosperous and wealthy, covered the Mediterranean with their fleets, and its shores with their factories. Tyre in the course of time became the dominant city, and under her supremacy were founded the Phoenician colonies in Greece, Sicily, Africa, and Spain. The wealth of her merchant princes had often tempted the cupidity of the despots of Asia. Salmanassar, the Assyrian conqueror of Israel, directed his attacks against Tyre, and continued them for five years, but was finally compelled to raise the siege. Nabuchadonosor was more persevering, and succeeded in capturing the city, after a siege that lasted thirteen years.

The old town, situated on the continent, was never rebuilt; but a new Tyre rose from its ruins. This occupied the area of a small island, described by Pliny as two miles and a half in circumference. On this confined space a large population existed, and remedied the want of extent by raising story upon story, on the plan followed by the ancient inhabitants of Edinburgh. It was separated from the main land by an armlet of the sea, about half a mile in breadth and about eighteen feet deep. The city was encircled by walls and fortifications of great strength and height, and scarcely pregnable even if accessible. The citizens were bold and skilful, and amply supplied with arms, engines, and other warlike munitions.

Apparently, no monarch ever undertook a more hopeless task than the capture of Tyre, with the means of offence possessed by Alexander. But no difficulties could daunt him. Without a single ship, and in the face of a formidable, navy, he prepared to take an island fortress with his land forces. His plan was to construct a mound from the shore to the city walls, erect his battering rams on the western end, there effect a breach, and carry the town by storm.

Materials were abundant; the whole shore was strewed with the ruins of old Tyre; and the activity of the leader was well seconded by the zeal of his troops. The work advanced rapidly at first. The waters were shallow, and the loose and sandy soil easily allowed the piles to reach the more solid strata below. But as the mole advanced into deeper water the difficulties of the undertaking became more evident. The labour of construction was greater, the currents more rapid, the progress slower, and the annoyance given by the enemy more effectual.

Missiles, discharged from the engines erected on the wall, reached the work in front; *triremes*, properly fitted out, attacked it on both flanks. The men employed found it difficult to carry on the labour, and at the same time to defend themselves. Engines were therefore raised on the sides of the mounds, to resist the *triremes*; and two wooden towers were built at the extreme end, in order to clear the city walls of their defenders. These were hung in front with raw hides, the best defence against the enemy's fire-darts.

To counteract these measures, the Tyrians constructed a fire ship, filled with the most combustible materials, and towed it to the mound. They then laid it alongside of the wooden towers, and there set fire to it. When the flames had taken effect, a general attack was made by the Tyrian fleet in front and on both sides. The Macedonians, blinded by the smoke, and enveloped in flames, could offer no effectual resistance. The Tyrians ascended the mound, destroyed the engines, and directed the progress of the flames. Their success was complete, and in a few hours the labours of the Macedonians were rendered useless.

Alexander possessed perseverance as well as ardency of character. He recommended the construction of the mound on a larger scale, so as to admit more engines and a broader line of combatants. In the interval he varied his labours by making a short excursion against the robber tribes of Mount Lebanon. This was not a service of great danger, but the necessity of pursuing the robbers into the recesses of their mountains, occasioned the following adventure, which Plutarch has recorded upon the authority of Chares.

Lysimachus, his preceptor in earlier days, had accompanied Alexander into Asia. Neither older nor less valiant than Phoenix, he claimed a right to attend his former pupil on all such expeditions. Night overtook the party among the wilds of Anti-Libanus; the rugged ground compelled them to quit their horses, but the strength of the old man began rapidly to sink under the united effects of age, fatigue, and cold. Alexander would not forsake him, and had to pass a dark and cold night in an exposed situation. In this perplexity he observed at a distance a number of scattered fires which the enemy had lighted: depending upon his swiftness and activity, he ran to the nearest fire, killed two of the barbarians who were watching it, seized a lighted brand, and hastened with it to his party. They soon kindled a large fire, and passed the night in safety. In eleven days, he received the submission of most of the mountain chiefs, and then descended to Sidon.

He was convinced by this time that he could not entertain any reasonable hope of taking Tyre without the co-operation of a fleet. Winter had now set in, and he had every reason to hope that the Phoenician fleets would return, and as usual, spend that season in their own harbours. He was not disappointed; the kings of Aradus, of Byblus, and Sidon, returned home, and finding their cities occupied by Alexander, placed their fleets at his disposal. A few ships also joined from other harbours. Thus, the king suddenly found himself master of more than a hundred sail. This number was soon after more than doubled by the junction of the kings of Cyprus, with a hundred and twenty ships of war. These were Greeks, but their seasonable arrival was too welcome to admit of reproaches for past misconduct; all was forgotten, and their present appointments confirmed.

CHAPTER 7

Third Campaign, B.C. 332

The siege of Tyre occupied the first five months of this year, supposing it to have commenced in November, B.C. 333, but if it did not commence till December, the capture did not occur till the end of June, 332. The Tyrians were surprised and dismayed when Alexander came with his formidable fleet in sight of their city. Their first impulse was to draw out their vessels and give battle; but the enemy's superiority disheartened them. Their next care was to prevent their own fleet from being attacked. To ensure this they sunk as many *triremes* in the mouths of their two harbours as would fill the intervening space,

The island, now a peninsula, was in shape a parallelogram, with its longest sides exposed to the north and south; the western end threw out a small promontory to the north, and in the curve thus made was the principal harbour, secured by strong piers, and a narrow entrance; off this Alexander stationed the Cyprian fleet, with orders to keep it closely blockaded. In rough weather the fleet could take refuge in the northern angle, between the mound and the shore. The opposite side was occupied by the Phoenician fleet, which thence watched the southern harbour.

This was the only use derived from the mound, as the city walls in front of it were 150 feet high, and of proportional solidity. Had not this wall defied the battering ram, the Tyrians had ample time and room to triple and quadruple their defences on that single point. It does not appear, however, that the mound ever reached the walls, or that an assault was made from that quarter. The camp was now filled with smiths, carpenters, and engineers, from Rhodes and Cyprus, who constructed huge rafts, on which battering rams and other engines were erected, and exposed the whole circumference of the walls to attack.

But it was found that these enormous masses could not approach close enough to allow the engines to be plied with effect, as the outermost foundations of the wall were protected by a breastwork of huge stones, placed there to break the violence of the waves. The Macedonians, therefore, with great labour and loss of time, had to remove these unwieldly obstacles and to clear the ground. The vessels employed in this service experienced every species of active annoyance from the Tyrians. Small boats with strong decks slipped under their sterns, and cutting their cables, sent them adrift.

And when Alexander had protected his working vessels with a line of boats similarly decked, the Tyrian divers eluded their vigilance and cut the cables close to their anchors. Chain cables were finally substituted, and the work proceeded. Ropes were fastened to immense masses, and they were drawn to the mound and sunk in deep water between its western end and the wall. It was probably these stones that, in aftertimes, converted the island into a peninsula.

At this period the Tyrians made an attempt to regain their naval superiority. They secretly prepared three *quinqueremes*, three *quadriremes*, and seven *triremes*; these they manned with their most skilful and active sailors, and with their best armed and boldest warriors. The intention was to surprise the Cyprian fleet; the time chosen midday—when the sailors usually went ashore, and the watches relaxed their vigilance. Then the Tyrian ships quietly glided one by one from the inner harbour, formed their line in silence, and as soon as they came in sight of the Cyprians, gave a gallant cheer and plied every oar with zeal and effect. The first shock sent down three *quinqueremes*, and in one of them, Pnytagoras, a Cyprian king; the rest, partly empty and partly half manned, were driven ashore, where the victors prepared to destroy them.

Alexander's tent was pitched on the shore not far from the station of the Phoenician fleet. He, like the rest, probably in consequence of the heat, used to retire to his tent at noon. On this day his stay had been much shorter than usual, and he had already joined the Phoenician fleet, when the alarm was given of the Tyrian sally. The crews were instantly hurried on board, the greater number ordered to station themselves off the southern harbour, to prevent another sally from that quarter, while he, with all the *quinqueremes* and five *triremes*, moved round the western end of the island as rapidly as the crews could row.

The Tyrians, who from the walls viewed this movement, and recognised Alexander by his dress and arms, saw that if he succeeded in doubling the point and gaining the entrance into the northern harbour before their ships returned, their retreat must inevitably be cut off. One universal cry was therefore raised, and ten thousand voices called upon the detached party to return; and when the combatants, in the moment of their triumph, disregarded sounds easily to be mistaken for cheers of applause and encouragement, signals were displayed on every conspicuous point. These were at length observed, but too late for the safety of the ships.

A few regained the harbour, the greater number were disabled, and a *quinquereme* and the three quadriremes were taken without being damaged. The crews abandoned them and swam to the shore. The loss of lives was, therefore, trifling.

The attempts to batter down the walls were no longer liable to be interrupted by the Tyrian Navy, but great difficulties still remained; for the besieged, from their commanding position on the walls, could seriously annoy the men who worked the engines. Some they caught with grappling-hooks, and dragged within the walls; others they crushed with large stones or pierced with engine darts. They also threw hot sand on their nearer assailants; this penetrated the chinks of their armour, and rendered the wearer frantic with pain. Diodorus adds, and he could not have invented the tale, that from their fire-casting engines they threw red-hot iron balls among the dense masses of the besiegers, and seldom missed their aim.

The attack on the eastern and western sides had already failed, when a more vulnerable part was found in the southern wall; a small breach was there made, and a slight assault by way of trial given. The ensuing day was devoted to preparations for the final effort; every ship was put in requisition and furnished with missiles, its proper place assigned, and orders given to attack at the preconcerted signal.

The third day was calm and favourable for the intended assault: two rafts, carrying the most powerful engines and battering rams, were towed opposite the vulnerable spot, and soon broke down a considerable portion of the wall. When the breach was pronounced practicable the rafts were withdrawn, and two ships of war, furnished with moveable bridges, brought up in their place. The first was manned by the guards, commanded by Admetus; the second, by the Companion infantry, commanded by Coenus; Alexander was with the guards. The ships were brought close to the wall, the bridges successfully thrown across, and Admetus, at the head of the forlorn hope, scaled the breach, and was the first to mount the wall; in the next moment he was pierced by a lance and died on the spot; but Alexander and his friends were close behind, and made their ground good. As soon as some turrets with the intervening wall had been secured, the king advanced along the battlements in the direction of the palace, where the descent into the city seemed easiest.

In the meantime, the fleets had made two successful attacks from opposite quarters; the Cyprians had forced their way into the northern, and the Phoenicians into the southern harbour. The crews landed on the quays, and the city was taken on all sides. Little mercy was shown, as the Macedonians had been exasperated by numerous insults, by the length and obstinacy of the defence, and the serious loss they had suffered; for more men were slain in winning Tyre, than in achieving the three great victories over Darius. The Tyrians also had, in the time of their naval superiority and of their confidence, cruelly violated the laws of war. A vessel, manned by Macedonians, had been captured and taken into Tyre. The crew were brought upon the walls, slaughtered in cold blood, and thrown into the sea, before the eyes of their indignant countrymen.

In revenge, eight thousand Tyrians fell by the sword when the city was stormed, and thirty thousand were sold as slaves. The king, the magistrates, and the principal citizens, had taken refuge in the temple of Hercules, or, more properly speaking, of Moloch. These all received pardon and liberty. It is to be hoped that superstition alone did not cause this distinction; and that the, authorities proved that the law of nations had been violated not under their sanction, but by the excesses of a lawless mob. Tyre had not tyrannically abused her supremacy over the other Phoenician states, and they actively interfered in behalf of her children in the day of distress. The Sidonians alone saved fifteen thousand from the victor's wrath; nor is it probable that any captives were carried out of Phoenicia.

The capture of Tyre was, perhaps, the greatest military achievement of Alexander; and had he spared the citizens when he had won their city, it would be a pleasing task to dwell upon the spirit, vigilance, self-resources, perseverance, and contempt of death, displayed by him during his arduous enterprise. But his merciless consignment of the wives and children of the merchant-princes of the eastern world to a state of slavery, and to be scattered in bondage among barbarian masters, sadly dims the splendour of the exploit, and leaves us only to lament that he did not act in a manner more worthy of himself and of the dignity of the captured city. It is no excuse to allege in his behalf, that it was done in accordance with the spirit of his age; for Alexander, in feelings, in natural talents, and by education, was far beyond his contemporaries, and his lofty character subjects him to be tried by his peers, according to the general laws of humanity.

A curious anecdote connected with the siege, and illustrative of ancient manners and superstitions, is recorded by historians. The Carthaginians, in one of their campaigns against the Sicilian Greeks, had seized and carried away a valuable statue of the Grecian Apollo. This god of the vanquished had been selected as a gift worthy of the acceptance of the mother city, and had been placed at the footstool of Moloch in his Tyrian temple. The Grecian god, in this state of degradation, was naturally suspected of rejoicing at the approach of his countrymen; and the morbid feelings of some Tyrians deluded them so far, as to lead them to imagine that he had appeared to them in their sleep, and announced his intention to desert.

The case was brought before the magistrates, who could not discover a more effectual mode of allaying the popular apprehensions than by binding the disaffected statue, with golden chains, to the horns of Moloch's altar. The Tyrian's patriotism was not doubted. To his custody, therefore, his fellow god was consigned.

One of Alexander's first cares, on entering the temple, was with due ceremony to release the statue from its chains, and to give it the new name of Phil-Alexander.

The sacrifice to Hercules, the ostensible cause of the war, was celebrated with due pomp; and the vessels sailed, and the troops marched, in solemn procession. The usual festivities followed, accompanied by gymnastic contests, and the whole was closed by the favourite lamp race. The *quinquereme*, which he had himself taken, the sole trophy of his naval wars, was dedicated with an inscription in the temple of Hercules. So also, was the battering-ram with which the walls had been first shaken. Its beam probably was formed of the trunk of one of the magnificent cedars of Lebanon.

Mitford says:

Arrian relates, as a report generally received, and to which he gave credit, that, soon after the Battle of Issus, a confidential *eunuch*, a principal attendant of the captive queen of Persia, found means to go to her unfortunate husband. On first sight of him, Darius hastily asked, if his wife and children were living. The *eunuch* assuring him, that not only all were well, but all treated with respect as royal personages, equally as before their captivity, the monarch's apprehension changed. The queen was generally said to be the most beautiful woman in the Persian empire. How, in the usual concealment of the persons of women of rank throughout the eastern nations, hardly less in ancient than in modern days, this could be done, unless from report of the *eunuchs* of the palace, Arrian has not said; but his account rather implies that her face had been seen by some of the Grecian officers.

Darius's next question, however, was said to be, Was his queen's honour tarnished, either through her own weakness, or by any violence? The *eunuch* protesting with solemn oaths that she was as pure as when she parted from Darius, and adding that Alexander was the best and most honourable of men, Darius raised his hands towards heaven and exclaimed, 'O Great God, who disposest of the affairs of kings among men, preserve to me the empire of the Persians and Medes, as thou gavest it; but if it be thy will that I am no longer to be king of Asia, let Alexander, in preference to all others, succeed to my power.'

The historian then adds his own remark, 'so does honourable conduct win the regard even of enemies.' This, which Arrian has judged not unworthy of a place in his *Military History of Alexander*, is obviously not, like numberless stories of private conversations related by Diodorus, and Plutarch, and Curtius, and others, what none who were likely to know would be likely to tell; but, on the contrary, what no way requiring concealment, the *eunuch* would be rather forward to relate: so that, not improbably many Greeks, and among them some acquainted with his character, and able to estimate his veracity, might have had it from himself.

I have transcribed the above anecdote from Mitford, and added his judicious observations; and I regard the second embassy from Darius as the effect of the impression made upon his mind by the *eunuch's* communication. It arrived in the camp before the fall of Tyre. The ambassadors were empowered to offer, on the part of Darius, ten thousand *talents* as the ransom of his family, one of his daughters in marriage, and, as her portion, all Asia to the west of the Euphrates.

These proposals were as usual submitted to the consideration of the Macedonian council, and Parmenio unhesitatingly said, "Were I Alexander, I would conclude the war on these terms, and incur no further risk."

The king said "so would I, were I Parmenio, but as I am Alexander, another answer must be returned."

This, in the direct form, was to the following purpose:

"I want no money from you, nor will I receive a part of the empire for the whole; for Asia and all its treasures belong to me. If I wished to marry your daughter, I can do it, without asking your consent. If you wish to obtain any favour from me, come in person and ask for it."

This answer convinced Darius that negotiations were useless. He, therefore, renewed his preparations for another struggle. The siege of Tyre had lasted seven months, but no attempt to relieve it had been made from any quarter. It is difficult to say what prevented the Carthaginians from aiding the mother city, which, with their maritime superiority, they could so effectually have done. Rumours of civil dissensions and wars in their own territories have been alleged, but history fails us as to particulars. Carthaginian ambassadors were found in Tyre, but they do not seem to have interfered between the belligerents.

Palestine, with the adjoining districts, submitted to the conqueror. The patrimony of David and the city of Goliah equally acknowledged his sovereignty, and Ace, Ashdod, and Ascalon, neither lifted a spear nor drew a sword. Gaza alone, under the government of Batis, a *eunuch*, dared to resist, and remain faithful to its king amidst the general defection. The city was built on a mound, and situated on the edge of the desert that separates Egypt from Syria. The fortifications were good, and the vicinity furnished no materials for the construction of works. Batis took into pay a body of Arabs from the desert, on whose ferocity, if not skill, he could depend.

Alexander threw up a mound against the southern side of the city, on this he mounted part of the engines and battering rams with which Tyre had been overthrown. But the labour was great, as the sandy soil gave way under the works, and there was no timber to be procured. The city walls encircled the outer edge of the mound before described. Hence, they were liable to be undermined, and the miners were set to work.

As Alexander was one day sacrificing with the sacred wreath round his brows, and was cutting the hair off the victim's forehead, one of those carnivorous birds, which in eastern cities are half tame, and were then probably well acquainted with the nature of a sacrifice, happened to hover above the king's head, and drop a small stone upon his shoulder. The omen was judged important, and, according to Aristander, foreboded the eventual capture of the city, but personal danger to the king, if he exposed himself during that day.

In obedience to the warning, the king retired beyond the reach of missiles. But the besieged sallied at the moment, and were preparing to burn the engines. Alexander, thereupon, either forgot, or despised, the caution, and hurried forward to repel the assailants. He succeeded, but was struck by an arrow discharged from a catapult; it penetrated his shield and breast-plate, and sunk deep into his shoulder.

His first feeling on receiving the wound was joy, as it implied the veracity of Aristander, and the consequent capture of the town. But the wound was severe and painful, and was not easily healed. Soon after, the wall was battered down and undermined in various places, and an assault given. The breaches still required scaling ladders, but the emulation of the Macedonians was great, and the place was carried by storm. The first to enter the city was Neoptolemus, one of the Companions and an Æacides. The garrison refused quarter, fought to the last, and were all put to the sword.

Gaza possessed a good harbour, and was a considerable emporium for the productions of Arabia. Among the booty, great stores of frankincense, myrrh, and other aromatics, fell into the conqueror's hands. The sight of these brought an anecdote of his boyish days to the recollection of Alexander. Leonnatus, his governor, had one day, observing him at a sacrifice throwing incense into the fire by handfuls, thus admonished him, "Alexander, when you have conquered the country where spices grow, you may be thus liberal of your incense; in the meantime, use what you have more sparingly."

He now sent his governor large bales of spices, and added the following note.

Leonnatus, I have sent you frankincense and myrrh in abundance, so be no longer a churl to the gods.

Here also he found many of the specimens of the arts and productions of the east. He selected some of these as presents for Olympias, and his favourite sister, Cleopatra, the Queen of Epirus.

According to Josephus, Alexander marched, with hostile intentions, from Gaza to Jerusalem, nor did he invent the account, as it is also given in the Book of Maccabees. The question, as to the truth of the statement, has been debated with more virulence than the case required. The description given by Josephus is highly wrought—and interesting, as giving a vivid picture of Jewish habits, he writes:

Alexander, having destroyed Gaza, hastened to ascend to Jerusalem. Jaddeus, the high priest, learning this, was alarmed and terrified, as he knew not how to meet the Macedonian king, irritated by his former disobedience. He, therefore, ordered the people to make their supplications, and sacrificing to God, besought him to protect the nation and deliver it from the impending danger. God appeared to him in a vision, as he was sleeping after the sacrifice, and told him to be of good cheer, to crown the city with garlands, to throw open the gates, to go forth to meet the Macedonians, with all the priests in their sacerdotal robes, and with the people in white garments, and not to fear, as God would provide for their defence.

Jaddeus rose from sleep, and rejoicing in spirit, communicated the divine message to the people. He then performed all that he was commanded to do, and awaited the arrival of the king.

On learning his approach to the city, he went forth attended by the priests and people, so as to give the procession a sacred character, distinct from the habits of other nations. The spot where the meeting took place was at Sapha, or The Watchtower, so called because Jerusalem and the Temple are thence visible. But the Phoenicians and Chaldæans, who followed the king, and expected him in his anger to allow them to plunder the city and put the high priest to death with every species of torture, witnessed a far different scene.

For when Alexander from a distance saw the multitude in white garments, and the priests in front with their variegated robes of fine linen, and the chief priest in his hyacinthine dress embroidered with gold, and bearing on his head the *cidaris*, with its golden *diadem*, on which was inscribed the name of God; he advanced alone, prostrated himself before the holy name, and was the first to salute the high priest. But when the Jews with one voice had saluted and, encircled the king, the Syrian kings and the rest of his retinue began to doubt the soundness of his intellects.

Parmenio then ventured to draw near and ask 'Why he, before whom all prostrated themselves, paid that honour to the high priest of the Jews?' he answered, 'I did not prostrate myself before him, but before the God with whose priesthood he has been honoured. For while I was as yet at Dium, in Macedonia, I saw him in the same dress in my dreams. And as I was deliberating in what manner I should conquer Asia, he exhorted me not to hesitate, but to cross over with confidence, as he would be a guide to the expedition and deliver the Persian empire into my hands. As, therefore, I have seen no other in a similar dress, as this spectacle reminds me of the vision in my sleep, and of the exhortation, I conclude that my expedition was undertaken under Divine Providence, that I shall conquer Darius, put an end to Persian domination, and succeed in all my plans.'

After this explanation, Alexander took the high priest by the right hand and entered the city, while the priests ran along on both sides. He then went up to the temple and sacrificed to God according to the directions of the high priest, and highly honoured both him and the other priests. Then the Book of Daniel, and the prediction that Greek was destined to overthrow the Persian empire, were shown to him. From it he concluded that he was the person signified, and being much delighted, dismissed the multitude.

Thus Josephus:—it might easily be shown that the time fixed by him is a mistake, but of the occurrence of the visit there can be entertained no rational doubt. The behaviour of Alexander is the same as in all other similar cases, and according to his maxim—"to pay the highest reverence to the priesthood of every country, and to invoke the gods of every nation." It is also incredible that Alexander, who was detained nine months on the sea coast, and whose curiosity as a traveller was equal to his ambition as a warrior, did not visit a city of the importance and magnitude of Jerusalem, and a temple and priesthood, the fame of which was great, at least on the adjacent coast. But when we have the direct testimony of the people most concerned, that he did not in this instance act contrary to his usual habits, it is too much to call upon us to disbelieve the positive testimony, merely because other writers have omitted to notice the occurrence.

Perhaps the only stain on the character of Ptolemy, the son of Lagus, is his cruelty to the Jews, and if, in oppressing them, he was guilty of violating the privileges conferred upon them by Alexander, we have a sufficient reason why he passed over the circumstance in silence. That such was the case may almost positively be inferred from the fact stated by Curtius, that while Alexander was in Egypt, the Samaritans revolted and put the Macedonian governor to a cruel death. For this conduct they could have no other cause than the superior favour shown to their enemies the Jews; for before they had been the first to acknowledge the power of Alexander.

We read in ancient and modern historians of the difficulties to be encountered by armies in marching across the desert from Gaza to Pelusium, and of the great preparations necessary for such a hazardous enterprise; but Alexander encountered no similar difficulties, and his army passed in safety between the "Sirbonian Bog" and "Mount Casius old," without suffering from thirst or being swallowed in quicksands. At Pelusium, which he reached in seven days, he found Hephæstion, who had conducted the feet from Phoenicia.

One hundred and ninety-four years had elapsed since the conquest of Egypt by Cambyses, but the Egyptians had never been willing slaves to their masters. Their revolts had been numerous, bloody, and even successful. After enjoying a turbulent independence for more than sixty years, they had been reunited to the empire by the late king Ochus, aided by a large Greek force. But their wounds were still green; and hatred against Persia was as strong a motive to revolution, as affection to Macedonia could have been.

Sabaces, the *satrap*, with all the disposable troops, had fallen at Issus. His lieutenant, Mazaces, was powerless, and in the hands of the natives. He, therefore, made a grace of necessity, and attempted no resistance. Thus, Alexander took quiet possession of this most ancient and once powerful kingdom, without throwing up a mound or casting a spear.

From Pelusium he advanced up the country along the eastern branch of the Nile, and first visited Heliopolis, and then Memphis, the capital of Lower Egypt. Here he remained for some time, and according to his usual policy offered sacrifices to the Egyptian gods. Even Apis was duly honoured, and an effectual pledge thus given to the natives, that thenceforward their superstitions were to be respected. Public games and festivals followed; and competitors in athletic contests, in music, and poetry, flocked from the remotest parts of Greece, to contend for the prize of excellence before a Macedonian monarch, seated on the throne of Sesostris.

At Memphis, he embarked upon the Nile, and sailed down the Canopic branch. From it he passed into the Mareotic lake, where he was struck with the advantages of the site on which Alexandreia was afterwards built. The lake Mareotic was then separated from the sea by a solid isthmus, broadest in the centre, and narrower at both ends. In front was the island of Pharus, which offered a natural protection for vessels, between itself and the isthmus. The advantages of the situation were so striking, that the ancient Egyptians had posted a body of troops on the isthmus in order to prevent merchants, whom they held in abhorrence, from frequenting the road. Around this military post a small town called Rhacotis had grown, but before Alexander's visit it was fallen into decay.

The disciple of Aristotle was not ignorant that there was no safe harbour at any of the numerous mouths of the Nile, and that the navigation along the shallow and dangerous coast was consequently much impeded. He was struck with the capabilities of the spot on which he stood, nor did he rest until the skilful engineers, by whom he was always attended, had drawn the ground-plan of the future queen of the East.

So eager was the king to witness the apparent result of their plans, that for want of better materials the different lines were marked out with flour taken from the provision-stores of the army. These lines were soon effaced by the clouds of water fowl which rose from the bosom of the lake and devoured the flour. Aristander being consulted on the occasion, foretold from this very natural phenomenon, that it would be a mighty city, abundantly supplied with the necessaries of life.

During his visit to Ephesus, Alexander had observed and admired the taste displayed by Dinocrates, the architect, in rebuilding the temple of Ephesus. From that moment he engaged him in his service, and to him was now committed the work of planning and superintending the erection of the future capital of Egypt. Ample funds were placed at his command, and a great city started into mature existence on the borders of the Libyan desert, without struggling through the previous stages of infancy and childhood.

Here he was visited by Hegelochus, his admiral in the Ægean, who came to announce the dissolution of the Persian fleet, the recovery of Tenedos, Lesbos and Chios, and the capture of the Persian leaders. This result naturally followed the defection of the Phoenician fleets, and gave the empire of the sea to the Macedonians. Carthage, which alone could have disputed it, shrunk from the competition, and remained motionless in the west.

His next adventure, for his actions resemble more the wildness of romance than the soberness of history, was the visit to the Ammonian Oasis. Perseus, in his expedition against Medusa and her fabled sisters, and Hercules after the victory over Busiris, were said to have consulted this Libyan oracle. These were heroes whom he was anxious to rival, and from whom he could trace his descent. He, therefore, determined to enter the western desert, and, like his great ancestors, inquire into the future at the shrine of Jupiter Ammon.

The fate of the Army of Cambyses, which had perished in the attempt to reach the temple, buried, as tradition reported, beneath a tempest of moving sand, could not deter Alexander. Cambyses was the contemner of religion, the violator of the gods of Egypt. The devoted troops sought the holy shrine for the acknowledged purpose of pollution and destruction. But their guides through the desert must have been natives. Many of these, in a case where their religion was so deeply concerned, might be found willing to conduct the *infidels* into pathless wilds, and to purchase the safety of the sanctuary at the expense of their own lives.

Besides, all the warriors of Egypt had not fallen in one battle, and the islands of the desert would be the natural refuge of the boldest and noblest of the band. Probably, therefore, human agency, as well as physical causes, combined in preventing the return of a single messenger, to announce the fate of sixty thousand men.

Alexander, on the contrary, was hailed as the deliverer of Egypt, who honoured the gods whom the Persian insulted, and who sought the temple in order to consult the deity, and thus add to the celebrity of the oracle.

Escorted by a small and select detachment, he set out from Alexandreia, and marched along the seashore until he arrived at Parætonium. Here he supplied the troops with water, turned to the south, and in eleven days arrived at the Ammonian Oasis.

The Macedonians were prepared to expect miracles on this expedition, and certainly, according to their own account, were not disappointed. When threatened with thirst, they were relieved by sudden and copious showers of rain, and when a south wind, the terror of the wanderer in the deserts of northern Africa, had arisen, and obliterated all traces of the paths, and the very guides confessed their ignorance of the right way, two ravens appeared to the bewildered party, and guided them in safety to the temple.

This, perhaps, admits of an explanation; for a raven in the desert would towards nightfall naturally wing its way to its accustomed roosting place. But what can be said for Ptolemy, who writes that two large serpents, uttering distinct sounds, conducted them both to and from the temple? Is it to be supposed, that the sovereign of Egypt, drawing great sums from the consulters of the oracle, was guilty of a pious fraud, for the sake of raising its fame, and multiplying its votaries? If this cannot be admitted, we must have recourse to the mystic theories of Bryant, according to whom both the Ravens and the Serpents were only the symbolical names of Egyptian priests.

Later writers pretend to give in detail conversations supposed to have taken place between the king and the priests, and the royal questions and the divine answers. But they are proved guilty of falsehood by the testimony of the original historians, who agree in stating that Alexander alone was admitted into the innermost shrine, and that when he came out, he merely informed his followers that the answers had been agreeable to him.

He much admired the beauty of this insulated spot, surrounded by a trackless ocean of sand, and not exceeding six miles in diameter either way. It was covered with olives, laurels, and shady groves of palm trees, and irrigated by innumerable bubbling springs, each the centre of a little paradise, fertilized by itself. In the middle stood the palace of the chief, inclosing within its buildings the residence of the god. At some distance was another temple, and the celebrated springs which cooled with the ascending and warmed with the departing sun, were at midnight hot, and icy-cold at noon. Imagination aided the Macedonians in verifying this natural miracle, although probably the change of temperature belonged to the judges rather than to the waters.

According to Ptolemy, he returned across the desert to Memphis. Here he was welcomed by the deputies of numerous Greek states, who all succeeded in the various objects of their mission. He also renewed with great splendour the feasts, games, and spectacles, and offered a public sacrifice to the Olympian Jove. Nor did these festivities interfere with his active duties, for during his stay at Memphis he settled the future civil and military government of Egypt. Doloaspis, a native, was appointed governor of the central part; Apollonius of the side bordering on Libya; Cleomenes of the vicinity of Arabia.

These two were ordered not to interfere with the duties of the local magistrates, to allow them to administer justice according to the ancient laws of the country, and to hold them responsible for the collection of the public revenues. Memphis and Pelusium were occupied by strong Macedonian garrisons, the rest of the country was guarded by Greek mercenaries. The army was supported by a fleet, but the commanders in chief by sea and by land were independent of each other. Arrian says:

> He thus divided the government of Egypt among many, from being struck with the natural defences of the country, so that it did not appear safe to commit the entire command to one man;—and the Romans—taught, as I think, by the example of Alexander, to be on their guard with respect to Egypt-never appointed its proconsul from the senatorian, but from the equestrian rank.

The history of Egypt, for the last twelve hundred years, is the best commentary upon the policy of Alexander and the observations of Arrian; for, during that period, it has been either an independent government, or held by rulers whose subjection has been merely nominal.

Alexander was desirous of visiting Upper Egypt, of viewing the magnificent ruins of the hundred-gated Thebes, and the supposed palaces of Tithonus and Memnon. But Darius was still formidable, and the remotest provinces of the East were arming in his defence. The king, therefore, reluctantly postponed his examination of the antiquities on the banks of the Nile, and directed, his march to Syria.

CHAPTER 8

Fourth Campaign. B.C. 331

With the spring the army moved from Memphis, and arrived a second time at Tyre, where Alexander received numerous communications from Greece, concerning the operations of Agis, King of Sparta. The Lacedæmonians had not concurred in the general vote of the confederates, according to which Alexander had been appointed captain-general. They were consequently justified in attempting to dissolve the confederacy, as the confederates were justified in compelling them to submit to the general decision.

But both Philip and Alexander had avoided war with them, and now they, unable to remain passive any longer, took up arms, and invited the southern Greeks to form a new confederacy under their ancient leaders of Sparta. Darius had supplied them with money, which they employed in bribing the chief magistrates of the republics, and in hiring mercenary soldiers. The Arcadians, Eleians, and Achæans, joined them; some of the mountain tribes in Thessaly excited disturbances; and had Athens acceded, all Greece, with the exception of Argos and Messenia, would apparently have disclaimed the Macedonian supremacy.

But Athens, if deprived of the leading place, cared little whether it belonged to Sparta or Macedonia, and we have the positive testimony of Æschines, that Demosthenes remained inactive at this critical period. The great patriot went still further, for when the Athenians had sent ambassadors in the public ship *Paralus*, to wait on Alexander at Tyre, these Paralians, as Æschines calls them, found a friend and emissary of Demosthenes in constant communication with the Macedonian king, who was also said to have received a letter full of fair words and flattery from the great orator.

Under these circumstances, Alexander released the Athenian prisoners, sent money to Antipater, and a powerful fleet into the Peloponnesus.

The Homeric principle, that there could be no heroes without continual feasting, was regularly acted upon by Alexander. At Tyre, previous to entering upon the grand expedition to Babylon, a public sacrifice to Hercules was celebrated, and the whole army feasted. They were also entertained with music and dancing, and tragedies were represented in the greatest perfection, both from the magnificence of the scenery and the spirit of emulation in those who exhibited them. Plutarch, from whom we derive this information, does not say whether the Tyrians had a public theatre or not.

Probably a city so much frequented by Greeks as Tyre was not without one. It is impossible that the great body of the people in modern times should take the same lively interest in theatrical representations as the Greeks did; their theatres were invariably scenes of contest either between rival poets or rival actors; party spirit entered deeply into the business of the stage, and large sums of money were lost or won according to the sentence of the judges.

In the present case, the spectacles had been got up at the expense of the Kings of Cyprus. Athenodorus and Thessalus, the two greatest tragic actors of the day, were brought to compete with each other. Pasicrates, the King of Soli, risked the victory upon Athenodorus, and Nicocreon, King of Salamis, upon Thessalus. We are not told whether the two actors played in the same piece;—probably not, and each had to choose his favourite character. Alexander's feelings were interested in the contest, as Thessalus was his favourite; he did not, however, discover his bias, until Athenodorus had been declared victor by all the votes; then, as he left the theatre, he said:

I commend the judges for what they have done, but I would have given half my kingdom rather than have seen Thessalus conquered.

The above anecdote proves the warmth of his feelings, the following fact the steadiness of his affections. He heard that his misguided friend, Harpalus, was a fugitive at Megaris. His plans, whatever they were, had miscarried, and his associates had deserted him. Alexander sent to request him to return, and to assure him that his former conduct would not be remembered to his disadvantage. Harpalus returned, and was restored to his situation. It was a dangerous experiment;—and it failed, for on a subsequent occasion he acted in the same manner, only on a much larger scale. His reappointment was, however, an error of the head and not of the heart.

All the necessary preparations had been completed, and the army quitted the shores of the Mediterranean, and marched to the Euphrates. There were three main passages over that river, which all at different periods bore the common name of Zeugma, or the bridge. The most ancient was the Zeugma at Thapsacus, where Cyrus, Alexander, and Crassus passed into Mesopotamia. This was opposite the modern Racca. The next was the Zeugma of the contemporaries of Strabo, at Samosata. The third was the Zeugma of later writers, and was the passage opposite the modern Bir.

Two bridges had been partly thrown across beforehand; these were completed as soon as the army arrived, and all passed into Mesopotamia. Mazæus, a Persian general, who rather watched than guarded the passage, retired with his 3,000 horse without offering any resistance. According to Pliny, Alexander was struck with the advantages of the site of the modern Racca, and ordered a city to be built there; it was called Nicephorium, and by its vicinity soon exhausted the less advantageously placed Thapsacus. In the Middle Ages it became the favourite residence of Haroun al Rashid.

At this point Alexander had to decide upon the future line of advance. He could either follow the example of the younger Cyrus, and march down the left bank of the Euphrates, or cross Mesopotamia, ford the Tigris, and enter Assyria from that quarter; he preferred the latter, because it was better furnished with necessaries, and not equally

99

exposed to the heat of the sun.

Not a single stage or action in Mesopotamia is indicated by Alexander's historians, although he crossed the Euphrates in July—and the Tigris not before the end of September. The royal road from Nicephorium followed the course first of the Bilecha, and then of one of its eastern tributaries up to Carræ, the Haran of the Scriptures. Thence it intersected the channels of the numerous streams which, flowing from Mount Masius, fertilise the rich territory of which Nisibis was the capital. Here the army might halt, and furnish itself with necessaries to any amount. Hence also Alexander could rapidly move to any selected point upon the Tigris, and cross it before the enemy could bring any considerable force to bear upon him.

Darius, in the meantime, had assembled all the forces of the East under the walls of Babylon. Having ascertained the direction of the enemy's march, he moved to the Tigris, and crossed over into Assyria. The whole army then advanced up the left bank of the river, until the royal road turned to the right in the direction of Arbela; it then crossed the Caprus or Little Zab, and reached Arbela, where the baggage and the useless part of the army were deposited.

Darius conducted the combatants to the River Lycus or Great Zab. These alone consumed five days in traversing the bridge thrown over this river. Perhaps military men may, from this fact, make a gross calculation of their numbers. The same bridge was, in later times, traversed by the Persian Army which captured Amida in the reign of Constantius, in three days. Ammianus Marcellinus was a distant spectator of their passage.

Darius then advanced to Gaugamela, or the Camel's House, so called from the camel which had borne Darius, the son of Hystaspes, in his retreat from Scythia. It was situated not far from the River Bumadus, the modern Hazir Su. Here the immense plain of Upper Assyria, stretching northward between the Gordyoean mountains and the Tigris, presented the field of battle best calculated for the operations of a Persian Army:

Darius selected his own ground, and every hillock and other obstacle that could interfere with the movements of cavalry were carefully removed; light troops were then sent forward to observe rather than contest the passage of the Tigris.

Alexander had reached this river in the vicinity of Beled or Old Mosul. The season was favourable, as all the rivers that flow from Mount Taurus are lowest in autumn; and no enemy appeared on the opposite bank; yet the army encountered great difficulties in the passage, both from the depth and force of the current, and the slippery nature of its bed. The cavalry formed a double line, within which the infantry marched with their shields over their heads, and their arms interlinked. In this manner they crossed without the loss of lives. Their entrance into Assyria was signalised by an almost total eclipse of the moon. This, according to the calculation of astronomers, occurred on the night of the 20th of September.

The soldiers were alarmed, and feared its disastrous influence; but Aristander soothed their agitated minds, by saying that it portended evil to Persia rather than to Macedonia. It is not easy to discover on what principle this explanation was founded; for, as the sun, the glorious Mithra, was the patron god of Persia, that kingdom could scarcely be supposed to sympathize with the labours of the moon; but Aristander was an able man, as well as a diviner, and boldly affirmed, that the sun properly belonged to the Greeks, and the moon to the Persians; on the same principle, he saw in the ensuing battle an eagle hovering over Alexander's head, and pointing upwards, announced the fact to the soldiers.

It is a curious historical coincidence, that the Battle of Arbela, the greatest victory achieved by the Macedonian arms, and the defeat at Pydna which proved fatal to their empire, were both preceded by eclipses of the moon, and that the victor in each case knew how to convert the incident to his own purposes. Alexander as well as Paulus Æmilius offered sacrifices to the sun, moon, and earth, to the regular motions of which they knew the phenomenon to be attributable.

For three days the army marched down the left bank of the Tigris without seeing an enemy; on the fourth, the light horsemen in front announced the appearance of a body of Persian cavalry in the plain; they did not wait to be attacked, and were pursued by Alexander himself and a chosen body of horse. He failed to overtake the main body, but captured a few whose horses were inferior in speed; from them he discovered that Darius was encamped as before described, and ready to give battle. It is evident from the above account and from the authority of other historians, that the whole country to the west of the field of battle had been driven, and that no inhabitants remained from whom any information could be derived.

The army halted for four days on the spot where the king received the long-desired intelligence; this short repose was granted in order to enable the soldiers to recover from their fatigues, and to prepare themselves for the ensuing contest. Part of even this brief relaxation from active duty was employed in forming an intrenched camp for the protection of the baggage and non-combatants.

At three o'clock on the morning of the fifth day he recommenced his march at the head of his combatants, who bore nothing but their arms, his intention to arrive in front of the enemy at daybreak, but the distance was miscalculated, as the day was far advanced, when on surmounting a range of hillocks, he saw the interminable lines of the Persians drawn up in order of battle. The intervening space was still four miles.

Here he commanded a halt, and proposed the question to the leading officers hastily called together, whether they should immediately advance or postpone the battle till the next morning. The great majority were adverse to delay, but Parmenio, whose experienced eye had already discovered the traces of the levelling operations, was for encamping on the spot, and carefully examining the ground, as he suspected various parts in front of the enemy's lines to be trenched and staked. His prudent advice prevailed, and the army encamped on the brow of the low hills, under arms, and in order of battle.

Then the king in person, escorted by a strong body of light troops and cavalry, examined every part of the field as narrowly as circumstances would allow. On his return to the main body, he again called his officers together, and told them, it was needless for him to exhort men whose own courage and past deeds must prove the strongest incitement; but he earnestly besought them to rouse the spirits of those under their command, and impress upon their minds a sense of the importance of the impending combat, in which they were to contend, not for Syria, Phoenicia, and Egypt, as before, but for all Asia and for empire. For this purpose, every captain of horse and foot ought to address his own troop and company; every colonel his own regiment; and every general in the *phalanx* his own brigade.

The men, naturally brave, needed not long harangues to excite their courage, but to be simply told, carefully to keep their ranks during the struggle, to advance in the deepest silence, to cheer with a loud and clear voice, and to peal forth the shout of victory in the most terrific accents. He requested the officers to be quick in catching transmitted orders, and in communicating them to their troops, and to remember that the safety of all was endangered by the negligence and secured by the laborious vigilance of each individual.

The generals, as at Issus, told their king to be of good cheer, and to rely with confidence upon their exertions. The men were then ordered to take their evening meal, and to rest for the night.

It is said that Parmenio, alarmed by the immense array of the Persian lines, and by the discordant sounds of the congregated nations, borne across the plain like the hoarse murmurs of the agitated ocean, entered the king's tent at a late hour, and proposed a night attack. The answer was (for Parmenio was not alone) "it would be base to steal a victory, and Alexander must conquer in open day and without guile."

While the Macedonians were thus snatching brief repose, the Persians were kept all night under arms, as they had been during the greatest part of the preceding day; this alone was sufficient to break down the spirits of the men and to jade the horses. But Darius had chosen and prepared his ground, and could not change it without throwing his whole line into confusion.

His order of battle, described on paper, fell into the hands of the Macedonians. The troops were arranged according to their nations, under their own *satraps*, in the following manner:—

On the left were the Bactrians, Dahæ, Persians, (horse and foot intermingled,) Susians and Cadusians. These last touched the centre.

On the right were the Syrians, Mesopotamians, Medes, Parthians, Sacæ, Tapeiri, Hyrcanians, Albanians, and Sacasenæ. The last touched the centre.

The centre, commanded by Darius himself, was composed of the Royal Kinsmen, the Immortals, the Indians, the expatriated Carians, and the Mardian archers.

Behind, a second line was formed of the Uxians, Babylonians, Carmanians, and Sitacenians.

In front of the left wing were drawn up 1,000 Bactrians, and all the Scythian cavalry, and 100 scythe-armed chariots. In front of Darius, and facing Alexander's Royal Troop of Companion Cavalry, were placed 15 elephants and 50 of the war-chariots. In front of the right wing were posted the Armenian and Cappadocian cavalry, and 50 more of the chariots. The Greek mercenaries were drawn up on both sides of Darius, opposite to the Macedonian *phalanx*, as they alone were supposed capable of withstanding the charge of that formidable and dreaded body.

With this list of nations before us, it is absurd to impute the victories of Alexander to the effeminacy of the Medes and Persians. The bravest and hardiest tribes of Asia were in the field: Bactrians, Scythians, and Dahæ, with their long lances, barbed steeds, and steel panoplies; Sacæ and Parthians, mounted archers, whose formidable arrows proved in after ages so destructive to the legions of Rome; Armenians, Albanians, and Cadusians, whom the successors of Alexander failed to subdue; and Uxian and Mardian mountaineers, unrivalled as light troops and skirmishers. Arrian computed their united numbers at 1,000,000 of infantry, and 40,000 cavalry. Supposing the infantry did not exceed one fourth of that number, there would still remain troops enough to bear down and trample the Macedonians under foot.

But the great mass was without an efficient head; their nominal chief could not bring them to co-operate, as there was no principle of cohesion between the different parts. The sole point of union was the royal standard: as long as that was visible in the front of battle, it cannot be said that the Persian *satraps* ever forgot their duty; but if the king fell, or still worse, if the king fled, all union was dissolved, all efforts against the enemy instantly ceased, and a safe retreat into his own province at the head of his own troops became the object of every *satrap*. In attaining this object no distinction was made between friend and foe, all who obstructed the escape were indiscriminately treated as enemies. Cyrus had betrayed the fatal secret to the Greeks, Xenophon had made it public, and Alexander proved the truth of the maxim, "if the commander in chief of an oriental army be killed or forced to fly, all is gained."

The king's sleep was deeper and longer than usual on the morning of this decisive day; nor did he awake till Parmenio entered his tent to announce that the troops were all under arms and expecting his presence. Parmenio asked why he slept like a man who had already conquered, and not like one about to commence the greatest battle of which the world had hitherto heard? Alexander smiled and said, "In what light can you look upon us but as conquerors, seeing we have no longer to traverse desolate countries in pursuit of Darius, and he does not decline the combat?"

Alexander was neither tall nor large, but, with more than ordinary power of limb, possessed great elegance of figure; the many portraits on coins yet extant, give assurance that his countenance was of the best models of masculine beauty; his complexion was fair, with a tinge of red in his face; his eye was remarkable for its quickness and vivacity, and defied imitation; but a slight inclination of the head to one side, natural to him, was easily adopted by his courtiers, and even by many of his successors. His dress and arms on this memorable day are described by Plutarch, and deserve attention.

He wore a short tunic of the Sicilian fashion, girt close around him, over that a linen breastplate, strongly quilted; his helmet, surmounted by the white plume, was of polished steel, the work of Theodectes; the gorget was of the same metal and set with precious stones; his sword, his favourite weapon in battle, was a present from a Cyprian king, and not to be excelled for lightness or temper; but his belt, deeply embossed with massy figures, was the most superb part of his armour; it was given by the Rhodians, and Helicon, at an advanced age, had exerted all his skill in rendering it worthy of Alexander's acceptance; if we add to these the shield, lance, and light greaves, we may form a fair idea of his appearance in battle.

The army was drawn up in the following order: on the extreme right were the Companion cavalry, in eight strong divisions, under the immediate command of Philotas; the right wing of the *phalanx* was commanded by Nicanor, the son of Parmenio; the left by Craterus; the cavalry of the left wing was composed of the Thessalians and Greek confederates; Parmenio commanded the left, Alexander the right wing. This was the main battle,

Behind the *phalanx* a second line of infantry was formed, with orders to face to the rear if any attack were made from that quarter.

On the right flank of the main battle, and not in a line with it, but in deep column behind the royal troop of Companion cavalry, were placed half the Agrians, half the archers, and all the veteran mercenaries. The flank of this column was covered by the Prodromi, Pæonian, and mercenary cavalry, under the command of Aretas. Still more to their right Menidas commanded another body of mercenary cavalry. The left flank of the main battle was protected in a similar manner, by the Thracians of Sitalces, the Odrysæ, and detachments from the confederate and mercenary cavalry.

In front of the Companion cavalry were the rest of the Agrians and archers, and a body of javelin men. The number of Alexander's forces amounted to forty thousand infantry, and seven thousand cavalry. The necessity of the unusual arrangement of his troops is obvious from the circumstance that Alexander, on his own extreme right, was opposite Darius, who occupied the Persian centre. The Macedonian Army was certain, in that great plain, of being enveloped within the folding wings of their adversaries. Hence it became necessary to be prepared for attack in front, on both flanks, and from the rear.

Alexander, either to avoid the elephants and the scythe-armed chariots, or to turn the right of the Persian centre, did not lead his line straight forwards, but caused the whole to advance obliquely over the intervening ground. Darius and his army adopted a parallel movement. But as Alexander was thus rapidly edging off the ground, levelled for the use of the chariots, Darius ordered the Bactrians and Scythians, who were stationed in front of his left wing, to wheel round and attack the enemy's right flank, in order to prevent the extension of their line in that direction.

Menidas and the mercenary cavalry rode forth to meet their charge, but were soon overpowered by the numbers of the enemy. Then all the cavalry under Aretas was ordered up to the support of Menidas. These also were roughly handled, as the barbarians were not only in greater force, but the complete armour of the Scythians made it very difficult to make any impression upon them. The Macedonians, however, stood their repeated charges, and by keeping their own squadrons in close order, succeeded in driving them back.

Then the chariots were driven against Alexander and the right wing of the *phalanx*. But these, as usual, made no impression, for the greatest part of the horses and drivers were killed in the advance by the javelin men and the Agrians; who even ran between these once-dreaded machines, cut their traces, and speared the drivers. The few that reached the line were allowed to pass through to the rear, where they were easily captured by the grooms and royal attendants. Not a word is said of the operations of the elephants. Their attack must, therefore, have proved as unsuccessful as that of the chariots.

The two main bodies were still at some distance, when Darius ordered his line to advance. Alexander observing this, commanded Aretas, with all the cavalry and infantry of the flank column, to charge the left wing of the enemy, who were now wheeling round, while instead of meeting Darius with his line, he advanced in column, and as soon as his leading troops had broken through the first line of the barbarians, he directed the whole force of the Companion cavalry, and the right wing of the *phalanx*, to the open interval. There he pierced and divided the Persian line, and then attacked the left centre of Darius in flank. His great object was to break through the Kinsmen and Immortals, and reach that monarch.

The close combat did not last long. The Persian cavalry were thronged, and in the press their missiles were of no avail against the Macedonian lances. The infantry also broke and fled before the bristling pikes of the *phalanx*, which nothing could withstand on the levelled surface of the plain. Aretas and his troops were equally successful, and routed the enemy's left wing; so that in this quarter the victory of the Macedonians was decisive. I wish it were possible to believe that Darius, as recorded by Curtius and Diodorus, behaved with courage and spirit. But the testimony of Arrian is explicit:—

Fearful as he was before hand, he was the first to turn and fly.

The result was by no means the same in other parts of the field. The three brigades, attached to the left wing, had not been able to accompany the rest of the *phalanx*, in the great charge, but had halted for the protection of the troops to the left, who were in great danger of being defeated. An immense gap was thus opened between the separated parts, and the Indians and the Persian cavalry passed unmolested through the interval, and reached the baggage where the army had slept the preceding night. The Persians slew many of the camp attendants, and were busied in plundering, when the second line of the *phalanx* faced round, attacked them in the rear, slew many, and compelled the rest to fly.

The Persian right wing, where the Sacæ, the Albanians, and Parthians were stationed, wheeled to the left at the beginning of the battle, and attacked Parmenio on every side. Their success at one time was so decided, that the veteran general was forced to dispatch a messenger, in order to inform Alexander of his dangerous situation, and of the necessity of instant aid. One great object of Alexander's ambition was to capture the Persian monarch on the field of battle; and that object, at the moment he received the message, was apparently within his grasp; but he did not hesitate between his duty and inclination, and instantly ceased from the pursuit, and with the Companion cavalry galloped towards the enemy's right wing. He had not proceeded far when he met the Persian and Parthian cavalry in full retreat.

It was impossible for them to avoid the contest, and a desperate engagement took place. The Persians and Parthians fought manfully, when not the victory, but their own lives, were the stake, and many of them broke through the Macedonian squadrons and continued their flight without turning round. In this encounter sixty of the Companion cavalry were killed, and Hephæstion, Coenus, and Menidas, wounded.

In the meantime, the Thessalian cavalry, already, perhaps, feeling the benefit of the king's victory in the relaxed efforts of their assailants, renewed their exertions, and Alexander arrived in time to witness their final charge and the enemy's flight. He immediately turned round and resumed the pursuit of Darius. At the bridge, over the Lycus, night overtook him. There he rested for a few hours, and again setting out at midnight, in the course of the following day reached Arbela, forty miles from the field of battle. Darius, however, was not there, but all his treasures and equipage fell into the victor's hands, and a second chariot, bow, and spear, were added to the former trophies.

Thus terminated this famous battle, the success of which was principally due to the gallantry of the Companion cavalry and Alexander himself. We have no means of ascertaining their number, but it is evident that it had been much increased since the last battle. Their labour and consequent fatigue were enormous, and they alone lost five hundred horses from wounds or over-exertion.

It would be idle to speak of the number of men who fell on both sides. Perhaps we may infer from Arrian, that a hundred Macedonians of rank were slain. As the Lycus was not fordable, and Alexander obtained early possession of the bridge, the whole Persian Army was evidently at his mercy Hence Arrian, who estimates the Persian loss of lives at three hundred thousand, states the number of prisoners to have been far greater. Their king had brought them into such a position between the River Tigris, the Gordyæan mountains and the Lycus, that they had no choice between victory and death, or captivity.

Darius fled from the field of battle, not down the Tigris towards Babylon, but across Mount Zagrus, probably by the pass of Kerrund. He was joined in his flight by the Bactrians, two thousand Greek mercenaries, and the surviving remains of the Royal Kinsmen and body guard. These formed an escort strong enough to conduct him to Ecbatana. He did not dread an immediate pursuit, as Babylon and Susa would naturally attract the first notice of the victor.

Alexander marched from Arbela, and in four days arrived at a town called Memmis by Curtius, Ecbatana by Plutarch. There he viewed and admired the perpetual flames which from time immemorial have issued from a gulf or cavern in the vicinity of the modern Kerkook. The place was also remarkable for its fountain of liquid naphtha, of so combustible a nature, that the Greeks concluded it was the fabled drug with which Medea anointed the robes that proved fatal to the Corinthian princess. The natives, eager to show its powers to the foreigner, formed a long train in front of the king's lodgings, and as soon as it was dark set fire to one end, when the whole street burst into an instantaneous blaze. Such spots were highly venerated by the worshippers of fire. Near the burning fountain were built a temple in honour of the great Persian goddess Anaitis, and a palace, once the favourite residence of Darius, the son of Hystaspes.

Thence he advanced through a submissive country to Babylon, the imperial seat of Semiramis and Nabuchadonosor. This mighty city had once given law to all the nations of the East, but was now rapidly declining in wealth, and importance, and the marshes of the Euphrates were yearly recovering their lost dominions. The Persians had been severe taskmasters to their more civilized neighbours. Cyrus had treated them kindly, but the rebellion against the first Darius had been followed with heavy penalties, and the partial destruction of their massy fortifications. His son Xerxes proved a tyrant to them, he plundered their shrines, slew the chief priest of Belus, took away the golden statue of their god, and partly destroyed his great pyramidical temple.

When Herodotus visited the city about one hundred and twenty years before Alexander, he found all the signs of a declining and falling people.

The Babylonians, therefore, hailed the change of masters with joy, and poured forth in crowds to meet the conqueror. Mazæus, the Persian *satrap*, and the military commander of the citadel, headed the procession. The Chaldæans, in their sacred robes, and the native chiefs, followed in order; and all, according to the customs of the East, bore presents in their hands. The first care of Alexander was to restore the shrines destroyed by Xerxes, and even to rebuild the temple of Belus in all its original magnificence. The immense revenues attached to its establishments by the piety of the Assyrian kings were restored to the priests, to whom the management of the funds, and the superintendence of the building, were entrusted. He then offered a sacrifice to Jupiter Belus, according to the regular forms of the Chaldæan religion.

Mazæus was restored to his *satrapy*, but his authority was limited to the civil government, and the administration of justice. The command of the troops and the receipt of the revenue were entrusted to two Macedonians.

Having arranged the affairs of Assyria, and its dependant provinces, Alexander marched eastward to Susa. Thither he had dispatched one of his officers from the field of battle. On the road he met a deputation, accompanied by the son of the Susian *satrap*, who bore a letter from the Macedonian officer, announcing the important intelligence, that the Susians were ready to surrender their city and citadel, and that the treasures were in safe custody.

Abulites the *satrap* came forth to meet Alexander on the banks of the Choaspes, the modern Kerah, and conducted him into the most ancient palace of the monarchs of Asia. This had been a favourite seat of the Persian dynasty, on account of its central situation between Persia, Media, and Assyria, nor had Persepolis or Pasargada been more favoured with their presence and regard. Its citadel was a *gaza*, or treasury, where the surplus revenues of Asia had been accumulating for ages.

According to Herodotus, all the coin that remained, after defraying the regular expenses of the year, was melted into earthen jars. When the metal had cooled, the jars were broken, and the bullion placed in the treasury. Again, when the annual disbursements exceeded the regular income, or some extraordinary expenses from war or other causes took place, bullion, according to the emergency, was recoined and sent to circulate through the provinces. Alexander found fifty thousand *talents* of silver thus treasured up in the citadel of Susa. Three thousand of these were immediately sent to the sea-coast, in order to be forwarded to: Antipater, for the expenses of the Lacedæmonian war, and the pacification of Greece. The same sum, wisely expended by Darius at the commencement of the war, would have retained Alexander to the west of the Hellespont.

The conqueror drew a strong line of difference between the Susians and the nations hitherto visited by him. He paid no honours to the indigenous gods, but celebrated his arrival with Grecian sacrifices, gymnastic games, and the lamp race. Probably he regarded the Susians as a component part of the dominant tribes of Media and Persia, whose supremacy it was his object to overthrow. The Susians, originally called Cissians and Cossæans, were a peaceful people, described, since history has recorded facts, as always subject to the ruling nation. But, according to their own traditions, their monarch, in the Homeric ages, was the king of kings, and their city was the capital of Tithonus, whose ever-blooming bride was Aurora, destined to witness the gradual decay and imbecility, not only of her once youthful husband, but of many successive dynasties of the lords of the East.

Their citadel, in the days of Æschylus and Herodotus, still bore the name of Memnoneium, and these two great antiquaries, as well as Strabo, regard the Susians or Cissians as possessing a far better right than the Egyptians to claim the dark-visaged auxiliary of Priam as their countryman.

At Susa also, in the gardens of the palace and on the banks of the Ulai or Choaspes, the Prophet Daniel had seen those visions which so clearly describe the career of Alexander, and the destruction of the Persian empire. Nor is it the least striking circumstance connected with the history of Susa, that—when her citadel has tumbled into dust—when her palaces have disappeared—when the long lines of Persian, Greek, Parthian, and numerous other dynasties have passed away, and left not a vestige of their magnificence and glory to attest their former existence—a small temple still commemorates the burial-place of Daniel, and the wilderness of Shus is annually visited by thousands of Israelites, who, from the remotest periods, have ceased not their pilgrimages to the tomb of the Prophet.

Aristagoras the Milesian, when exciting the Spartan king to invade Persia, had concluded his picture by saying:

When you have taken Susa, you may vie with Jupiter himself in wealth.

Nor were the Macedonians disappointed; for, in addition to the gold and silver, they found other valuables of inestimable price. But, what was as gratifying to Alexander's own feelings, he there found many of the trophies which Xerxes had carried away from Greece;—among others, the bronze statues of Harmodius and Aristogeiton, the supposed liberators of Athens. He selected these as the most appropriate present for the Athenians. They returned in safety to their original pedestals, where they still remained in the days of Arrian. The fact is worth being recorded, because it both proves that Xerxes was an admirer of the fine arts, and that Alexander was in his own conscience so guiltless of a wish to tyrannise, that he scrupled not to honour these celebrated tyrannicides.

Abulites was reappointed *satrap*, and a Macedonian garrison and governor left in the citadel. His next march was against Persia Proper, which henceforward I shall distinguish by its Grecian name, Persis. He set out from Susa, and crossed first the Coprates, the modern Abzal, and then the Pasi-tigris, the modern Karoon, both large and navigable rivers. On crossing the latter, in the vicinity of the modern Shuster, he entered the Uxian territory. The Uxians of the plain were a peaceful race, who lived in obedience to the laws of the empire. But their kinsmen of the hills were robbers and warriors.

The royal road between Susa and Persepolis passed through a defile in their possession. The command of this had enabled them to make the great king tributary, and a certain sum was regularly paid to these bandits, whenever the king passed from one capital to the other. They now sent a message to Alexander, announcing that he should not pass unless he paid the customary gratuity. He told them briefly "to attend next day at the defile, and receive their due."

As soon as the messengers had departed, he took his guards and eight thousand chosen infantry, and entered into the mountain gorges. Craterus was ordered to conduct the rest of the army along the royal road. Alexander, guided by Susians, arrived by night at the chief villages of the Uxians, and surprised the inhabitants in their beds. Many of these were slain, a few escaped up the mountains, and their flocks and herds were driven away.

Thence he hurried to the pass, where the Uxians had assembled their whole effective force. They were panic-struck on seeing Alexander coming from the hills upon their rear, and the main army at the same time advancing along the road, and broke and fled in all directions. Some were killed, others threw themselves over precipices, and all were taught in a very short time that the sovereignty of Asia had passed into very different hands. It was not without difficulty that they were allowed to retain their mountain fastnesses, on engaging to pay a tribute. Ptolemy adds, that they owed their safety to Sysigambis, the mother of Darius, who interfered in their behalf.

Did the present rulers of Central Asia behave with the spirit and decision of Alexander, some hopes might be entertained of the civilization of that part of the world, the inhabitants of which form only two great divisions, the robber and the robbed the bandits of the desert and the mountains, and the half-starved cultivators of the plains.

The geography of Persis is peculiar and strongly marked. From Media it is separated by the continuous ridge of Mount Zagrus, and from its own sea-coast by another nameless ridge, which, parting from Mount Zagrus near the sources of the River Tab, takes a south-eastern direction, and breaks into numerous branches before it enters Carmania. The country enclosed between these two ridges was, from its position, called Coelè, or Hollow Persis, and formed the most fertile district of the kingdom. Its vales were numerous, and these were irrigated by various streams, of which the principal were the Medus, the Araxes, and the Cyrus.

The Medus and Araxes, flowing down from different parts of Mount Zagrus, united their streams, and, after passing under the walls of Persepolis, were either expended in the irrigation of the great vale, or, as at present, discharged their waters into an inland lake. The Cyrus has not yet been identified with any modern stream, but will be found, according to ancient authorities, considerably to the east of Persepolis.

In Alexander's time, two roads appear to have existed between Su-siana and Persis, one leading to the sea-coast, and thence turning to the left across the nameless ridge into the great vale, the other follow-ing the course of the modern Tab up to the strong pass called by the ancients the Persian Gates, by the moderns Kelat Suffeed, (the Castle of the Dæmons). Parmenio with the baggage was ordered to take the lower road, while Alexander with the effective force marched to The Gates.

Persis was wealthy and populous, and the inhabitants must have been aware that the invader had in deed and word distinguished their case from that of the subject nations. According to this distinction, the Persians alone had been guilty of all the outrages against Greece. They, as the dominant power, had assembled their slaves, and driven them forwards to the work of destruction. They were, therefore, personal enemies, and to be humbled as well as subdued. The *satrap* Ariobar-zanes, therefore, had no difficulty in arming forty thousand men for the defence of the passes.

These are defended at one point by a lofty rock, abrupt and pre-cipitous on all sides. The summit is a small plain, supplied with copi-ous springs, and impregnable if faithfully defended. These Gates, and the hills on both sides, were occupied by the *satrap*'s forces, and a fortified camp commanded the narrowest gorge. Alexander marched into the defile, and reached the foot of the rock. Then Ariobarzanes gave the signal for attack, and the Macedonians were overwhelmed with stones and missiles of every description, not only from the front, but also from both flanks. The success of the Persians was for the time complete, and their enemies retired before them for the space of nearly four miles.

Alexander then summoned a council, and examined prisoners as to the existence of any road by which the pass could be turned. Some were found who promised to guide the army, by mountain paths and precipitous ways, into the plain of Persis. The king's plans were soon formed. He ordered Craterus, with the main body, to encamp at the mouth of the pass, and to make a vigorous attack from the front, as soon as he should understand, from the sound of the trumpets, that the king had gained the rear.

With the evening twilight he led out the rest of his troops, en-tered the mountains, and, having followed the guides for six miles, sent Amyntas, Philotas, and Coenus forward, with orders to descend into the plain, and throw a bridge over the river, which, he understood, intervened between the pass and Persepolis. Then putting himself at the head of the guards, the brigade of Perdiccas, the most active archers and Agrians, and the royal troop of the Companion cavalry, he turned to the right over high mountains and difficult paths, and in succession surprized three posts of the enemy, without allowing a single individual to escape in the direction of the *satrap*'s camp.

At break of day, he found himself in the rear of the pass and of the fortified camp. He attacked and carried the latter with his usual impetuosity, and drove out the Persians—surprised and panic-struck, and more anxious to fly than eager to fight. In front they were met by Craterus, and driven back upon Alexander, who pressed close upon their rear. In their despair they attempted to regain their camp, but this was already occupied by Ptolemy, the son of Lagus, with three thousand men. Hemmed in, therefore, on all sides, the greater part were cut to pieces. A few, with Ariobarzanes, escaped up the sides of the mountains. It is not mentioned that the rock was taken; probably it was deserted in the general panic, or surrendered to the victor when its further defence could have no rational object.

On the road between the defiles and Persepolis, the king met a messenger from Tiridates, the governor, desiring him to hasten his advance, as the Persian soldiers were threatening to plunder the royal treasury. Thither, therefore, he hurried at the head of his cavalry, found the bridge across the river completed, and reached Persepolis in time to save the treasures.

According to Diodorus and Curtius, the city, with the exception of the palace, was given up to the Macedonians, who plundered it with all the license usually granted to soldiers when towns are taken by storm. The palace, according to Arrian, was deliberately committed to the flames, to avenge the destruction of Athens, the conflagration of the temples of the Grecian gods, and the other evils inflicted by Xerxes on Greece. Parmenio attempted in vain to dissuade the king from the commission of this outrage.

Among other arguments, he represented how unseemly it was in him to destroy his own property, and how such conduct must naturally incline the Asiatic nations to regard him more as a passing depredator than as their future and permanent sovereign; but the spirit of Achilles predominated over the voice of justice, generosity, and prudence, and the palace of the Achæmenidæ, at the gates of which the deputies of a hundred nations used to bow and listen to their destiny, was reduced to ashes.

It is impossible to say, whether the after tale of the revelry and excess, and of the influence of the Athenian Thais, in producing this catastrophe, was invented as a palliation or exaggeration of the monarch's conduct. By the Greeks at home the action would be hailed as a deed of laudable vengeance and retributive justice, but perhaps it was wisdom to whisper among the Eastern nations that it sprung from the wild excess and excitement of the moment, and not from the cool and deliberate resolution of their conqueror.

Previous to the destruction of the palace, the victor entered it, and examined the whole with the care and attention justly due to the taste and magnificence displayed in its erection. He entered the presence chamber—and seated himself on the throne of the king of kings. There can be no doubt that such a sight must have been a source of the greatest pride and exultation to every Greek who possessed a single spark of national feeling. Demaratus, the Corinthian, who was one of the royal Companions then present, burst into tears, with the exclamation:

What a pleasure have the Greeks missed who died without seeing Alexander on the throne of Darius!

At the entrance of the palace stood a colossal statue of Xerxes. This, probably by the Greek soldiers, had been thrown down from its pedestal, and lay neglected on the ground. Alexander, on passing it, stopped and addressed it, as if it had been alive:

Shall we leave you in this condition on account of the war you made upon Greece, or raise you again for the sake of your magnanimity and other virtues?

He stood a long time as if deliberating which he should do, then passed on, and left it as it was. Both these anecdotes are given by Plutarch.

The ruins of the palace of Persepolis are still to be seen near Istakar, on the right bank of the united waters of the Medus and Araxes. Travellers speak of them with admiration—not unmixed with awe. Many pillars still remain standing, a melancholy monument of the wealth, taste, and civilization of the Persians, and, in this instance, of the barbarian vengeance of the Greek.

The winter had already set in, but the activity of Alexander was not to be repressed; at the head of a chosen detachment, he invaded the mountain tribes, known by the names of Cossæi, Mardi, and Paro-etacæ, pursued them into their hill villages during the most inclement season of the year, and thus compelled them to submit to his authority.

He also visited Pasargada, built by the elder Cyrus, on the spot where he had finally defeated the Median Astyages. The treasures and citadel were delivered up without resistance, and made the third *gaza* which fell into his hands. Conscious that he had not treated the inhab-itants of Persis like a generous conqueror, he did not venture to leave the treasures within the province. An immense train of baggage-horses were therefore laden with the spoils of Persepolis and Pasargada, and attended the motions of the army, which, after remaining four months in Persis, set forward again in pursuit of Darius.

That monarch had hitherto lingered at Ecbatana, where, instead of manfully preparing to renew the contest, he had been indulging idle hopes that some untoward accident might befall Alexander in his visits to Babylon and Susa, and in his conquest of Persis.

CHAPTER 9

Fifth Campaign, B.C. 330

Alexander advanced from Persepolis, and on the road heard that the Cadusians and Scythians were marching to the assistance of Dar-ius, who, according to the report, was to meet the Macedonians and give them battle. On hearing this, he separated his effective force from the long train of baggage that attended him, and in twelve days en-tered Media; here he learned that the report respecting the Cadusians and Medians was false, and that Darius was preparing to fly to the Up-per Provinces. On this he quickened his pace, and when within three days' march of Ecbatana, met Bisthanes, the son of Ochus, the late king; from him he received certain information that Darius had com-menced his flight five days before, with 6,000 infantry, 3,000 cavalry, and with 7,000 *talents* taken from the Median treasury.

Alexander soon after entered Ecbatana, the modern Ispahan, and the capital of the second imperial nation of Asia. This city, like Perse-polis, is situated on a river that finds no exit into the sea, but is lost in sandy deserts. Its own natural stream was too scanty to supply the great plain through which it flowed and the wants of the rising city. Semiramis, therefore, or one of those great Assyrian monarchs, whose names have perished, but whose works remain, had with incredible labour, and by perforating a mountain, conducted a much larger river into the plain. This, at present, is called the Helmund.

The spot where the rock is perforated is about three days' journey to the south-west of Ispahan. The climate of this capital is most delightful and healthy. The hottest day in summer is tempered by the mountain breezes, and instead of relaxing, braces the human frame; hence it was the favourite summer residence of the ancient monarchs, from the elder Cyrus to the last of the Sassanidæ. The plain on which it is situated is unrivalled for its fertility, and capable of supplying a countless population with abundant provisions. Polybius describes the city as infinitely surpassing its sister capitals in wealth and magnificence; and Herodotus writes, that the citadel alone, within which was enclosed the palace of Dejoces, the founder of the second Median monarchy, was equal in circumference to Athens.

Here terminated the services of the Thessalian and Confederate cavalry, that had served Alexander with so much valour, fidelity, and success. Addition to their full pay and to the booty accumulated during the four campaigns, they received, as a further proof of their leader's approbation of their conduct, a gratuity of 2,000 *talents* to be divided among them.

Their war-horses were purchased by the king, and a body of cavalry appointed to escort them to the sea-coast, whence they were to be conveyed in ships to Euboea. Liberty was given to all who might wish to enter the Macedonian service, and many preferred the dangers and excitements of a warrior's life to the comforts of a peaceful and wealthy home.

Six thousand Macedonians and a strong body of horse were left in garrison at Ecbatana. The treasures of Persepolis and Pasargada, were deposited by Parmenio in the citadel, and entrusted to the care of Harpalus. Parmenio, after arranging affairs at Ecbatana, was ordered to lead the mercenaries, the Thracians, and all the cavalry but the Companions, by a circuitous route, through the territory of the Cadusians into Hyrcania.

Alexander himself, with the Companion cavalry, the greater part of the *phalanx*, the archers, and the Agrians, went in pursuit of Darius. Two roads lead from Ispahan to the north-eastern provinces of the empire, one through Yezd, and thence along the eastern edge of the Great Desert into Khorasan; the other, which is most frequented, through Kashan or Natunz, along the western edge of the Great Desert, to the pass of Khawar (the Caspian gates), and thence along the southern foot of Mount Taurus into Khorasan.

As Darius was conveying a heavy treasure with him along this latter road, Alexander entertained a hope that he might be able to overtake him before he reached the gates. He pressed forwards, therefore, with extraordinary rapidity, so that not only a great part of the infantry were compelled to fall behind, but many horses perished from fatigue and heat. In eleven days, he reached Rhagæ, placed by Strabo about thirty miles south of the Caspian gates, and consequently not to be confounded with the Rey of the Middle Ages, which is more than fifty miles to the northwest of them.

Here he was informed that Darius had already past the defile. Despairing, therefore, of overtaking him with his tired troops, he halted five days at Rhagæ, to refresh his army and reassemble the stragglers. During his short stay he appointed a Persian nobleman, by name Oxydates, to be *satrap* of the important province of Media. Alexander had found him a prisoner in the citadel of Susa, and this very dubious test was looked upon as a sufficient recommendation for his fidelity at least.

He resumed his march, and in the course of the second day passed through the Caspian gates, and reached the edge of a small desert to the east of them. Here he had halted, and parties had been sent in different directions to procure forage and provisions, when Bagistanes, a Babylonian nobleman, and Antibelus, the son of Mayæus, came and informed him that Nabarzanes, the commander of the royal guards, the *satraps*, Bessus, of Bactria, Barsaentes, of the Drangæ, Brazas, of the Arachosians, and Satibarzanes, of Areia, had seized the person of their sovereign and were keeping him in confinement.

Alexander, without a moment's delay, or even waiting for the return of the foraging parties, selected the ablest and most active of the infantry, and with these and the Companion cavalry, bearing nothing with them but their arms and two days' provisions, hastened forward to rescue, if possible, the unhappy Darius from the hands of traitors. The party marched all night, and did not halt till next day at noon.

With the night they again resumed their march, and with the dawn reached the spot where Bagistanes had left the *satraps* encamped. Here he procured further information, that Darius was confined in a covered waggon, and Bessus recognised as chief, by the Bactrian cavalry and all the barbarians—except the Persian Artabazus and his sons, who, together with the Greek mercenaries, had remained faithful, but being too weak to prevent the treason, had separated from the traitors, and retired to the mountains on the left; that the supposed plans of the conspirators were, if Alexander pursued closely, to deliver Darius and thus obtain favour—but if he did not, to assemble all the forces they could collect, and assert the independence of their several *satrapies*— in the meantime obeying Bessus as their leader.

Alexander reposed for the whole of that day at the place where he procured this information, for both men and horses were exhausted by the continued exertions. At night the march was again resumed, and continued until the next day at noon, when they arrived at a village, where the *satraps* had encamped during the preceding day, for they also marched by night. Here he questioned the inhabitants, whether there were no shorter road than the one along which the enemy was proceeding, and heard that there was, but across a desert and without water.

He immediately ordered guides, and as the foot could no longer keep up with him, he dismounted 500 of the cavalry and gave their horses to the same number of infantry officers and others, distinguished for their strength and agility: these men were, of course, to act again as foot-soldiers, should such service become necessary. Nicanor and Attalus were ordered to select the most active of the remaining troops, and to pursue the enemy along the main road, while the main body, under Craterus, was to follow slowly and in battle array.

The king himself, with the Companion cavalry, and mounted infantry, set out early in the evening, advanced five-and-twenty miles during the night, and at break of day had the satisfaction of seeing the troops of the *satrap* marching in disorder, and mostly without their arms. The very sight of Alexander put the greater number to flight, and when a few of those who offered resistance had been cut down, all fled. Bessus and his companions attempted for a time to hurry forward the vehicle in which the unfortunate Darius was confined; but, on discovering that the victor was rapidly gaining upon them, Barsaentes and Satibarzanes wounded him fatally, and left him to expire by the roadside.

He had breathed his last before Alexander came up, who thus lost an opportunity of showing how generously he could treat his rival, when fortune had decided the contest in his favour. The assassination took place in the month of July, B.C. 330, and the scene was probably the plain to the southwest of the modern Damgan. Arrian's estimate of the character of Darius is, in my opinion, so judicious, that I shall content myself with translating it freely. He says:

This was the end of Darius, who, as a warrior, was singularly remiss and injudicious. In other respects, his character is blameless, either because he was just by nature, or because he had no opportunity of displaying the contrary, as his accession and the Macedonian invasion were simultaneous. It was not in his power, therefore, to oppress his subjects, as his danger was greater than theirs. His reign was one unbroken series of disasters. First occurred the defeat of his *satraps* in the cavalry engagement on the Granicus, then the loss of Æolia, Ionia, both Phrygias, Lydia, Caria, and the whole maritime coast as far as Cilicia; then his own defeat at Issus, followed by the capture of his mother, wife, and children, and by the loss of Phoenicia and all Egypt. At Arbela, he was the first to commence a disgraceful flight, where he lost an innumerable army, composed of barbarians of almost every race.

Thenceforth he wandered from place to place, a fugitive in his own empire, until he was at last miserably betrayed by his own retinue, and loaded, king of kings as he was, with ignominy and chains. Finally, he was treacherously assassinated by his most intimate connections. Such was the fortune of Darius while living. After his death he was buried with royal honours, his children were brought up and educated by Alexander—in the same manner as if their father had been still king, and the conqueror married his daughter. At his death he was about fifty years old.

Alexander then entered Hecatompylos, the ancient capital of Parthia Proper. It received its Greek name from being the centre where many roads met, and is probably the modern Damgan. Here he rested until he had re-collected and refreshed the army, scattered and exhausted by the extraordinary rapidity of the pursuit. Nicanor, the son of Parmenio, who had held one of the most confidential commands during all the campaigns, and who had of late undergone great fatigue, sunk under the exertion, and soon after died.

Alexander now prepared to invade Hyrcania. This province situated between Mount Taurus and the south-eastern shores of the Caspian Sea, contained the greater portion of the modern Mazanderan, and the whole of Astrabad and Jorgan. The country between Mount Taurus and the Caspian is low, marshy, and covered with excellent timber, well adapted for ship building. Thus, it forms a striking contrast to the elevated steps of Media, Khorasan, Carmania, and Persis.

The mountain passes being beset by the bandit tribes, the king divided his army into three bodies.

He himself led the most numerous and active division over the mountains, by the shortest and most difficult paths. Craterus, with two brigades of the *phalanx*, and some archers and cavalry, was ordered to make a circuit to the left through the territories of the Tapeiri, who have bequeathed a name to the modern Tabaristan. Erigyius, the friend of his youth, who had been much brought forward of late, conducted the main body along the royal road leading from Hecatompylos to Zadra-Carta, probably the modern Sari. The three divisions were equally successful, and re-united in the plains of Hyrcania.

They had not, however, fallen in with the Greek mercenaries of Darius, who had been one object of this combined movement. While the army was thus encamped, Artabazus and his three sons presented themselves before Alexander, and brought with them Autophradates, the *satrap* of the Tapeiri, and deputies from the Greek mercenaries. His *satrapy* was restored to Autophradates; and Artabazus and his sons were received with great distinction and honour, both on account of their high nobility and of their fidelity to their unhappy sovereign. The Greek deputies, who came to seek some terms of pacification, were briefly told that none could be granted, and that they must submit themselves to the judgment of the king.

This they promised to do, and officers were sent to conduct them to the camp. In the meantime, he himself marched westward into the country of the Mardi, who inhabited the lofty mountains to the north-west of the Caspian Gates, and in the vicinity of the modern Tehran. This nation, into whose mountain fortresses no enemy within the memory of man had ever penetrated, submitted after a slight resistance, and were commanded to obey the orders of the *satrap* of the Tapeiri. If Alexander had known as much of the heroic poetry of the East as of the West, he would have prided himself on having traversed the regions, and conquered the enemies, which had already conferred an immortal name on Rustan, the Hercules of Persia.

On his return from this expedition, he found the Greek mercenaries, and ambassadors, from various states, who had continued to the last in the court of The Great King. Among others, deputies from Lacedæmon and Athens proved how busy of late the intrigues between the southern Greeks and Darius had been. These were imprisoned, but the envoys from Sinopè and Carthage were dismissed. In the case of the Greek mercenaries, a distinction was drawn. Those who had entered the Persian service previous to the decree constituting a captain-general to lead the Greeks into Asia, were dismissed. Pardon was offered to the rest, on condition of entering into the Macedonian service. These willingly accepted the alternative, and were placed under the command of Andronicus, who had conducted them into the camp, and interested himself in their behalf.

Alexander then moved to Zadra-Carta, where he remained fifteen days, which were partly devoted to public sacrifices, festivities, and gymnastic games.

Thence he marched eastward through Parthia—and arrived at Susia or Susa, a city of Areia, the modern Khorasan. Satibarzanes, the *satrap*, came and made his submission; and, although he had been one of the actual murderers of Darius, was restored to his government. An officer and forty horsemen were sent to escort him to Arta-Coana, his chief city, and to announce to all that he was recognised as *satrap* by the victor. Many Persians came over to Alexander, while remaining at Susia, and informed him that Bessus wore the upright tiara, and the robe with the intermingled white and purple stripes, distinctions in Persia peculiar to the king of kings—that he had assumed the name of Artaxerxes, and claimed the sovereignty of all Asia—that he was supported by the Persians who had taken refuge in Bactria, as well as the majority of the Bactrians—and that he was in daily expectation of being joined by a strong body of Scythian auxiliaries.

This important intelligence determined Alexander immediately to enter Bactria. He had already collected his forces and was preparing to march, when suddenly it was announced that Satibarzanes had put the officer and the escort of cavalry to death, and was collecting an army at Arta-Coana—with the intention of supporting Bessus and making war upon Alexander. As this was the first breach of faith, committed by any Persian nobleman admitted into his service, Alexander, with his usual promptitude, returned instantly, reached Arta-Coana in the evening of the second day, and by his celerity confounded the plans of the *satrap*, who fled and left his accomplices to the mercy of the victor.

Arta-Coana was probably the city which, by the later Greeks, was called the Areian Alexandreia. The latter was undoubtedly the modern Herat, and the struggle between its native and Greek name was long and doubtful:—even as late as the fourteenth century it was called Skandria by the Persians. It was situated on the river Aries, which according to ancient authors ended either in the desert or a lake;— although modern maps prolong its course into the Tedjen or Ochus, which, to say the least of it, is extremely improbable.

Alexander, having been thus forced to return to Arta-Coana, did not resume his original route into Bactria, but changed his plan. Probably the inclination shown by the Areians to rise in arms rendered it imprudent to advance into Bactria, while Areia on the right and Sogdiana on the left flank were hostile. After suppressing the Areian revolt, he therefore marched into Drangiana against Barsaentes, the *satrap*, the accomplice of Satibarzanes in the murder of Darius, and probably in the late revolt. The assassin fled into the eastern provinces; and, being there seized and delivered to Alexander, was ordered to be executed for his treason.

While the army was encamped in this province, a conspiracy was discovered, which ended in the execution of the two most powerful men in the army. Arrian's account is brief and consistent, and therefore deserves to be inserted:

> Here the king discovered the treason of Philotas, the son of Parmenio. Both Aristobulus and Ptolemy write that his guilty intentions had been mentioned to Alexander even as early as the visit to Egypt; but that the information appeared incredible to the king, on account of the friendship which, from their earliest years, had subsisted between him and Philotas, and of the honours with which he had loaded both the father and the son. Ptolemy, the son of Lagus, writes that Philotas was brought before the assembled Macedonians, that Alexander was vehement in his accusations, and that Philotas spoke in his own defence; that witnesses were brought forwards and convicted Philotas and his accomplices, both by other clear proofs and by his own confession, that he had heard that a conspiracy was forming against Alexander. He was thus convicted of having concealed the matter from the king, although he had had to wait upon him twice a day in the royal tent. Philotas and his accomplices were, therefore, pierced to death by the darts of the Macedonians.

One of the Roman emperors complained, with equal humour and truth, that baffled and detected conspiracies are always supposed never to have existed; and that the only chance a sovereign had of being believed in such a case, was to allow the traitors to execute their designs. It is not to be wondered, therefore, that the republicans of Greece have depicted this most unhappy and melancholy occurrence in the colours best adapted to blacken the character of Alexander. According to them, Philotas was put to the rack, tortured, and blasted by the withering look of his sovereign, while yet hanging upon the wheel; and a confession of guilt, thus extorted, was pressed against him when brought before the Macedonian assembly. For these atrocities, however, there does not appear the slightest foundation. The facts of the case, as far as they can be extracted from the different accounts, appear to have been as follows.

Dymnus, an officer of no great rank or authority, had attempted to induce his friend Nicomachus to join in a conspiracy against the life of Alexander. Nicomachus pretended to enter into the design, and drew from Dymnus the names of the leaders in the plot. He then without delay mentioned the whole affair to his brother Cebalinus, who, as the other's motions would probably be watched, was to discover the affair. But Cebalinus, finding it difficult to procure personal access to the royal presence, accosted Philotas, who was in daily attendance, and requested him to transmit the circumstances to the king.

Philotas agreed to do so. But Cebalinus, naturally surprised that no inquiry took place, and that neither he nor Nicomachus had been summoned to give evidence, waited again on Philotas, and asked if he had made the communication. The answer given by Philotas was, that Alexander had been too busily engaged all day, but that he would certainly mention it next morning. This also was passing without any inquiries, when the brothers, either suspicious of the integrity of Philotas, or fearful lest the discovery should reach the king by some other channel, applied to Metron, one of the royal pages, who instantly laid the whole affair before Alexander.

Nor was any delay safe, as according to Dymnus the very next day was fixed for carrying the plot into execution. Alexander himself examined the informers, and sent a detachment of the guards to seize Dymnus; but they failed to bring him alive before the king. He either slew himself, or by his extreme resistance compelled the guards to slay him. His conduct in either case was conclusive of his guilt, and proved that his patrons, whoever they might be, had rightly judged of his fitness for the desperate service on which he had entered.

The clue being thus broken, it was natural that suspicions should fall upon the great officer whose most culpable negligence had thus endangered the life of his sovereign; and he was brought to trial before the great jury of the Macedonian Army. According to Curtius, the assembly in peace, and the army in war, had alone, under the Macedonian constitution, the power of inflicting capital punishment.

Philotas was a brave and gallant man, of expensive habits, fond of pleasure, affecting Persian magnificence in his equipage, retinue, and mode of living. It is said also that among private friends, and even to his mistresses, he was wont to speak in a disparaging tone of the abilities and achievements of Alexander—call him *the boy*—and claim for himself and his father the whole glory and renown of the Macedonian victories. Indulgence in conversation of this description, equally absurd and indecorous, must have tended to foster, if not produce, in his mind feelings of contempt and disregard for his sovereign.

"Make yourself less conspicuous, my son," was the wise but ineffectual counsel of his father. His insolent demeanour could not escape the personal observation of the quick-sighted monarch, nor were there wanting those who carefully repeated in the royal presence the arrogant language of Philotas. Thus was the king's confidence in the son of Parmenio shaken; and the vain youth had the mortification of seeing Craterus, his personal opponent, entrusted, during the two last campaigns, with every separate command of importance. A preference so marked must naturally have increased his discontent, caused him to regard himself as overlooked and aggrieved, and made him a willing participator in any desperate schemes.

He had been left behind in Parthia, to celebrate the funeral obsequies of his brother Nicanor, and had not long rejoined the camp before the discovery of the plot took place. It is not unlikely that Parmenio also paid the last honours to that gallant youth; and both the veteran general, we may easily believe, and Philotas felt that, while royal favour had passed away, the casualties of war were pressing heavy on their family—for the youngest brother Hector had also perished.

One fact is certain—Parmenio had refused to obey orders. Alexander had commanded him to advance from Media, through Cadusia, into Hyrcania. And the king's western march into the territories of the Mardi was apparently undertaken for the sake of giving him the meeting. But neither Parmenio nor his troops appear to have quitted the walls of Ecbatana.

Had Alexander fallen by the hand of Dymnus, or some such *desperado*, Philotas, the commander of the Companion cavalry, would undoubtedly have been entitled to the command of the army; and as Ecbatana and the treasures were in the power of Parmenio, the empire would have been completely at the disposal of the father and son. The Macedonian nobles were a turbulent race, who scrupled not, on what they conceived adequate provocation, or even prospect of personal advantage, to dip their hands in the blood of their sovereigns.

Of the eight immediate predecessors of Alexander died only two a natural death; one fell in battle; five perished by the blow of assassins. Without taking these things into consideration, it is impossible to understand the difficulties of the young king's position, or to form a just estimate of his character. In the present instance his conduct was most constitutional, for all authors agree in the three following points:— that the trial was public, that a majority of the assembled Macedonians pronounced the sentence of condemnation, and that this majority carried their own sentence into execution.

The most painful and difficult question remained—to decide the fate of Parmenio. Diodorus writes that he also was condemned by the assembly; but his authority is not sufficient in this case. Arrian says:

> Perhaps, it seemed incredible to Alexander that the father should not have been a participator in the plots of the son. Even were he not an accomplice, he might prove a dangerous survivor, exasperated by the death of his son, and so highly honoured, not only by Alexander and the Macedonians, but by the whole body of mercenaries in the army, whom, both on ordinary and extraordinary occasions, he had commanded with the greatest applause.

It was decreed that he should die. Polydamas, one of the Companions, was dispatched to Media, with a letter from the king to Sitalces, Menidas, and Cleander, the lieutenants of Parmenio, ordering them to put their chief to death. The headquarters of the army were then in Drangiana, the modern Zarang or Zaringe of the Arab geographers, situated on the northern bank of the great River Heermund, the ancient Etymander. This, on the map, is five hundred and sixty miles from Ecbatana or Ispahan; yet Polydamas, according to Strabo, mounted on a dromedary, crossed the desert, and reached the city in eleven days. The generals obeyed, and Parmenio died.

Three sons of Andromenes—Amyntas, Attalus, and Simmias— were also brought to trial, principally on account of the great intimacy and confidence that had always subsisted between the eldest of them and Philotas. The danger of these young men had been much increased by the conduct of Polemon, a fourth brother, who, on hearing of the apprehension of Philotas, deserted to the enemy. Amyntas, however, made a powerful defence before the assembly, repelled the charges, and was acquitted. He then asked the assembly's permission to go and seek his fugitive brother. It was granted. He went in search of him, found him, and persuaded him to return and submit to the law.

If any doubts remained before, they were removed by this open and sincere behaviour of Amyntas. Alexander, the Lyncestian, who had now been three years in custody, was also tried, condemned, and executed by the great jury of the assembly. Demetrius, one of the generals of the bodyguard, soon after fell under suspicion of having been deeply implicated in the treason of Philotas. He was, therefore, consigned to safe custody, and Ptolemy, the son of Lagus, the personal and early friend of Alexander, promoted to fill the vacancy.

It is clear that this affair must have rudely shaken the unlimited confidence with which Alexander had hitherto treated his friends, and that henceforth he judged greater caution necessary. The command of the Companion cavalry, so superior both in rank and gallantry to all the rest, was no longer trusted to one individual. It was separated into two bodies, and Cleitus was appointed to the command of one, and Hephæstion of the other division.

From Drangiana Alexander marched up the Heermund, and arrived among a peaceful and civilized nation, that once had borne the name of Agriaspæ, but were then called Euergetæ or Benefactors. This honourable appellation had been bestowed upon them by Cyrus the Great, whose army, exhausted by hunger and fatigue, in returning from an expedition, were relieved and refreshed by the active kindness of this tranquil and agricultural people. Alexander treated them with marked attention, both on account of their excellent character, and from respect for the first Cyrus, whom he held in great admiration.

He offered them an increase of territory, which, with the exception of a small corner, they had the moderation to refuse. Probably they were an Assyrian colony, attracted by the copious streams of the Heermund, and the delightfulness of the climate. Even as late as the tenth century, Ebn Haukal describes the vale of the Heermund as populous, and covered with cities. From Bost to the lake Zurrah, it was intersected with canals, like the land of Egypt. At present the cultivated strip on both sides the river is very narrow.

From the Agriaspæ the king marched eastward, and as he advanced, received the submission of the Drangæ, the Drangogæ, and the Arachosians. While he was thus employed, Satibarzanes made an irruption into Areia at the head of 2,000 Bactrian cavalry, granted to him by Bessus, and succeeded in organising a formidable insurrection. The Persian Artabazus, Erigyius, and Caranus, were sent back to suppress this, and Phrataphernes the Parthian *satrap*, was ordered to invade Areia from the west. Satibarzanes stood his ground, and fought a well-contested battle; nor had the barbarians the worst, until Erigyius with his own hand slew their general, piercing him in the face with his lance. The Asiatics then fled, and Erigyius had the honour of being the first Macedonian in Asia, who carried away what the Romans would have called the "*Spolia Opima*," the arms of a commander in chief, won in single combat by an opponent of the same rank.

Alexander, with the main army, still continued their advance, and toiled over the mountains of Candahar in deep snow, and with great labour. They then approached the southern foot of the great range of mountains, which hitherto they had called Taurus, but to the eastern part of which they now, in compliment to the king, gave the name of Caucasus.

The more accurate geographers, however, call it Paropamisus. There Alexander founded and called after his own name a city, which, as I shall have occasion to show in describing the march from Bactria into India, could not have been far from the modern Cabul. Here he remained for two months, until the severity of the winter had relaxed.

CHAPTER 10

The Sixth Campaign, B.C. 329

With the spring the army moved from its winter quarters, and in fifteen days crossed the main ridge of mountains that separated the southern provinces from Bactria. Aristobulus writes that nothing grew on these hills but pines and the herb silphium, from which the *laser-pitium* of the Romans, and the *benzoin* of the Orientals was extracted. This drug, so highly prized by the ancients, is, according to naturalists, the modern *asafoetida*; if so, taste must have strangely altered during the last 2,000 years. The hills, however, were well inhabited by pastoral tribes, whose flocks and herds grazed the silphium, a nourishing and favourite food.

On reaching Adrapsa, on the northern side, the Macedonians found the whole country laid waste by Bessus and his supporters; their hope was to prevent the advance of Alexander by this system of devastation. But, in Arrian's simple style:

> Alexander advanced nevertheless, with difficulty, indeed, on account of the deep snow, and in want of all necessaries, but still he advanced.

When Bessus heard that the king was not far off, his heart failed him, and he and his associates crossed the Oxus and entered Sogdiana. Seven thousand Bactrian cavalry, who had hitherto followed his banner, refused to abandon their country, disbanded and returned to their several homes. The Macedonians soon after captured Bactria and Arnus, the two chief cities, and effectually relieved themselves from all their difficulties. Thus, Memnon's plan may be said to have been fairly tried, by Bessus, and to have utterly failed; in fact, the only case where such a system can succeed, is where there is some great barrier within which the invaded can defy the attack of the invader.

Bactria, the modern Balk, and once called Zariaspa, was built on the banks of a considerable stream, which flowing down from the Paropamisus, entered the Oxus about a day's journey to the north of Bactria, In the days of the Arabian geographers, the whole of its waters were expended in irrigation, long before its junction with the Oxus; and this probably is its present state. Balk, although fallen from its regal magnificence, is still a considerable city. The whole district followed the fate of the capital, and submitted to the conqueror, who appointed Artabazus to the vacant *satrapy*:

He then prepared to cross the Oxus and pursue Bessus into the Transoxiana of the Romans, the Mawaralnahr of the Arabians; but the Thessalian and confederate troops, who had volunteered at the commencement of the last campaign, had been sickened by the snow, the cold, and the hunger to which they had been lately exposed; Alexander, therefore, seeing the state of their minds, gave them leave to return home. At the same time a scrutiny took place among the Macedonian soldiers, and all whom age, wounds, or other infirmities, had rendered either unable or unwilling to encounter further hardships, were sent home with the Thessalians.

According to Aristobulus—and he is on the whole the best authority even in our days—the Oxus, of all the rivers of Asia, was inferior to the great Indian rivers alone; its sources were supposed not to be far from those of the Indus and the Ganges—and its termination in the Caspian. This last assertion has been universally adopted as a truth, and the map of Asia, to this day, traces an imaginary course for the Oxus or Jihoon from the vicinity of Urgantz to the shores of the Caspian

But the waters of the Oxus never had, as I believe, any other termination than the lake Aral. In the tenth century, Ebn Haukal, in the thirteenth, Edrisi, describe it as falling into that lake. Abulghazi Khan certainly does assert that one branch did once pass under the walls of Urgantz; if so, it must have been an artificial canal, which, when the labour of man ceased to be bestowed upon it, soon was closed. Ancient geographers looked upon the mouth of the Ochus or modern Tedgen, as the main branch of the Oxus, although modern observations have proved that there is no communication between them.

Aristobulus, who could not be mistaken in this point, describes the Oxus as six *stadia*, or something less, (according to the measure adopted by the companions of Alexander,) than half a mile broad. This great stream presented a formidable obstacle to the northern progress of Alexander. Many attempts were made to construct piers on the bank, but as it consisted of a loose sandy soil, the short piles formed from the stunted timber to be procured in the vicinity, were swallowed, and no solid work could be constructed. The king, however, was not to be baffled by these untoward circumstances; floats were formed, supported on hides, either inflated, or stuffed with hay and rendered waterproof; and on these frail barks the whole army was ferried across in the course of five days.

As soon as the Macedonians had gained the right bank, Spitamenes, *satrap* of Sogdiana, and Dataphernes, two of the leading Persians who had hitherto adhered to Bessus, sent messengers to Alexander, promising, were a small force with a respectable commander sent to strengthen their hands, to deliver up Bessus, whom they had already placed under arrest. Ptolemy, the son of Lagus, was sent forwards, with a small but select force, and his account of the transaction must certainly be regarded as the most authentic.

He advanced with great rapidity, and in four days traversed a space equal to ten ordinary marches. On approaching the enemy, he was informed that Spitamenes and Dataphernes, scrupled actually to deliver Bessus into the hands of the Macedonians, but that the pretender to the empire of Asia was left almost destitute of troops in a walled village. Thither Ptolemy proceeded, and made himself master of the person of Bessus without encountering the slightest resistance. As soon as he had thus successfully executed his commission, he wrote to the king for instructions as to the manner in which he was to conduct the prisoner into his presence. The answer was, to deprive him of his arms, to place a rope round his neck, and thus conduct him to meet Alexander.

Ptolemy obeyed, and when the king appeared, drew his prisoner to one side of the road. Alexander, when opposite, stopped his chariot,

and asked Bessus why he had seized, bound, and murdered his kins-
man and benefactor, Darius? The unfortunate man answered, that it
was not his individual deed; that all the *satraps* had concurred with
him in the necessity of the measure, and that their common object
was to secure the favour of Alexander. This excuse, false certainly in
its latter part, was not received. Bessus was publicly scourged, while a
herald announced to all the nature of his offence, and was sent to Bactria, there to await his final doom. Alexander then marched onwards,
and arrived at Maracanda, the modern Samarcand.

Many readers may imagine that the Macedonians had now been
conducted into sandy deserts and barren regions, where all was desolate, and the necessaries of life could scarcely be procured; but the
contrary was the case, for, according to the Arabian geographers, who
were intimately acquainted with every part of the country, there cannot under the sun be found more delightful spots than in Mawaralnahr, between the Oxus and Jaxartes, the Jihoon, and the Sihoon. The
valley, Al Sogd, (whence the Greek Sogdiana,) with Samarcand at its
upper and Bokhara at its lower end, is in an especial manner celebrated by them, as one of the terrestrial paradises. Ebn Haukal, the great
traveller and geographer writes:

> In all the regions of the earth, there is not a more delightful and
> flourishing country than Mawaralnahr, especially the district of
> Bokhara. If a person stand on its ancient citadel and cast his eyes
> around, nothing is visible on any side but beautiful green and
> luxuriant herbage, so that he might imagine the green of the
> earth and the azure of the skies to be blended with each other;
> and as there are verdant fields in every quarter, so there are villas
> interspersed among them.

The same author writes:

> It is said, that in all the world there are not more delightful plac-
> es than the *sogd* (vale) of Samarcand, the *rood* Aileh, (near Bal-
> sora,) and the *ghouteh* of Damascus; but the *ghouteh* of Damascus
> is within one *farsang* of barren and dry hills, without trees, and
> it contains many spots which are desolate and without verdure.
> A fine prospect ought to be such as completely fills the eye, and
> nothing should be visible but sky and green. The River Aileh
> affords this kind of prospect for one *farsang* only, and the ver-
> dant spot is either surrounded by or opposite to a dreary desert.
> But the vales, and buildings, and cultivated plains of Bokhara,

extend above thirteen *farsangs* by twelve, and the *sogd*, for eight days' journey, is all delightful country, affording fine prospects, and full of gardens, orchards, villages, cornfields, villas, running streams, reservoirs, and fountains, both on the right and left hand. You pass from cornfields into rich meadows; and the *sogd* is far more healthy than the *rood* Aileh and the *ghouteh* of Damascus, and its fruit is the finest in the world.

Alexander remained for some time in this delightful region, where he remounted his cavalry, as the loss of horses of every kind had been great during the winter operations, and the passage of the Paropamisus. In an attack on a hill fortress, the position of which is doubtful, as Arrian places it near the Jaxartes, Curtius, between the Oxus and Maracanda, he received a severe wound from an arrow, which splintered a portion of one of the bones of his leg, and long incapacitated him from active duty. He could not, however, remain quiet until the wound was thoroughly healed, but caused himself to be carried in a litter wherever he judged his presence necessary. A dispute took place, consequently, between the cavalry and infantry;—to which belonged the privilege of carrying their wounded king. This Alexander decided with his usual judgment, by devolving the duty alternately on both parties.

All Transoxiana had now acknowledged his authority, and every important city had admitted a Macedonian garrison; he himself had advanced to the Jaxartes or Sihoon, and fixed upon the site of a new town, to be called Alexandreia, which he expected would in time prove a great and flourishing city, when suddenly the Sogdians and Bactrians rose up in arms and expelled or massacred most of the Macedonian garrisons.

There can be no doubt of the connexion of Spitamenes and the other accomplices of Bessus with this insurrection; their reception from Alexander was probably not very cordial, nor do we read of any re-appointments to their governments, as had invariably been the case on previous occasions. It appears also to me, that Alexander deeply erred in ordering Bessus to be scourged publicly for his crimes. That lord belonged to the highest order of nobility, and was entitled to great privileges.

Xenophon informs us, that when Orontes had been condemned to death for his treachery to Cyrus the Younger, and was in the act of being led to execution, all men prostrated themselves before him, as usual. It may be inferred that the feelings of the Persians were as much outraged by the degrading punishment of Bessus, as those of the English nobility would be, were they to see a Duke of Norfolk or Northumberland flogged by the hands of the common hangman through the streets of London.

Alexander had summoned an assembly, to be composed of all the leading men in the country. The object probably was to settle the government and the collection of the revenues on the plan most agreeable to the men of influence. But Spitamenes, an able and active man, took occasion from this to convey private intelligence to all summoned, announcing that the object of the invader was to seize and massacre them all. The consequence was the general revolt, in which the people in the immediate vicinity of Alexander and his army joined.

The inhabitants of these provinces were not only more warlike than the nations hitherto subdued, but connected by blood and international communication with the powerful Scythian tribes to the north of the Jaxartes and to the east of Sogdiana and Bactria, who, as afterwards plainly appeared, had promised to aid Spitamenes and his associates. The emergency, therefore, was such as to call forth all the energies of Alexander.

The inhabitants of the populous vale on the left bank of the Jaxartes—called in modern times the districts of Fergana and Al-Hash—had taken refuge in seven fortified cities. The walls were formed of indurated earth or mud, being the same materials still used in that country for like purposes.

Alexander, having ordered Craterus to march against Cyropolis, the chief city, (probably the modern Chojand,) proceeded in person to Gaza, one of the towns. The troops formed a circle round it—with the archers, slingers, and dartmen in the rear. These, while the soldiers were marching to the escalade, cleared the walls of their defenders, by the clouds of missiles which they discharged; the ladders were then applied, and the Macedonians mounted the walls. The men were put to the sword, the women and children were spared. The army was then led to the next town, which was fortified in the same manner—and captured by the same means. Next day, a third city experienced the like fate.

While the infantry were thus employed, the cavalry was sent to watch two other cities, lest the inhabitants, taking warning from the fate of their neighbours, should seek refuge in the desert or among the mountains, where pursuit would be impossible. The inhabitants of these, as Alexander had foreseen, learning the fate of the others from the smoke of the conflagration, and from chance fugitives, attempted to escape in a body, but were overtaken by the cavalry and mostly cut to pieces.

Having thus captured five towns in the short space of three days, the king joined Craterus under the walls of Cyropolis, the capital. This town had been founded by the great Cyrus, as a barrier against the Scythians. Its fortifications were more formidable, and it was garrisoned by eighteen thousand of the bravest barbarians of the vicinity. Engines were, therefore, constructed, and preparations made to batter down the walls, and form breaches in the regular way.

But as he was carefully examining the walls, he discovered the channel of a stream, which in winter ran through the city, but was then dry. The aperture between the wall and the bed of the torrent was large enough to permit the entrance of single soldiers. He himself, with a few others, creeped into the city by this inlet, while the attention of the besieged was fixed upon the operations of the engineers. The party having thus gained entrance, rushed to the nearest gate, broke it open, and admitted the guards, the archers, and Agrians, who had been drawn up in front of the gate for the very purpose. The garrison, surprized, but not dismayed, bravely charged the assailants, and nearly succeeded in expelling them.

Alexander himself received a stunning blow from a stone, on the nape of his neck, and Craterus was wounded by an arrow. The Macedonians at last drove the garrison from the streets and the market place into the citadel. But as this was not supplied with water, ten thousand men surrendered at discretion in the course of the following day; and the seventh and last city followed their example. The prisoners were divided among the soldiers, in order to be conveyed out of the country—it being Alexander's fixed resolution not to leave in Sogdiana a single individual who had been actively engaged in this insurrection.

The necessity of these rapid and energetic measures became manifest, when the right bank of the Jaxartes was seen crowded by Scythian cavalry, eager to render assistance to the insurgents.

These Scythians, so much extolled by the sophists, and even poets, of Greece and Rome, for their virtues and the happy simplicity of their lives, have, in all recorded ages, been the curse of the civilized world. Issuing in all directions from the steppes of Tartary, they have spread ruin and desolation over the fairest portions of our globe. Their habits and practices have been the same for five-and-twenty centuries, and under the various names of Cimmerians, Trerians, Scythians,

Getæ, Tochari, Parthians, Goths, Huns, Mongols, Zagataians, Tatars, Turks, and Turkomans, they have never ceased to be the scourge of agricultural Asia and Europe; nor will anything ever stay this plague but the introduction of European arts and sciences among the peaceful inhabitants of, the banks of the great Asiatic rivers. Alexander had already come in contact with their kindred tribes, to the west of the Euxine—and he was now destined to hear their taunts from the right bank of the Jaxartes.

He was then engaged in founding and fortifying that Alexandreia which was named by the Greeks *Eschata* or *Extreme*. This city is probably the modern Aderkand on the left bank of the Jaxartes, at the eastern end of the fertile district of Fergana. Ebn Haukal says:

It enjoys the warmest climate of any place in the district of Fergana. It is next to the enemy, and is twice or thrice as large as Awash. It has an ancient citadel, and suburbs, with groves and gardens, and running streams.

The army was engaged for three weeks in fortifying this limitary town. The termination of the labour was celebrated by the usual sacrifices and their accompanying festivities. The soldiers competed for prizes in horse races, chariot races, and other trials of skill, strength, and activity. The colonists, for the new city, were selected indifferently from Greeks, barbarians, and Macedonians.

But each returning day presented to the view of Alexander the hated Scythians on the opposite bank. They even shot their arrows across, as the river was not broad in that quarter, and dared the Macedonians to the combat, telling them that if they came over, they would soon be taught the difference between the Scythians and the Asiatic barbarians.

Exasperated by these and similar taunts, Alexander ordered floats and rafts, supported by inflated skins and stuffed hides, to be constructed, for the purpose of conveying the troops across. But the sacrificial omens were pronounced by the diviners to be most inauspicious. Aristander and his companions were probably alarmed for the honour and safety of the king. They must have known that the Jaxartes was the river which, under the name of Araxes, the great Cyrus had crossed previous to his fatal defeat by the Scythian Massagetæ. The narrow escape also of the first Darius, and the consequent irruption of his pursuers into Thrace, had rendered the Scythian name terrible in Greece.

The diviners, therefore, persisted in reporting bad omens; and

Alexander, angry and indignant as he was, dared not (nor would it have been wise) to disregard their answers. The Scythians, however, still continued to line the opposite bank, and he also persevered in consulting the omens, He had no other choice he could not march back into Sogdiana and Bactria to suppress the rebellion, and leave the Scythians to cross the river without molestation. His perseverance succeeded, and Aristander at length pronounced the omens favourable for the expedition, but that great personal danger to the king was portended.

By this answer, probably, he hoped to sooth the angry feelings of Alexander, while he calculated that the great officers, supported by the voice of the army, would interfere and prevent operations likely to prove fatal to their sovereign. But Alexander declared that he would run every risk rather than be braved and baffled by the Scythians as the first Darius had been.

There is no reason to suspect any collusion between him and the diviners. If any did exist, it was probably between the great officers and the latter. Aristander's declaration was, "that he could not falsify the omens, because Alexander wished them different."

The army was drawn up on the edge of the river ready to embark. Behind the troops were placed the engines, from which missiles of every kind were discharged, in order to dislodge the enemy from the opposite bank, and leave room for the soldiers to land. The Scythians were terrified by the execution done by the powerful catapults, especially when they saw one of their chief warriors actually transfixed through shield, breastplate, and back-piece, by an engine-dart. They, therefore, retired beyond the reach of the missiles. The trumpets instantly gave the signal, and the floats pushed from the shore, headed as usual by Alexander in person.

The first division consisted of archers and slingers, who kept the enemy at a distance, while the second division, consisting of the *phalanx*, were landing and forming Alexander then ordered a troop of the mercenary cavalry, and four troops of heavy lancers, to advance and charge. The Scythians not only stood their ground, but wheeled round the flanks of this small body, and severely galled the men with their missiles, while they easily eluded the direct charge of the Macedonian horse.

As soon as Alexander had observed their mode of fighting, he distributed the archers, Agrians, and other light troops, between the ranks of the cavalry. He then advanced, and when the lines were near, ordered three troops of the Companion cavalry, and all the mounted dartmen, to attack from the flanks, while he formed the remainder into columns, and charged in front. The enemy were thus prevented from executing their usual evolutions, for the cavalry pressing upon them on every side, and the light troops mingling among them, made it unsafe for them either to expose their flanks or to turn suddenly round. The victory was decisive, and a thousand Scythian horsemen were left dead on the field.

The pursuit was across a parched and sandy plain, and the heat, for it was in the middle of summer, was great and overpowering. Alexander, in order to allay the thirst from which, in common with the whole army, he suffered excessively, drank some brackish water, which, either from its own noxious qualities, or from the overheated state of the king, nearly proved fatal to him. The pursuit which, as usual, was led by himself, was instantly stayed, and he was carried back to the camp more dead than alive. Thus, the credit of Aristander was preserved.

Soon after an embassy arrived from the Scythian king, imputing the late hostilities to bandit tribes, that acted without the authority of the great council of the nation, and professing the willingness of the Scythian government to obey the commands of Alexander. The apology was accepted, and the ambassadors received with kindness. The rumour of this victory and of the consequent submission of the Scythians, hitherto regarded invincible, proved highly advantageous in repressing the further progress of the insurrection. The Macedonians, either from ignorance or flattery, called the Jaxartes the Tanais, and boasted that their victorious king had passed into Europe through the north-western boundaries of Asia.

This victory over the Scythians was very seasonable, as soon after the news arrived of the heaviest blow that befell the Macedonian arms during the whole war.

While Alexander was detained on the Jaxartes, Spitamenes, at the head of the insurgent Sogdians, had marched to Maracanda, gained possession of the city, and besieged the Macedonian garrison in the citadel. Alexander, on hearing this, dispatched to the assistance of the besieged a reinforcement of Greek mercenaries, consisting of fifteen hundred infantry and eight hundred cavalry. To these were added sixty of the Companions. The military commanders were Andromachus, Menedemus, and Caranus. But these were ordered to act under the direction of Pharnuches, a Lycian, skilled in the language of the country, and accounted an able negotiator. Perhaps Alexander thought that, as the insurrection had principally been caused by a misconception, Pharnuches would be more likely to suppress it by explanations, than military men by the sword.

As soon as Spitamenes heard of their approach, he raised the siege of the citadel, and retired down the River Polytimetus towards the royal city of Sogdiana. The Polytimetus is the modern Kohuk, and the royal city is Bokhara, called by Ptolemy Tru-Bactra. Spitamenes was pursued by the Greeks, who, in their eagerness to expel him entirely from Sogdiana, followed him into the territory of the Scythian nomads, who possessed the great steppe between the Sogd and the lake Aral. Its present inhabitants are Uzbeks. The invasion of their territories roused the tribes of the desert, and six hundred chosen horsemen joined Spitamenes.

Inspirited by this accession of strength, greater in name even than reality, the Persian halted on the edge of the desert, and prepared to give his pursuers battle; and the tactics, which the genius and activity of Alexander had repeatedly baffled, proved successful against commanders of less skill and vigour.

Spitamenes neither charged himself, nor awaited the Macedonian charge; but his cavalry wheeled round them in circular movements, and discharged their arrows into the centre of the infantry. When the Greek cavalry attacked, the Scythians easily eluded them by the greater swiftness and freshness of their horses. But the moment the assailants halted or retired, the Scythians again returned and resumed the offensive. When many Greeks had been thus wounded and a few slain, the generals formed the whole into a square, and retreated in the direction of the Polytimetus, in the vicinity of which a wooded ravine seemed likely to protect them from the enemy's missiles.

But, on approaching the river, Caranus, the commander of the cavalry, without communicating with Andromachus, the commander of the infantry, attempted to cross, and thus give the cavalry at least a chance of safety. The infantry being thus deserted by their only protectors, broke their ranks, and hurried in disorder, and without listening to the voice of their officers, to the bank of the river. And although this was high and precipitous, and the river itself far larger than the Thessalian Peneius, they rushed down the bank and into the stream, heedless of consequences.

The enemy were not slow in taking advantage of this disorder; their cavalry rode into the river, and, while some crossed, took possession of the opposite bank, and drove such of the Greeks as reached it back into the stream—others pressed from the rear, and cut down those who were entering the water; large parties stationed themselves on each flank, and showered their darts and arrows upon the helpless Greeks, who, being thus surrounded on all sides, took refuge in a small island. But here they were equally exposed to the arrows of the barbarians, who did not cease to discharge them until they had destroyed the whole. Only forty of the cavalry, and three hundred of the infantry, returned to Maracanda from this scene of slaughter.

According to Aristobulus, Pharnuches, as soon as the service appeared dangerous, wished to yield the command to the generals, alleging that his commission extended only to negotiate, and not to fight. But Andromachus and Caranus declined to take the command, in opposition to the letter of the king's commission, and in the hour of danger, when nothing but great success could justify their assumption of it. The victory of Spitamenes was, therefore, partly insured by the anarchy and consequent indecision of the Macedonians. The conqueror returned to Maracanda, and again invested the citadel.

When Alexander received information of this serious defeat—the loss in which, from the constitution of a Greek Army, cannot be stated at less than five thousand men—he took with him one half of the Companion cavalry, the guards, the Agrians, the archers, and the most active soldiers of the *phalanx*, and, after a march of ninety miles, arrived at Maracanda on the morning of the fourth day. Spitamenes did not await his approach, and retired as before to the desert. Alexander pressed him hard in his retreat, until he arrived at the scene of the late disaster. The sight of his slaughtered soldiers, with whose fate he deeply sympathized, arrested the pursuit, and the dead were buried with due honours.

He then turned his wrath against the inhabitants in the vicinity, who had aided Spitamenes in the work of destruction, and overran the whole country, until he arrived at the spot where the Polytimetus, large as it was, sunk into the sands of the desert.

★★★★★★★★★★

Such also was its termination in the days of the Arabian geographers, and such probably it is now, although on modern maps we see its stream conducted into the Oxus.

★★★★★★★★★★

After this act of vengeance, Alexander conducted his troops across the Oxus, and spent the winter at Bactria. As the Sogdians were still in arms, it is evident that some causes, of which we have been left ignorant, caused this retrograde march.

During the short intervals between his almost incessant military operations, Alexander had of late, when appearing in his civil capacity, partially adopted the Persian dress and regal costume. This gave serious offence to many Macedonian veterans, who could ill brook to see the barbarian *cidaris* on the brow of an Heracleid prince, or his limbs enveloped in the loose folds of the Median robe. In their opinion, it not only betrayed a degrading sympathy with the feelings of the vanquished, but also foreboded a determination to claim the privileges, and exert the unlimited authority, possessed by his predecessors on the throne of Cyrus. They had long ago, therefore, regarded this tendency to innovation with a jealous eye.

On the other hand, the Persian nobility were naturally scandalised at the rude and boisterous manners of the Macedonian officers, who, claiming almost an equality with their sovereign, pressed into his presence without any of those tokens of respect and reverence which the Orientals in all ages have regarded as necessarily connected with the support of kingly authority. They thought themselves, therefore, entitled to remonstrate with Alexander upon the rude manners of his court, and press him to adopt some of those ceremonies, the absence of which would be certain in the end to draw upon him the contempt of his eastern subjects.

Nor could a man of Alexander's talents and knowledge ever suppose, that the innumerable millions of his acquired empire were to be governed by the brute force of his few Macedonians. He was therefore, as we shall hereafter see, more anxious to amalgamate than to keep separate the Greek and Persian races. But this could not be done without sacrifices on both sides, and a mutual approximation to each other's habits.

Of all the practices of the oriental courts, the ceremony called by the Chinese *kotou*, which enforces prostration at the feet of the sovereign, is the most repugnant to European feelings. Something similar, but not requiring so humiliating a posture, was necessary on approaching the presence of the Persian King of Kings. It consisted most probably of a low inclination of the body, as we read that a sturdy Spartan once satisfied the master of the ceremonies, and at the same time his own conscience, by dropping a ring, and stooping down to pick it up again in the royal presence.

The Greeks in general regarded the ceremony as idolatrous, and as a species of adoration due only to the gods. When, therefore, it was proposed to pay the same outward respect to Alexander, it could only be done by asserting, that he was as much entitled to divine honours as Dionysus, Hercules, and the Dioscuri, Castor and Pollux.

As far as can trace, Alexander never attempted to claim any other homage as a divinity; nor do I find, from any respectable authority, that he ever asserted himself to be the son of Ammon. That such a tale was whispered in the camp, and published both in Europe and Asia, there is no doubt; but it will be difficult to show that Alexander treated it otherwise than as an excellent subject for witty sayings and good jokes.

Arrian's account of the first attempt to introduce the adoration, or *Greek 3*, is so descriptive of the feelings and opinions upon the subject, that I cannot do better than translate it.—It ought to be premised, that the court of Alexander was frequented by many literary characters, eager to see the new world opened to their observations, and to gain the favour of the king. Among these, Anaxarchus, a philosopher from Abdera, and Agis, an Argive poet, whose verses, according to Curtius, were inferior to the compositions even of Choerilus, were supposed more eager to gratify their great patron than to uphold their own dignity and independence.—

It had been agreed (says my author) between the king, the sophists, and the most respected Medes and Persians, to introduce the subject of adoration while the wine was going round. Anaxarchus commenced by saying—'that Alexander could with far greater justice be deemed a divinity than Dionysus and Hercules, both on account of the numerous and splendid actions performed by him, and because Dionysus was Theban, having no connection with the Macedonians, and because Hercules was an Argive, equally unconnected with Macedonia, except through the family of Alexander, who was an Heracleid. It was also more proper for the Macedonians to distinguish their own sovereigns by divine honours, especially when there could not be a doubt that they would honour him as a god after his departure from among men. Much more just would it be, then, thus to honour him while living than after his death, when all such distinctions would be unavailing.'—

When Anaxarchus had advanced these and similar arguments, those to whom the proposition had been previously communicated applauded his speech, and wished immediately to commence the adoration. The majority of the Macedonians, although hostile to the ceremony, remained silent; but Calisthenes took up the question and spoke—

'O Anaxarchus, Alexander in my opinion is worthy of every honour which, without exceeding due bounds, can be paid to a man; but a strong line of distinction has been drawn between divine and human honours. We honour the gods in various ways—by building temples, erecting statues, exempting ground consecrated to them from profane uses; by sacrificing, pouring libations, and composing hymns in their praise—but principally by adoration. Men are kissed by those who salute them; but the divinity, seated aloft, beyond the reach of the touch of man, is honoured by adoration. The worship of the gods is also celebrated with dances and sacred songs.

Nor ought we to wonder at this marked line of difference, for even different gods have different honours paid to them, and those assigned to deified heroes are distinctly separated from those paid to the divinity. It is unbecoming, therefore, to confound all these distinctions, and to swell men by excessive honours beyond their fair proportion, and thus, as far as depends upon us, by granting equal honours to men, degrade the gods to an unseemly humiliation. Even Alexander himself would not tolerate the conduct of any private individual, who might attempt by illegal suffrages and election to arrogate royal honours to himself; with much greater justice will the anger of the gods be excited against those men, who either themselves arrogate divine honours, or permit others to claim such for them.

'But Alexander beyond comparison is, and has the reputation of being, the bravest of brave men, the most princely of kings, and the most consummate general. And you, O Anaxarchus, who associate with Alexander for the purpose of being his instructor in philosophy, ought to be the first in enforcing the principles laid down by me, and in counteracting the contrary.

'In you, therefore, it was highly unbecoming to introduce this proposal, and to forget that you are the companion and adviser, not of a Cambyses or a Xerxes, but of the son of Philip, by birth a Heracleid and an Æacide, whose ancestors emigrated from Argos to Macedonia, and whose family, for successive generations, has reigned over Macedonia, not by tyrannical force, but according to the laws. No divine honours were paid by the Greeks even to Hercules while living, nor yet after his death until the oracle of Delphi had enjoined them to worship him as a god.

'But if we are to adopt the spirit of barbarians because we are few in number in this barbarous land, I call upon you, O Alexander, to remember Greece; and that the whole object of your expedition was its welfare, and to subject Asia to Greece, not Greece to Asia. Consider therefore whether it be your intention after your return to exact adoration from the Greeks, who of all men enjoy the greatest freedom, or to spare the Greeks, and impose this degradation on the Macedonians alone; or, finally, to be honoured by the Greeks and Macedonians as a man and a Greek, and only by the barbarians according to their own fashion?

'But since it is said that Cyrus, the son of Cambyses, was the first who was adored among men, and that from his time this humiliating ceremony has continued among the Medes and Persians, recall to your memory, that the Scythians, poor and independent, chastised his pride—that the insolence of Darius was checked by their European countrymen-that Xerxes was brought to a proper sense of feeling by the Athenians and Lacedemonians—Artaxerxes by Clearchus and Xenophon with the ten thousand—and Darius by Alexander, not yet adored.'"

Thus far I have transcribed the words of Arrian—Calisthenes, (he proceeds to say,) by these and similar arguments, excessively annoyed Alexander, but spoke in unison with the feelings of the Macedonians. The king, observing this, sent round to inform them, that the adoration or prostration was not expected from them. As soon as silence had been restored, the Persians of the highest rank rose and performed the ceremony in order. Leonnatus, one of the companions, as a Persian was performing his salaam without much elegance, ridiculed the posture of the performer as most degrading. This drew upon him at the time the severe animadversion of Alexander, who however again admitted him to favour.

The following account has been also recorded. Alexander pledged the whole circle in a golden cup, which was first carried to those with whom the ceremony of the adoration had been previously arranged. The first who received it, drained the cup, rose up, made his adoration, and was kissed by Alexander; and the cup thus passed in succession through the whole party. But when it came to the turn of Calisthenes to pledge the king, he rose up, and drained the cup; but, without performing the ceremony, approached the king with the intention of kissing him.

Alexander at the moment was conversing with Hephæstion, and had not observed whether Calisthenes had performed the ceremony or not; but Demetrius, the son of Pythonax, one of the Companions, told him, as Calisthenes was approaching, that he had neglected the ceremony; the king, therefore, refused the salute, on which the philosopher turned on his heel and said, "Then I return the poorer by a kiss."

It is evident from this account, that the divine honours respecting which the southern Greeks so extravagantly calumniated Alexander, were no more than the prostration or bending of the person, which the etiquette of the Persian court exacted from all subjects on approaching the royal presence. Whether it was prudent in Alexander to show an inclination to require it from the Macedonians is another question. He evidently was a great admirer of the writings of Xenophon, who had highly eulogized his perfect prince for the supposed institution of this and other ceremonies. The question was agitated at this period with great heat, and was productive of bitter animosities between the two parties, and finally terminated in the greatest calamity of Alexander's life.

Cleitus, called by Plutarch Cleitus the Black, was the brother of Larnicè, the lady who had actually nursed the infant Alexander, although the superintendence had been entrusted to her mother Hellænicè. Alexander's attachment to his nurse had extended to her family, and when his two foster brothers had fallen by his side in battle, Cleitus became the favoured representative of the family. During the first four campaigns, he had been the commander of the royal troop of the Companion cavalry, whose especial duty it was to guard the king's person on the day of battle.

We have already seen how well he performed his duty in the battle on the Granicus, and how his services had been rewarded with the command, after the death of Philotas, of half the Companion cavalry. The importance of this office may be inferred from the circumstance mentioned by Arrian, that Perdiccas, when dividing the *satrapies* of the empire among the great officers, reserved to himself the command of the Companion cavalry, "which was in fact the regency of the whole empire." Cleitus, therefore, was not only the confidential friend of

Alexander, but one of the highest officers in the Macedonian camp.

While Alexander continued in his winter quarters at Bactra, the day came round which the Macedonians held sacred as the festival of Dionysus or Bacchus. The king had hitherto religiously observed it with all the due sacrifices and ceremonies; but on the present occasion he neglected Dionysus, and devoted the day to the Dioscuri, Castor and Pollux.

The ancient Persians, whose origin was probably Scythian, were deep drinkers. Darius, the son of Hystaspes, caused it to be recorded in his epitaph, that, among other laudable qualifications, he could bear more wine than any of his subjects. Alexander, unfortunately for himself, preferred the deep carousals of the barbarians to the sober habits of the Greeks, and his winter quarters were often characterized by prolonged sittings and excessive drinking. Like many other men, the king appears to have found it more easy to practise abstemiousness as a general rule, than temperance on particular occasions.

On this day, the conversation had naturally turned upon the exploits of Castor and Pollux, and many of the guests, certainly not without reason, affirmed that their deeds were not to be named in comparison with the achievements of Alexander. Others of the company were not more favourable to the pretensions of Hercules, and both parties agreed that envy alone prevented men from paying equal honours to living merit. Cleitus, who had ere now testified his contempt for the barbaric innovations of Alexander, and the baseness of his flatterers, being much excited by wine, exclaimed that he would no longer allow the exploits of the deified heroes of ancient days to be thus undervalued; that the personal achievements of Alexander were neither great, wonderful, nor worthy to be compared to the actions of the demigods; that alone he had done nothing, and that his victories were the work of the Macedonians.

This argument was retorted by the opponents, as being equally applicable to the actions of Philip, the favourite hero of the veteran, while they insisted that, with the same means and with the same Macedonians, Alexander had infinitely surpassed his father in the magnitude and glory of his deeds. On this Cleitus lost all self-command, and began to exaggerate beyond measure the actions of the father, and to derogate from the honours of the son. He loudly reminded Alexander that it was he, one of Philip's veterans, who had saved his life, when he had turned his back to Spithridates, and he repeatedly extended his right hand in an insolent and boastful manner, calling out, "This hand,

O Alexander—this hand saved your life on that day!"

The king, who was also under the excitement of wine, unable any longer to endure the drunken insolence of an officer, whose especial duty it was to check all such conduct in others, sprung at Cleitus in his wrath, but was held back by the company. Cleitus, however, did not cease to utter the most insulting and irritating language. Alexander then loudly called for his guards, remonstrated with those who detained him, complained that he was as much a prisoner as Darius had been in the hands of Bessus, and that he was king only in name. With that he broke with violence from the hands of his friends, sprung forwards, tore a lance from a sentinel's hand, and thrust it through the unfortunate Cleitus, who fell dead on the spot.

Aristobulus writes, and it is the more probable account, that when Alexander first sprung from his seat and was restrained by his friends, others of the party hurried Cleitus out of the banqueting room, and that he even reached the quarters of Ptolemy, the son of Lagus, the commander of the guard. But as Alexander, in a paroxysm of phrenzy, was loudly calling him by name, he rushed back into the room with these words, "Here am I, Cleitus, for you, O Alexander!" and was instantly slain.

The sight of blood, and the completion of his insane vengeance, produced the natural and usual effect, and the king was immediately restored to reason. His first impulse was to place the shaft of the lance against the wall and to rush upon the point; but his friends prevented him, and conveyed him to his chamber, where he remained for three days, inconsolable, without eating or drinking.

Arrian says:

> I blame Cleitus severely for his insolence to his sovereign, and I pity the misfortune of Alexander, who thus proved himself the slave of two evils, wine and anger, by neither of which ought a temperate man to be overcome. But I praise Alexander for his subsequent conduct, as he became instantly conscious of having perpetrated an atrocious deed.

The majority of historians write:

> That he retired to his chamber and lay there lamenting and calling on Cleitus by name, and on his sister, Larnicé, his nurse, and saying how generously he, when grown up, had repaid her fostering care. Her sons had already fallen in battle in his

defence, and now he, with his own hand, had murdered her brother. He did not cease to call himself the murderer of his friend, and obstinately abstained for three days, not only from food and drink, but also from all attention to his person.

By degrees he allowed his friends to mitigate the violence of his grief, and especially listened to the consolations of Aristander, who imputed the misfortune to the immediate displeasure of Dionysus, who had thus severely punished the king for the neglect with which he had been treated. He, therefore, offered an extraordinary sacrifice to the Theban god, and was happy to impute the rash deed to the anger of a deity and not to his own infirmity of temper. It may be added, that the extreme irritation, and consequent phrenzy, displayed by Alexander on this melancholy occasion, may have partly been caused by the severe blow in the nape of the neck and back of the head, which he had received the preceding summer in the assault of Cyropolis.

Numerous recruits from southern Greece and Macedonia joined the winter quarters at Bactra, where probably also Alexander heard of the defeat of Agis, King of Sparta, and his Allies, by the regent Antipater. Curtius writes that the first information of the actual commencement of hostilities did not reach Alexander before his first visit to Bactra. And the expressions of Æschines, as to the situation of Alexander at that period, can only be applicable to his Bactrian and Sogdian campaigns.

A second embassy from the king of the Scythians brought valuable presents, and offered the daughter of their sovereign in marriage. Alexander received them kindly as before, but declined the honour of a Scythian connection.

To Bactra also came Pharasmanes, King of the Chorasmians, escorted by fifteen hundred cavalry. His object was to pay his respects to the conqueror of Asia, and to offer his services in guiding and provisioning the army, if the king wished to subdue the nations to the north and west of the Caspian Sea. Pharasmanes was treated with due honours, and told to place himself in communication with Artabazus, *satrap* of Bactria. Alexander declined his offers for the present, as he was anxious to enter India; but added that it was his intention at a future period to conduct a large naval and land force into the Euxine, where the co-operation of the King of Chorasmia would be thankfully received.

This Chorasmia, unknown to the ancient geographers, is the modern Kharasm, of which the present capital is Khiva, situated in the delta of the Oxus, not much inferior in population and magnitude to the delta of the Nile. Had Alexander known of its proximity to the Sogd, he would in all probability have paid it a visit.

But we cannot doubt that Pharasmanes represented it as far more distant than it really was, since he spoke of "his neighbours the Colchians and Amazons." This is also evident from the supposition of Alexander, that the king of Kharasm, on the lake Aral, could aid his operations in the Euxine.

The omission to trace the course and ascertain the termination of the great rivers Oxus and Jaxartes was contrary to Alexander's usual habits of research, and eagerness to extend the boundaries of the known world. For this, perhaps, two reasons may be given: the want of ship timber in Bactria and Sogdiana; and the king's expectation that his future operations in the Caspian would leave nothing obscure in that quarter.

Before he left Bactra, the unfortunate Bessus was brought before an assembly, condemned to have his nose and ears mutilated, and to be sent to Ecbatana to meet his fate in the great council of the Medes and Persians.

CHAPTER 11

Seventh Campaign, B.C. 328

Bactria and Sogdiana were still in a state of insurrection, as well as Margiana; Alexander, therefore, left Craterus with four lieutenants to subdue and pacify the Bactrians, while he himself a second time crossed the Oxus. He entered Sogdiana, and separated his army into five divisions; he himself commanded one, the others were led by Hephæstion, Perdiccas, Ptolemy, the son of Lagus, and Coenus. These, after scouring the country in all directions, and reducing the strong holds of the insurgents, united under the walls of Maracanda. Hence Hephæstion was sent to found a city at the lower end of the Sogd, and Coenus, supported by Artabazus, marched eastward towards the Massagetæ, in whose territories Spitamenes was said to have taken refuge.

Alexander himself marched northward, and subdued most of the insurgents, who still held out in that quarter. But Spitamenes, finding Sogdiana thus guarded against his operations, changed the scene of action. He persuaded 600 Massagetæ to join his Bactrian and Sogdian troops in an expedition into Bactria. They crossed to the left bank of the Oxus, took by storm a border fortress, and advanced within sight of the capital itself. With the assistance of the Scythians, he gathered together a large booty, principally flocks and herds, with which he prepared to return to the desert.

There happened to be then stationed at Bactra a few of the Companion cavalry and other soldiers, who were recovering their health and strength after wounds and illness. These, indignant at the insolence of the Scythians, sallied forth, and by the suddenness of their attack dispersed the enemy, and were in the act of returning with the rescued booty; but, not conducting themselves with sufficient attention to the rules of discipline, (as their most effective commanders were Peithon, master of the king's household, and Aristonicus, a minstrel—) they were overtaken and nearly all destroyed by Spitamenes.

Peithon was taken prisoner, but the minstrel fought and fell like a brave man—contrary (says Arrian) to what might have been expected from one of his craft. The observation of Arrian proves that the minstrels of his days were not the same characters as in the time of Alexander, Aristonicus was a minstrel who recited heroic poems to his harp—one of the ancient rhapsodists, who could fight as well as sing, use the sword as well as the harp.

When Craterus received information of this disaster, he pursued the Massagetæ with the greatest speed, and overtook them on the edge of the desert, but not before they had been reinforced by 1,000 of their mounted countrymen. A keen conflict ensued, in which the Macedonians obtained the advantage, but the vicinity of the desert prevented them from profiting by it.

At this time Artabazus, the Persian, wearied with the distracted state of his *satrapy*, asked permission to retire. This was granted, and Amyntas, the son of Nicolaus, appointed to succeed him. The successful resistance hitherto made by Spitamenes must have caused a strong sensation among his countrymen. In reading general history, two years seem scarcely an object of calculation, but to contemporaries they appear in a far different light, and a successful rebellion for that length of time is sufficient to shake the stability of the greatest empire. We find, consequently, that the Areians were disposed to revolt for a third time, at the instigation of their own *satrap*, Arsames, the successor of Satibarzanes; that the *satrap* of the Tapeiri had refused to attend when summoned to the camp; and that Oxydates, the Median *satrap*, was wilfully neglecting his duty.

Atropates, a Persian nobleman of the highest rank, was sent to

149

displace and succeed Oxydates; and Stasanor and Phrataphernes, the Parthian *satrap*, had been commissioned to seize Arsames. They had succeeded, and now brought the Areian *satrap* in chains to the camp. Stasanor, one of the Companions, and a native of Soli, was sent to succeed him as *satrap* both of Areia and the Drangæ; and Phrataphernes, to apprehend the Tapeirian *satrap*, and bring him into the camp.

Coenus, with a powerful force, still continued on the eastern frontier of Sogdiana, watching the proceedings of Spitamenes, whose activity was likely to be renewed by the appearance of winter, now setting in. He again persuaded the Massagetæ to join him in a plundering excursion into Sogdiana. This was not difficult, as they had no settled homes, but could easily, if invaded, remove their families, flocks, and herds, into the inmost recesses of eastern Tartary; they were not, therefore, much afraid to provoke the wrath of Alexander, and prepared to accompany Spitamenes and his troops with 3,000 horsemen.

Coenus was not taken by surprise, but led his troops to meet the invaders. A bloody contest took place, in which 800 of the Scythian cavalry were left on the field of battle; the survivors, accompanied by Spitamenes, fled back to the desert. The victory was decisive, and the Bactrians and Sogdians, who had hitherto adhered to the fortunes of Spitamenes, gave up the cause as lost, and surrendered to Coenus. This conduct was probably accelerated by their Allies of the desert, who, when the battle had proved unsuccessful, indemnified themselves for their loss by plundering the baggage of those whom they professed to aid.

On their return home they received the intelligence that the king himself was preparing to penetrate into their country. Alarmed by this report, and dispirited by their late defeat, they seized Spitamenes, cut off his head, and sent it as a peace-offering to Alexander. Thus perished the only Persian whose talents and spirit had rendered him formidable to the Macedonians. Upon this Coenus returned to the winter quarters at Nautaca, near Maracanda, where Craterus soon afterwards arrived to announce the pacification of Bactria.

While Alexander, at the commencement of this campaign, was encamped on the banks of the Oxus, two springs, one of water, another of oil, burst forth near his tent. The prodigy was mentioned to Ptolemy, the son of Lagus, who reported it to the king. Alexander sacrificed on the occasion, under the guidance of the diviners. Aristander said that the fountain of oil signified great labours, but victory also at the close of them.

Whatever may be our opinion as to the occurrence of the prodigy, we may be certain that Aristander's prediction was verified by the events of the campaign, and that probably, as it was the least glorious, so also it was the most toilsome of all the Asiatic campaigns.

The whole of the land was in arms; the Macedonians had to spread themselves in small bodies over the face of a country, which is capable of maintaining an immense population, provided, under a wise and beneficent government, the waters of the great rivers be judiciously diffused and carefully husbanded. At present it is in the hands of the most bigoted Mahometans in Asia; but in the tenth century, according to Ebn Haukal, Mawaralnahr alone could furnish 300,000 cavalry and 300,000 infantry for foreign service, without feeling their absence.

CHAPTER 12

Eighth Campaign, B.C. 327

Some strong places still held out. Alexander, therefore, with the first peep of spring, or rather as soon as the extreme severity of the winter had relaxed, led his army into Sogdiana, in order to besiege a precipitous rock, where, as in an impregnable fortress, Oxyartes, a Bactrian chief, had placed his wife and children, while he kept the field. When the Macedonians arrived at the foot of it, they discovered that it was inaccessible on every side, and abundantly provisioned for a long blockade. A heavy fall of snow increased the difficulties of the assailants, and the confidence of the barbarians, who were thus furnished with plenty of water.

This last observation by Arrian partly accounts for the total silence, as far as my researches have gone, of all the Arabian geographers and historians concerning this apparently impregnable and certainly indestructible fortress; for the rock, it appears, had no springs, and depended upon the heavens for its supplies of water; but at the time the Macedonians, perhaps, were ignorant of this circumstance, or Alexander would not wait until the hot weather set in.

He, nevertheless, summoned the place, and promised safety and protection to all, with liberty to return to their homes, on condition of surrendering the fortress. The garrison answered with little courtesy, that Alexander, if he wished to capture the rock, must furnish himself with winged men. When the king received this answer, he proclaimed through the camp, that the first soldier who ascended the rock, should receive twelve *talents*; the second, eleven; the third, ten; and so down to the twelfth, who was to receive one *talent*, or 300 *dareics*.

It is impossible for us in the present day exactly to appreciate the current value of any of the ancient coins, because that depended not only on the weight, but also on the comparative abundance or scarcity of the precious metals. The *dareic* was a gold coin of the purest kind, equal in weight to fifty Attic *drachmæ*, each of which is estimated as amounting to two pennyweights six grains of English troy weight; but we may form some idea of its real marketable value, when we read, that in the time of Xenophon one *dareic* a month was regarded as full pay for the Greek heavy-armed soldier.

We may, therefore, easily imagine the emulation that would naturally be excited among the Macedonians by this proclamation, which promised wealth and independence to the most successful, and a handsome competency to the twelfth in order. From the great numbers who presented themselves for this dangerous service, the three hundred best rock-climbers were selected; these were furnished with a sufficient number of the iron pegs used in fixing down the canvass of the tents, to be inserted where necessary in the interstices of the rock, and in the frozen snow. To each peg was attached a strong piece of cord, by way of ladder.

The climbers selected the most precipitous face of the rock, as being the most likely to be carelessly guarded, and commenced their labours as soon as it was dark. Thirty out of the three hundred lost their hold and footing, fell headlong, and sunk so deep into the snow, that their bodies could not be recovered for burial; the remainder succeeded in their perilous enterprise, and by break of day reached the top of the precipice; this was considerably higher than the broad platform occupied by the barbarians, who were not immediately aware of their ascent.

Alexander, therefore, again sounded a parley, and called on the garrison to surrender the fortress, as he had already procured the winged soldiers, with the want of whom they had before taunted him. The barbarians were astonished, on looking up, to see the summit occupied by Macedonian soldiers, who, according to orders, shook long pieces of linen in the air, to imitate the motions of wings. They, therefore, surrendered without further delay, and thus proved the truth of Alexander's favourite maxim, "That no place was impregnable to the brave nor secure to the timorous."

For although we need not suppose, according to the account, that the defenders were 30,000 in number, yet it is clear, that a few brave men could easily have overpowered an enemy without defensive arms, without a chance of being supported, and with their limbs necessarily benumbed by the cold and their excessive night fatigue. Among the captives were the family of Oxyartes, whose eldest daughter, Roxana, is said to have been, with the exception of the wife of Darius, the loveliest woman seen by the Macedonians during their Asiatic expedition.

The Bactrians held a middle place between the Persians and Scythians, partaking more of the polished manners of the former than of the rudeness of the latter. They still exist in Khorasan and Mawaralnahr, under the modified name of Bukhars. Wearied with the unceasing succession of new tribes of conquerors from the deserts of Tartary, they have for ages renounced the practice of arms, and, like the Armenians and other eastern nations, retain their industrious habits and peaceful occupations, as far as their barbarous masters will allow them. The Uzbek Tatars, the present sovereigns of these regions, call them Tajiks, or Burgesses, a name equally descriptive of their social and mercantile character. My author writes:

> They have, for the most part, large eyes, black and lively; their hair black and very fine; in short, they partake nothing of the deformity of the Tatars, among whom they inhabit. The women, who are generally tall and well-shaped, have fine complexions and very beautiful features.

The dazzling beauty of his young captive made a deep impression upon the victor, and the momentary passion ripened into a lasting attachment. But warrior as he was, and with the bad example of his model, Achilles, before his eyes, he scorned to take advantage of her unprotected state, and publicly solemnized his marriage with her. It is said that he consulted his two friends, Craterus and Hephæstion, upon the subject, and that Craterus strongly dissuaded him from an alliance so repugnant to Macedonian prejudices, while the gentler nature of Hephæstion saw no political reasons powerful enough to prevent his friend and sovereign from lawfully gratifying an honourable passion. I doubt the truth of the report—for I see no cause for supposing that the act was repugnant to the feelings of the Macedonians. Why should a Bactrian bride be more degrading to Alexander, than Illyrian and Thracian wives had been to Philip?

Oxyartes no sooner heard of the king's attachment to his child, than he immediately came into the camp without fear or ceremony, and was welcomed with all the demonstrations of joy and respect due to the father of the young queen.

The union with their countrywoman was regarded by all the natives as a compliment to themselves, and these regions of Upper Asia, as they were the most reluctant to submit, were also the last to shake off the Macedonian yoke.

Arrian's account of these two campaigns is not given with his usual clearness; he seems to have been wearied with recording the numerous marches and counter-marches necessarily made during this tedious and desultory warfare. Although, therefore, I have followed him in the preceding account, I am strongly inclined to believe that the rock, where Roxana and her family were captured, was not in Sogdiana but in Bactria, where Strabo has placed it; for what could a Bactrian chief have to do with Sogdiana, or why look for a refuge beyond the Oxus, when the Paropamisus, with its summits and recesses, presented a natural retreat for the insurgent Bactrians? If, therefore, it was in Bactria, there can be no doubt that it was the same hill fortress which was captured by Timour previous to his expedition into India, and the description of which answers exactly to the rock of Oxyartes. It ought to be added, that according to the tradition of the natives, it had been besieged in vain by the great Iskender, the name by which Alexander is still popularly known in all the regions visited by him.

We hear nothing in Arrian's regular narrative of the expedition into Margiana, although Alexander founded a city there, and Arrian mentions the River Epardus, among the Mardi, as one of those ascertained by the Macedonians to have its termination in the desert. As, however, we find in other places that the Paraetacae and the Mardi are continually confounded with each other, it may fairly be inferred that the Paraetacae, in the vicinity of Bactria, were the Mardi of Margiana. Curtius, although in a confused manner, mentions the march across the Ochus and the foundation of the city Margiana.

From these facts, I venture to assign the following probable route to Alexander. From Sogdiana he crossed the Oxus, and entered Margiana, a fertile district, surrounded on all sides by the desert, and watered by the modern Murg-ab, called Margus by Strabo, and Epardus by Arrian. According to the former writer, the Macedonians retained the native names of some rivers, gave names entirely new to others, and sometimes translated the native names into Greek.

To the last class plainly belong the Polytimetus or 'highly valuable', and the Epardus or the irrigator. Alexander built a city, called after himself, on the latter river, which soon fell into decay, but was restored by Antiochus, who gave it the name of Antiocheia Margiana. It still continues to be a large and flourishing city, under the modern appellation of Meru Shah-Ian.

From the banks of the Margus, he marched to the Ochus, the modern Tedgen, crossed it and entered the territory of the Parætacæ. Here also was a rock-fortress, something similar to the one already captured. It was called—according to Arrian—the rock of Chorienes. At the foot it was four miles in circuit, and the road leading from the bottom to the summit was more than a mile long. This was the only ascent, narrow and difficult of access, even were no opposition offered. A deep ravine separated the rock from the only rising ground, whence it could possibly be assailed with any prospect of success.

Alexander proposed to fill up this intervening gulf, and thus imitate on land what at the siege of Tyre he had already attempted by sea. The army was formed into two divisions. He himself superintended the operations of one half by day, while the other half, divided into three watches, worked by night under the inspection of Perdiccas, Leonnatus, and Ptolemy. But the work proceeded slowly, as the labours of the whole day did not advance the mound more than thirty feet, and the labours of the night not so much. The impatient soldiers, therefore, constructed long ladders from the tall pine trees, with which the hill was covered, and descended into the ravine.

Here, in proper places and at short intervals, they erected upright posts. The summits of these they connected by transverse pieces of timber, on which they placed hurdles, and finally earth, so as to form a broad and solid platform; on this again they erected covered galleries, which protected them from the enemy's missiles. The barbarians at first ridiculed the attempt, but the gradual approach of the platform brought them within reach of the Macedonian darts, which soon cleared a part of the rock of its defenders.

Chorienes, more astonished at the extraordinary exertions of the besiegers than having any immediate cause to fear the result, sent a messenger to Alexander, and expressed a wish to have a conference with Oxyartes. The latter, by permission, ascended the rock, and partly by affirming that no place could withstand the attack of Alexander, and partly by extolling his generous disposition, of which he, the speaker, was an example, persuaded Chorienes to submit himself to the good pleasure of the besieger. When the rock had been delivered up, the conqueror, escorted by a strong body guard, ascended and viewed, not without admiration, the natural defences of the place.

This celebrated fortress is, if I am not mistaken, the modern Kelat, the favourite strong hold and treasury of Nadir Shah. In description the two exactly correspond, nor is it probable that a place of the natural strength and importance of Kelat could have been passed over in silence by the historians of Alexander. During the siege, a heavy fall of snow had much incommoded the assailants, who were also badly supplied with provisions. Chorienes, therefore, to show his gratitude, as his strong hold and government had been restored to him, provisioned the army for two months, and distributed from tent to tent, corn, wine, and salted meat. He added, that this munificent donation had not exhausted one tenth of his regular stores.

Two chiefs, Austanes and Catanes, still kept the field in Parætaca. Craterus was sent against them, brought them to battle, slew Catanes, and brought Austanes prisoner to Bactra, where the whole army reassembled previous to the expedition into India. It would have been desirable to have heard more of Catanes, who, according to Curtius, was one of the early accomplices of Bessus, and bore the character of being deeply skilled in magic arts and Chaldæan lore. The spirit of resistance died with him, and all the northern provinces became tranquil.

Such, however, was the favourable impression made upon Alexander by the free spirit and gallant bearing of these barbarians, that he selected thirty thousand of their youth, probably all in their fifteenth or sixteenth year, who were to be taught the Greek language and Macedonian discipline, and to have the same dress and arms as the soldiers of the *phalanx*.

Alexander, like most other great warriors, was passionately fond of hunting. He even pursued the fox with great eagerness, when nobler game could not be found. But at Bazaria, which probably is the modern Bokhara, he found a royal park, which, according to the traditions of the natives, had not been disturbed for four generations. These parks, something similar to the forests of our Norman kings, were scattered over the face of the empire, and the animals bred therein reserved for the diversion of the monarch himself. A spot well supplied with wood and water was selected for the purpose, enclosed within lofty walls, and stocked with every species of wild beasts.

The younger Cyrus, according to Xenophon, possessed one of great extent round the sources of the Mæander, and we learn from St. Jerome, that, in his age, Babylon itself had been converted by the Parthian kings into a royal park. Julian, The Apostate, in his fatal expedition to the East, broke into one of these enclosures, and destroyed the wild beasts by the assistance of his army.

We may infer from the report of the natives, that the remoteness of the Bazarian chase had prevented the last four monarchs from visiting it. Alexander, therefore, anticipating considerable resistance, led a strong detachment of his army into the royal preserve, and declared war against its denizens-few of which probably had ever before heard the trumpet sound, or seen the broad and pointed blade of the hunting-spear. The king was in front and on foot, when an enormous lion, roused from the lair in which he had reposed for so many years undisturbed, faced his assailants and seemed inclined to select the king for his antagonist. The lion never attacks while running, walking, or standing. He first crouches and gathers his limbs under him, and thus gives ample warning of the intended spring.

Lysimachus, destined in time to be one of Alexander's great successors, had encountered a lion in single combat on the banks of the Euphrates, and had slain him, but not without receiving a dangerous stroke from the paw of the wounded brute, which had laid his ribs bare and seriously endangered his life. This gallant officer now stepped forward, placed himself in front of his king, but Alexander, jealous of the honour already acquired by his general, ordered him instantly to retire: saying "he could kill a lion as well as Lysimachus." His words were confirmed by the deed, for he received the animal's spring on the point of his hunting-spear with so much judgment and coolness that the weapon entered a vital part and proved instantly fatal. It was on this occasion that a Spartan ambassador, who had been deputed to wait upon him after the defeat of Agis, exclaimed, "Bravo, Alexander, well hast thou won the prize of royalty from the king of the woods!"

But the Macedonians, who were too sensible of the value of their sovereign's life to permit it thus to depend upon the critical management of a hunting spear, convened an assembly, and passed a decree, that thenceforward Alexander should not combat wild beasts on foot, nor hunt without being personally attended by a certain number of the great officers. Probably this was not the first time in which the king's life had been endangered by wild beasts. For Craterus consecrated, in the temple of Delphi, a hunting-piece in bronze—the joint workmanship of Lysippus and Leochares—which represented a lion and dogs—the king fighting with the lion—and Craterus hastening to his prince's assistance. These hunting parties were not only dangerous from the ferocity of the wild beasts, but also from the unskilful or rash

157

management of their weapons by the followers of the chase.

Thus, Craterus had his thigh pierced through by the lance of Perdiccas, while they were engaged in hunting the *ichneumon* on the banks of the Nile. Four thousand head of animals of various kinds were slaughtered in the great park at Bazaria, and the sport was closed by a public banquet, principally composed of the venison. It ought to be added, that even Curtius allows that the foolish story of the exposure of Lysimachus to a lion had no other foundation than the facts above recorded.

But there occurred, either during this or another hunting party about the same period, a circumstance which in its consequences had well-nigh proved fatal to Alexander.

It had been the policy of Philip to educate the sons of the Macedonian nobility in his own palace, both for the sake of their greater improvement, and probably of ensuring the loyalty and fidelity of their parents. In order more immediately to connect them with the court, some of the offices about the king's person were entirely committed to their charge. They acted as the royal chamberlains; as chief grooms they had the care of the horses from the door of the stable until the king and his own immediate retinue were mounted. They had also to attend him on hunting expeditions, probably to manage the dogs, and supply the king with fresh weapons.

The title of royal pages, therefore, will suit them better than any other in our language. Hermolaus, the son of Sopolis, one of these young gentlemen, had in the heat of a boar-hunt, forgotten his duty and slain the animal—perhaps unfairly, (for the laws of the chase in all ages and climes have been very arbitrary,)—certainly so as to interfere with the royal sport. The page was deprived of his horse, and ordered to be flogged; and it would appear this was the usual punishment for such offences. But Hermolaus regarded it as a personal disgrace, not to be effaced but in the blood of his sovereign. He persuaded Sostratus, the son of Amyntas, his particular friend among the pages, to enter into his designs. Sostratus succeeded in seducing Antipater, the son of Asclepiodorus, the *satrap* of Syria, Epimenes the son of Arses, Anticles the son of Theocritus, and Philotas the son of Carsis the Thracian, to become partners in the conspiracy.

The pages in turn watched the royal bed-chamber, and the young traitors agreed to assassinate the king on the night when it would be the duty of Anticles to watch. But Alexander did not enter his chamber on that night until the pages were changed. The cause assigned for his absence is curious. A Syrian female, an enthusiast and supposed to be divinely inspired, had attached herself to Alexander, and had so far ingratiated herself with the inmates of the palace, as to be allowed free ingress and egress at all hours of the day and night. It was often her practice to watch all night at the king's bedside. Her predictions also had been so successful, that either from policy or superstition great respect was paid to her person and attention to her advice. On this memorable night she met Alexander as he was retiring from the banqueting room to his chamber, and besought him with eagerness and earnestness to return and prolong the revelry till daybreak.

The king, who probably had never before received a similar exhortation from the prophetess, immediately replied, "that the gods gave wholesome counsel," and complied with the advice. It is more than probable that the Syrian, whose privileged habits enabled her freely to visit every place, had overheard the conversation of the pages, and had taken this strange mode of counteracting their treason.

Strange however as it must appear—it proved sufficient. For on the next day Epimenes communicated the plot to Charicles, the son of Menander, who immediately informed Eurylochus, the brother of Epimenes. The latter gave the same information to Ptolemy, the son of Lagus, who laid it before the king.

The conspirators were seized, put to the torture, confessed their own guilt, and named some accomplices. They were brought before the Macedonian assembly, where, according to some authors, Hermolaus spoke at length and apologised for his treason. His arguments were, that the Median dress and the attempt to enforce the ceremony of prostration, the drunken revelries and consequent somnolency of Alexander—were more than could be any longer tolerated by a freeman; and that he had done well in desiring to deliver the Macedonians from a tyrant who had put Philotas to death unjustly, Parmenio without even the forms of law, and who had murdered Cleitus in a fit of drunkenness.

But the assembly had no sympathy with the young regicide, who wished to screen his own vindictive passions under the cloak of patriotism and love of freedom. They therefore, condemned him and his associates to death, but in executing the sentence they did not use their darts, as in the case of Philotas, but overwhelmed the culprits with stones.

This conspiracy originated not in Macedonian but democratic principles, nor ought Alexander to have been astonished at the consequences of his own conduct. He was the patron of democracy in the Asiatic cities. He delighted in the conversation, and encouraged the visits, of the democratic philosophers of Southern Greece. Had he confined himself within these bounds, his conduct would have been as harmless as the coquetry of Catherine of Russia and of Frederick of Prussia, with similar characters in modern times. But he committed a serious mistake, in entrusting the most important part of the education of the royal pages to Calisthenes. This man had been a pupil of Aristotle; according to some writers he was his nephew; nor can it be doubted that he owed his situation in the court of Alexander to the recommendation of the Stagyrite.

He was an Olynthian by birth, rude of manner and bold of speech, of strong intellect and considerable eloquence. His principles were those of extreme democracy, nor perhaps had he forgotten the destruction of his country by Philip; at least it may be inferred from the following anecdote that he had not:

"Once at the king's table he was requested to pronounce an extemporaneous eulogy upon the Macedonians. This he did with so much eloquence, that the guests, not content with applauding him, rose up and covered him with their garlands. Upon this Alexander said, in the words of Euripides,

"'When great the theme 'tis easy to excel'

"But now, Calisthenes, show your powers in representing the faults of the Macedonians, that they may them and amend."

The orator immediately took the other side of the question, grossly abused the Macedonians, vilified Philip, whose successes he imputed to the divisions among the republican Greeks, and not to his own talents, and concluded with a quotation to this purpose

The wicked wretch through discord honour won.

By this he drew upon himself the implacable hatred of the Macedonians, and Alexander said, that " he had given a specimen not of his eloquence but of his malevolence."

Plutarch's account of this ill-judged exhibition is closed with the observation of Aristotle, that the eloquence of Calisthenes was indeed great, but that he wanted common sense.

It appears that he indulged in violent speeches, even in the presence of Aristotle, who is said to have answered one of them by simply repeating the Homeric line:

Short date of life, my son, these words forebode.

A quotation, perhaps, more applicable to the invective against the Macedonians and Philip—than it could be to any other speech. Of late he had lost ground in Alexander's favour, which had only induced him to become more insolent in his manners. He had repeatedly quitted the king's presence, with the following line of Homer on his lips

Patroclus died a better man than thou.

It is also recorded, that when asked by Philotas, whom the Athenians most honoured, he answered, Harmodius and Aristogeiton, because they slew one of the two tyrants and abolished the tyranny. Philotas then asked, where could the slayer of a tyrant obtain a safe asylum?

Calisthenes said:

If nowhere else among the Athenians, who had defended in arms the helpless Heracleidæ against Eurystheus, the then powerful tyrant of all Greece.

It is difficult for persons who form their general idea of a Greek philosopher from Plato, Xenophon, and Aristotle, to conceive the difference between these truly great men and the swarm of sophists, who in later times usurped the name of philosophers. Plato, Xenophon, and Aristotle were gentlemen in the most comprehensive sense of the word, the companions and friends of monarchs, and who knew how to respect the rights and privileges of others, without betraying their own dignity and independence. But the later sophist, the imitator of Diogenes, found it much easier to acquire the name of a philosopher by despising the decencies and even charities of life, and inculcating the doctrine of indiscriminate equality:—when I say *indiscriminate*, I mean that all distinctions except those of superior intellect and virtue, monopolised of course by the philosophers and their admirers, were to be contemned and set at nought.

Thus, Calisthenes was accustomed to say publicly, that Alexander had much more need of him than he had of Alexander—that the king's achievements were entirely at his mercy—and that his immortality did not depend upon the falsehoods propagated respecting his birth, but on what he, the historian of his actions, might choose to relate. Hermolaus was his favourite pupil, and strongly attached both to his person and doctrines.

It is not wonderful, therefore, that the conduct of the pupil should have excited suspicions against the preceptor. All the writers agree that the conspirators confessed that Calisthenes had always given a willing ear to their complaints against the king. Some add, that when Hermolaus was bitterly lamenting his punishment and disgrace, Calisthenes told him "to remember that he was now a man;" an expression, after such a castigation, liable to a very dangerous interpretation.

But I see no reason whatsoever to doubt the united testimony of Ptolemy and Aristobulus, who both wrote, that the pages had confessed that they had been incited and encouraged by Calisthenes in the prosecution of their plot. He was therefore seized and imprisoned. Respecting his end Aristobulus and Ptolemy disagree; the former says he died in custody, the other that he was first tortured and then hanged. On such a point the commander of the guard must be the best authority; but the account followed by Aristobulus was probably the one made public at the time.

I have dwelt the longer on the subject of Calisthenes, because his chains and death were regarded by his brethren of the long beard and short cloak, as an insult and an outrage committed against their order. He was regarded as a martyr to the great doctrine not of the equality but of the superiority of the self-styled philosophers to the kings of the earth, and his persecutor was loaded with slanders and calumnies, many of which are believed to this day.

Alexander left Amyntas governor of the regions between the Jaxartes and the Paropamisus, with 3,500 cavalry and 10,000 infantry. The spring had already passed away and the summer had set in, when he set out from Bactria to commence his Indian expedition. His troops for the last three years had been engaged in hard service, abounding more with blows than booty;—he proposed therefore to remunerate them for their past labours by leading them to attack more wealthy and less warlike nations.

He soon arrived at the northern foot of the Paropamisus, where, according to Curtius, he had already founded a city. Nor is this unlikely; for, according to Strabo, he founded eight cities in Sogdiana and Bactria, and one of them might well have been intended to command the southern end of the main pass over the mountains. The city Anderab, on the same site, still retains a considerable portion of Alexander's name. An old traveller writes:

> The town of Anderab is the most southern which the Usbeks
> possess at present, being situate at the foot of the mountains
> which separate the dominions of Persia and the Great Mogul

from Great Bukharia. As there is no other way of crossing those mountains towards India with beasts of carriage but through this city, all travellers and goods from Great Bukharia, designed for that country, must pass this way; on which account the *khan* of Balk constantly maintains a good number of soldiers in the place, though otherwise it is not very strong.

He then entered the defiles, and in ten days arrived at the Alexandreia which he had founded two years before. He had occasion to be displeased with the governor, whom he therefore removed; he also added new colonists to the city. But it did not prosper long under the name of Alexandreia. The probability however is, that the more ancient Ortospana, which the new city was to replace, recovered either its name or importance. For Strabo writes, that the main road from Bactra to the Indies, was across the Paropamisus to Ortospana; and Ptolemy has no Alexandreia in that neighbourhood, but a Cabura, also called Ortospana.

Cabura, without any real change, is the modern Cabul, the key of India in all ages, whether the invader is to advance from the west or the north, from Candahar or from Balk. The Paropamisian Alexandreia was, therefore, either the very same as Cabul, or must have been built in its immediate vicinity. The distance on the map between Anderab and Cabul, is about a hundred miles. Nor could the Macedonian Army, with its regular baggage, have crossed the intervening hills in less than ten days, for the road, such as it is, follows principally the beds of torrents; and Timour, who was ill, and had to be carried in a litter, on his return from India, was obliged, during this route, to cross one river twenty-six and another twenty-two times.

He then advanced to a city called Nicæa, where he sacrificed to Minerva, and ordered the *satraps* to the west of the Indus to come and meet him. Taxiles was the chief of these, and both he and the minor *satraps* obeyed, brought presents, and promised to give the king all the elephants which they possessed. Here he divided his army. Hephæstion and Perdiccas, with one division, were sent through the province of Peucaliotes, of which Peucela, was the capital, to the banks of the Indus, there to construct a bridge, and Taxiles and the other *satraps* were ordered to accompany them. Antes, the governor of Peucaliotes proved refractory, but was soon subdued, and his chief city, probably the modern Peishwar, was taken; the two generals then proceeded to execute their further orders.

Alexander, with the rest of the army, marched to the left, into the mountainous regions intersected by the western branches of the Indus. He crossed in succession the Choes, or Choaspes, the Euaspla and the Guræus. It is useless to attempt to follow him through these unknown regions; but his personal adventures were full of incident.

Between the Choes (which still retains its name, and must be crossed in travelling from Cabul to the Indus) and the Euaspla he besieged a city defended by a double wall. In the assault by which the outward wall was carried, Alexander was wounded by an arrow in the shoulder; the warriors of his army pronounced it slight, but their only reason for calling it so appears to have been that the point had not penetrated through. Leonnatus and Ptolemy were also wounded. The army, as usual in such cases, took ample vengeance for the king's wound. Craterus was left in this district, to complete its reduction, while Alexander moved into the country, between the Euaspla and the Guræus. The inhabitants of the first city approached by the Macedonians, set fire to it, and fled to the mountains; they were pursued and many overtaken before they reached their fastnesses.

In the pursuit, Ptolemy, the son of Lagus, saw the Indian king, surrounded by his guards, on one of the lower hills, at the foot of the mountains. He immediately led the few troops by whom he was accompanied to attack him. The hill was too steep for cavalry, he therefore dismounted and ascended on foot. The Indian seeing the small number of his supporters, so far from shunning the combat, advanced to meet the assailant: his weapon was a long and stout lance, and with this—without parting with the shaft—he struck Ptolemy on the breast; the point penetrated the breastplate, but did not reach the body, which probably was defended by thick quilting.

Ptolemy, in return, threw his lance, which pierced the Indian's thigh and brought him to the ground. But the Indians on the heights, who witnessed the fall of their chief, rushed down to save his arms and body from falling into the enemy's hands. Ptolemy must therefore have retired without the trophies of victory, had not Alexander himself arrived at the critical moment at the foot of the hill. He immediately ordered his guards to dismount, ran up, and after a severe and well-contested struggle, the arms and body of the Indian were borne away by the Macedonians. This was truly a Homeric combat, and had not the king himself been in the field, would have entitled Ptolemy to the second "*spolia opima*" won during this war.

It is worth observing, that both Erigyus and Ptolemy, who thus distinguished themselves, were the youthful favourites of Alexander. Erigyus unfortunately had died at the close of the last Bactrian campaign, to the great sorrow of the king Craterus, on whom devolved all separate commands of consequence, was ordered to build a new town on the site of the one burnt by these Indians. Alexander marched in the direction of a lofty mountain, where the neighbouring inhabitants were said to have taken refuge with their flocks and herds, and encamped at the foot of it.

Ptolemy was sent to reconnoitre, and brought back information that, as far as he could judge, the fires in the enemy's stations were far more numerous than in the king's camp. Alexander, concluding from this that a combination of various tribes had taken place, resolved to anticipate any intended attack. He took with him what he judged a sufficient number of troops, left the rest in the camp, and ascended the mountain. After having approached the enemy's fires, and reconnoitred their position, he divided his force into three columns; he himself led forward one, Leonnatus the other, and Ptolemy the third.

They all proved successful in the end, although not without much hard fighting, as the inhabitants of these districts were distinguished for their hardiness and valour. The booty was immense. Forty thousand prisoners, and two hundred and thirty thousand head of various kinds of cattle, were captured. Alexander, struck with the size and activity of the Indian oxen, selected the finest animals from the spoil, and sent them to Macedonia for the sake of improving the breed in his native dominions.

Thence he advanced to the River Guræus, which he forded with great difficulty, as the waters were deep and the current strong. Like all other mountain streams, its bed was formed of round slippery stones, which rendered it difficult for the soldier to keep his footing. The Guræus is probably the Suastus of Ptolemy, the modern Kamah or Cashgur. The country to the east was inhabited by the Assaceni or Affaceni, supposed to have been the ancestors of the modern Affghans. Their chief city was Massaga, a large and wealthy place; and which agrees both in name and position with the modern Massagour, not far from the left bank of the Kamah.

This capital was garrisoned by seven thousand Indian mercenaries, warriors by profession, and probably by caste, whose own country was far to the east. The inhabitants, supported by the mercenaries, advanced into the plain and gave battle to the Macedonians, but were defeated and driven into the city. There the resistance of the mercenaries became more effectual, and all attempts to carry the place by storm failed. The king, exposing himself as usual, was wounded in the leg by an arrow. In the meantime, the engines were brought up, and wooden towers constructed. The assailants in one of these had cleared the opposite wall of its defenders, when Alexander ordered a moveable bridge, similar to that with which he had captured Tyre, to be thrown across from the tower to the wall.

This was done, and the bravest of the guards rushed forwards; but unfortunately, their numbers and weight snapped the bridge in the centre, and they were all precipitated to the foot of the wall. Before they could extricate themselves, they were overwhelmed from above by every species of missiles, and the enemy sallied forth upon them through numerous posterns in the wall.

This loss was repaired; within four days another bridge had been flung from the tower to the wall. The garrison of mercenaries fought bravely, and as long as the governor lived showed no inclination to yield; but when he had fallen, by a dart discharged from an engine, they proposed to surrender on terms. The best were offered, provided they would enter into Alexander's service. They consented, quitted the city, and encamped on a hillock over against the Macedonian camp. Some misunderstanding, however, took place; either they mistrusted the promises of Alexander or were unwilling to join the foreign invaders; they therefore attempted to withdraw by night into the neighbouring cities.

But Alexander either anticipated their movements, or overtook them in their flight (for both accounts are given) and put them all to the sword. As Arrian gives no hint of any breach of faith on the part of Alexander, we may easily pass over in silence the charge adduced by other writers. He prided himself particularly on the extreme punctuality with which he observed all promises, and was never known to violate his pledged word. At the same time, it must be confessed that he was inexorable in punishing all those who either acted with bad faith themselves, or even neglected to fulfil their engagements from a suspicion that he intended to act with bad faith to them.

While engaged in the siege of Massaga, the king had detached a body of troops to invest Bezira and Ora. The latter was taken; but the inhabitants of the former, together with the whole population of the neighbouring province, took refuge on the celebrated rock Aornos, reported impregnable, and to have thrice resisted the arms of the famed and fabulous Hercules. Difficulties calculated to deter others only excited the energies of Alexander, who regarded the present as a fair opportunity of entering into competition with the great hero of Greece. And the contest was to be of that nature, that the meanest soldier in the army could judge of its final issue. It was not a matter of the slightest consequence whether the rock had been unsuccessfully besieged or not; for all rational purposes it was sufficient that the Macedonians were impressed with the belief, or even that the report was current, that his great ancestor had failed in capturing the supposed impregnable fortress.

The description given of the rock by Arrian is, that its circuit at the base was near twelve miles; that the lowest point was three quarters of a mile above the plain; and that on the summit there was a cultivated platform, plentifully irrigated by springs.

On encamping at its foot, Alexander was visited by some of the natives of the vicinity, who, as usual in similar cases, promised to betray the secrets of the stronghold and conduct the Macedonians to a spot where the operations for the final reduction of the place would be much facilitated. Alexander despatched Ptolemy, with an active party of men, to make the necessary circuit, under the guidance of these voluntary traitors, and to seize the spot described by them.

This was performed; and Ptolemy, by kindling a beacon-fire, indicated to the king his success and position. The post occupied appears to have been a detached summit, which considerably hampered the proceedings of the besieged. Alexander made an attempt to ascend from his side also, but was repulsed without much difficulty.

The enemy, encouraged by their success, then turned their forces against Ptolemy, who with difficulty maintained his position. In the course of the night Alexander conveyed, by the hands of another Indian traitor, a letter to Ptolemy, containing an order to make a vigorous attack from his position as soon as he saw the Indians assailed by himself. Alexander's object was to force his way and join Ptolemy. The simultaneous attack began with the dawn, and, after a severe contest, succeeded by mid-day; when the Indians, being attacked from below by Alexander, and from above by Ptolemy, retired and left the path open.

Thus, the Macedonian force was united on the point preoccupied by Ptolemy. But great difficulties still remained, for the summit thus occupied was separated from what may be termed the main body of the rock by an immense ravine. The victories of the Macedonians had, however, been achieved as much by toilsome labours as by discipline and valour; they therefore instantly began to fill up the intervening space.

In four days, under the immediate inspection of the king, the wonderful exertions of the army had advanced the mound, and the works erected on it, within bow-shot of the rock. Soon after, another detached summit, on a level with the great plain, was seized and occupied by a small party of Macedonians.

The Indians, finding themselves thus exposed to the enemy's missiles, sent a herald announcing their intention to surrender on terms, provided the assault was postponed. To this Alexander consented, but soon received information that the object of the Indians was to gain time, and to withdraw, under cover of the night, to their several homes. The king therefore withdrew all his outposts, and left the paths open. But as soon as he perceived that the enemy's outworks had been deserted—he scaled the rock, and the Macedonians, who first gained the summit, drew up their comrades by ropes, and thus achieved this memorable conquest.

The command of the fortress and province was entrusted to Sisicottus, an Indian whom he had found in the retinue of Bessus, and of whose fidelity he had received ample proofs. . . . The rock is not known to me from modern authorities, nor do I know of any traveller who has examined this remote corner. It is on the right bank of the Indus, close to the river; but I have no means of ascertaining its exact site. A traveller going up the right bank from Attock, could not fail to find it. . . . Here Alexander was informed that the king of the Assaceni, on retiring to the mountains, had turned out his elephants, thirty in number, to enjoy a temporary liberty in the rich pastures on the banks of the Indus. Alexander had already assembled a large troop of elephant-hunters around him, and with their assistance recovered all the animals but two, which were represented to have fallen over precipices, in their attempt to escape.

As the banks of the Indus were covered with forest trees, he cut down timber, built vessels, and embarked on the river. It was as the fleet was falling down the stream that he visited Nysa, the inhabitants of which claimed his protection, as being descendants of part of the victorious host of Dionysus, who had founded their city, and peopled it with the invalids of his camp. In proof of their assertion, they showed ivy, the Bacchic emblem, which, according to them, grew in no other part of India but their territories, and a mountain above their city, called Merus, or the Thigh, in remembrance of the miraculous birth of Dionysus.

Their chief, Acuphis, gave Alexander a description of their constitution, according to which the supreme power was lodged in a council of three hundred, consisting of the citizens most respected for age, rank, and abilities. Alexander was willing to believe their Bacchic origin, and that at last he had found traces of the two demigods who in remoter ages had preceded him in his present career. He therefore treated the Nysans with particular attention, and granted all their requests, on condition of being furnished with 300 horsemen as a military contribution, and a hundred (I must not spoil the Greek pun) of their *best men* as hostages.

At the last demand Acuphis smiled, and when asked to explain his mirth, replied, that Alexander was welcome to that number of the bad and vicious characters in Nysa, but wished to know how any city could be governed if deprived of a hundred of its best men. Alexander, pleased with the answer, took the cavalry, but remitted the hostages.

It is difficult to account for these and other traces of Hercules and Dionysus which are gravely recorded in the writings of Alexander's most trustworthy historians. The arms of Darius, the son of Hystaspes, had no doubt been carried to the Indus, and the rock Aornos might have been repeatedly besieged in vain by the Persians. Greeks also from Ionia, Doris, and Æolis might have been settled, according to a well-known Persian policy, on this distant frontier, and have carried with them the mysteries of Bacchus. Yet with all this it is difficult to believe that the Macedonians, who had traversed the most enlightened and civilized states of Asia without discovering one trace of Hercules and Dionysus, should thus find vestiges of the supposed expeditions of both heroes in the obscure corner between the river of Cabul and the Indus.

Might not some Macedonians have visited Nysa during the celebration of the festival of the Hindoo God Rama, and easily recognised his identity with their own Dionysus? The following passage from Bishop Heber's *Journal* in India is the best illustration of the subject:—

The two brothers, Rama and Luchmun, in a splendid *palxee*, were conducting the retreat of their army. The divine Hunnimân, as naked and almost as hairy as the animal whom he represented, was gambolling before them, with a long tail tied round his waist, a mask to represent the head of a baboon, and two great pointed clubs in his hands. His army followed, a number of men with similar tails and masks, their bodies dyed with indigo, and also armed with clubs. I was never so forcibly struck with the identity of Rama and Bacchus. Here were before me Bacchus, his brother Ampelus, the Satyrs, smeared with wine-lees, and the great Pan commanding them.

The Macedonian chiefs would gladly avail themselves of an opportunity to impress their sovereign with a belief that he had reached the boundaries of the conquests of Hercules and Dionysus, and that to surpass them by a few marches more to the east would be sufficient to satisfy the wildest dream of ambition. Acuphis and his companions could easily be induced to enter into a plan calculated to promote their own honour and advantage, and few in the army would venture to be very critical in their strictures respecting the claims of these self-styled Bacchi.

Even the interview with the king, as conducted by the deputies of Nysa, was far too theatrical not to have been studied. When ushered into the royal tent, they found him covered with dust, and in complete armour-helmet on head and spear in hand, being his usual costume during a march.

The deputies on seeing him were apparently overpowered with their feelings of awe and admiration, fell prostrate, and remained in that position without uttering a word, until they were raised by Alexander's own hand. It was then that they told their Bacchic tale, as before described.

Alexander, with the Companion cavalry and the flower of the *phalanx*, ascended Mount Merus and found it covered with ivy, laurels and dense groves of other trees: the Macedonians, delighted once more to see the green ivy plant, quickly formed it into chaplets for their brows, sung hymns to Bacchus, and invoked him by his numerous names. Alexander also offered a magnificent sacrifice to the god, and feasted the whole army.

According to some authors, many of the leading generals were seized at the termination of the banquet with the bacchanalian phrenzy, sallied forth in the height of their enthusiasm, and caused Mount Merus to re-echo the cries of Evoe, Iacche, and Lyæe. From Nysa, the whole army arrived at the bridge, already constructed by Perdiccas and Hephæstion. The whole summer and winter, as recorded from Aristobulus by Strabo, had been spent in the march from Bactria, and their late campaign among the mountains: With the commencement of spring, they descended into the plains.

CHAPTER 13

Ninth Campaign, B.C. 326

The region immediately to the east of the upper course of the Indus, was, at the period of Alexander's invasion, possessed by three leading chiefs;—Abissares, whose territories were on the left among the mountains; Taxiles, who ruled over the country immediately in front, between the Indus and the Hydaspes; and Porus, whose dominions were to the east of the Hydaspes, but who seems, from his military power, to have been an object of suspicion and alarm to his neighbours on every side. Taxiles, thus named either from his capital or from his office, immediately submitted, and with munificent presents hastened to meet the conqueror on the banks of the Indus.

The bridge gave a safe passage to the Macedonian Army, which for the second time thus found itself beyond the extreme limits of the Persian Empire. Arrian regrets that none of the historians of Alexander had described the construction of the bridge, although he concludes that it must have been supported on boats.

From the Indus the army marched to Taxila, the largest and wealthiest city between the Indus and the Hydaspes. Here time was allowed to the soldiers to recruit their strength and their health, after the late severe duty among the hills; and the king was so pleased with the liberality and generous kindness of Taxiles, that—far from depriving him of anything—he presented him with a thousand *talents*;—which drew from some discontented Macedonian the remark "that Alexander had apparently found no object worthy of his munificence before he entered India."

Abissares, the seat of whose government was probably the modern Cashmere, sent his brother with other ambassadors to make his submission, and to carry rich gifts to the king. Deputies also came from Doxares, the governor of a district, on the same errand. The stay of the army at Taxila was further marked by sacrifices, festivities, horse races, gymnastic contests, and other amusements calculated to revive the drooping spirits of the soldiers, who suffered excessively from the heavy rains, which had not ceased to fall since their entrance into India.

Although Alexander treated Taxiles with such distinguished honour and attention, he nevertheless stationed a Macedonian garrison

in his capital, and left there all the invalids of the army, while he conducted the rest to the Hydaspes, on the eastern bank of which Porus
had assembled his troops and prepared to dispute the passage.

According even to the modern laws of war, Alexander, after the
conquest of Darius and the Persians, was justified in requiring the
obedience of all the tribes which had formed component parts of
their empire. But—barbarous as our military code still continues to
be—we should in vain search its pages for a justification of a system of
aggression similar to that which Alexander was now directing against
the Indians. His conduct, however, must be examined, not on our
principles, but on those of his countrymen.

The Greeks held that they were naturally in a state of war with
all barbarians, and that nothing but a specific treaty could suspend
this natural hostility. Those nations, therefore, between whom and the
Greeks such treaties did exist, were termed *Enspondi,* and entitled to
international rights. All others were *Ecspondi,* and liable to be assailed,
despoiled, and enslaved without ceremony.

Even Aristotle writes that the Greek, from his superior virtue and
ability, had a natural right to seize and claim the services of the barbarians;—while, on the contrary, the barbarian who abused the chances
of war, and made a Greek his slave, was guilty of most unnatural conduct. It is not, therefore, surprising that the pupil of the Stagyrite felt
himself justified in exacting an acknowledgement of his supremacy
from all barbarians;—and in warning those who disputed his right, to
take the field and abide the decision of the sword.

Modern Europeans, with the exception of the Spaniards in Peru
and Mexico, have managed such matters with more delicacy and sem-
blance of justice—but the final result has been the same.

We are informed by Strabo, that the Macedonians marched in a
southern direction from the bridge across the Indus to the Hydaspes.
As there can be no doubt that the bridge was built in the vicinity
of Attock, we may be almost certain that the advance of the army
was along the main road leading from Attock to Jellick-pore, on the
Hydaspes, now called the Ihylun. The opposite bank of this noble
river was lined with the infantry and cavalry, the war-chariots, and
the elephants of Porus. Every spot, both above and below the main
road, that presented facilities for crossing was diligently guarded. The
invader divided his troops into numerous bodies, and sent them up
and down the stream, in order to confuse and distract the attention of
the Indians; but they were not to be thrown off their guard.

In the meantime, Alexander formed large magazines, as if he intended to remain encamped till the waters should decrease with the approaching winter:—for the rivers of northern India, like the Euphrates and Tigris, swell with the approach of the summer solstice, and shrink within their channels in the winter. The month of July still found Alexander on the right bank, when he had to view the Hydaspes rolling down a turbid and impetuous mass of waters, fourteen feet deep, and a full mile broad.

This obstacle alone might easily have been overcome; for the ships built upon the Indus had been taken to pieces and carried by land to the Hydaspes, and rafts and floats, supported on inflated hides, constructed in abundance. But what rendered the passage dangerous, was the line of elephants on the left bank. Alexander despaired of being able to form his cavalry after disembarking. He even doubted whether the horses would not precipitate themselves from the floats into the water, rather than face those large animals, the sight, smell, and voice of which were equally objects of alarm and abhorrence to the war-horse. The king, therefore, was compelled to steal a passage; and he effected this in the following manner.

He declared in public that it was his intention to wait for the falling of the waters—although his activity ceased not for a moment. For several nights in succession, he ordered large detachments of cavalry to parade the banks of the river, to sound their trumpets, to shout, sing *pæans*, and by outcries and dissonant clamours rouse the attention of the enemy. Porus for a time led his troops and elephants in a parallel line with these disturbers of his repose; but seeing that the alarms were not succeeded by any serious attempts to cross, he gradually ceased to regard them, or to harass his troops by useless night marches. When the vigilance of Porus had been thus lulled to sleep, Alexander prepared to put his plans in execution.

Ten miles above the camp he discovered a wooded promontory, round which the river made a considerable bend. About midway an island, covered also with wood, and uninhabited, divided the river into two main channels. He fixed upon this spot as well adapted for his purposes, because the woods and the island screened his operations from the view of the enemy. For the dangerous enterprise he selected five thousand cavalry and six thousand infantry.

Among the former were Scythians, Bactrians, and a thousand mounted archers from the Dahæ tribe; but the main strength was the formidable Companion cavalry. The infantry were the guards, two brigades of the *phalanx*, the Agrians, and the bowmen. The leading officers were Coenus, Perdiccas, Ptolemy, Lysimachus, and Seleucus, now mentioned for the first time, although destined to be the greatest of Alexander's successors.

Craterus, whom, next to Alexander, the Macedonians loved and admired, was left in command of the camp. His orders were, to remain quiet if Porus withdrew only a portion of his troops and elephants to meet the king, but if he marched away with the whole or greatest part, to cross immediately

The night was dark, the rain fell in torrents, and an Indian thunder-storm raged during the greatest part of the night. The enemy, therefore, could neither see nor hear the preparations on the right bank. The clashing of armour and the cries of the soldiers, as they embarked themselves and placed the horses on the floats, were alike drowned in the loud and incessant peals of thunder. According to Plutarch, many men were destroyed by the lightning; but it is worthy of observation that we do not read, in ancient histories, of the death of any great soldier from this cause.

Cased as their warriors were in polished steel, and with the point of the long lance raised aloft, they must, according to the theories of the present day, have been in imminent and peculiar danger when exposed in a thunder storm; yet they were apparently as safe as a modern lady in her robes of silk. Let better philosophers than I am explain the reason. With the dawn the storm ceased, and the embarkation was completed. The transports then pushed out into the river, and became visible to the enemy's sentinels as soon as they had passed the island before mentioned. These instantly gave the alarm, which rapidly passed from post to post, and was almost immediately communicated to Porus. But the Indian king knew not how to act.

The forces of Craterus were in front, and consisted apparently of the greatest part of the enemy's army; probably, therefore, he judged it to be a false attack, and that the real object was to induce him to quit his position. He therefore dispatched his son, with 2,000 cavalry and 130 war chariots, to reconnoitre and act according to circumstances. But these had to ride ten miles before they could arrive on the ground.

During the interval, Alexander and his vessels had reached what was imagined to be the opposite bank; here all were disembarked, the king as usual being the first to land. The cavalry formed regularly on the bank, and were followed by the infantry. But they had not advanced far before they discovered that they were on a second and larger island, separated from the left bank by a less considerable stream, but which, in consequence of the heavy rains, was swollen to the dimensions of a formidable river. The horsemen for a long time failed in discovering any ford, and fears were entertained that the troops would have to reembark and disembark a second time. At last, a place was found, where the infantry waded through with the water above their breasts.

They had, however, crossed this branch also, and were formed for the second time, before the young prince and his cavalry arrived. At first, Alexander mistook them for the vanguard of the Indian Army, and accordingly treated them with due respect; but as soon as he had discovered their actual numbers, and unsupported state, he charged them, at the head of the Companion cavalry, with his usual impetuosity. They also, as soon as they discovered that the king himself with a powerful force, had crossed, thought of nothing but of making their retreat good. They were eagerly pursued; 400 horsemen, and the young prince, were slain; and the chariots, unable to act in the miry and swampy soil, were all captured.

Porus, on hearing from the fugitives that the king, with the most effective part of his troops, had crossed, and that his son had fallen, left a few elephants and a small force to observe the motions of Craterus, and marched with all the strength of his army to give Alexander battle. He had with him 4,000 cavalry, 300 war-chariots, 200 elephants, and 30,000 infantry. These were all good soldiers, warriors by profession, well disciplined, and furnished with excellent arms, both offensive and defensive.

When he had arrived on an open plain, the soil of which was a firm sand, well adapted for the movements of his cavalry and chariots, he drew up his army in battle array, and waited the approach of the Macedonians. In front he placed the elephants, about a hundred feet distant from each other. Behind them were drawn up the infantry, not in an unbroken line, but with intervals behind each elephant. The cavalry were distributed between the two wings, and the war-chariots placed immediately in front of them. Arrian praises the arrangement; it was the very same which the Carthaginians, in later days, practised. Alexander, at the head of his pursuing cavalry, first came in sight of this formidable array.

He immediately halted his men, and waited for the arrival of the infantry. His object had been to surprise the enemy's camp, but the rapid and skilful movement of Porus had anticipated this; he was therefore obliged to content himself with making various demonstrations with his cavalry, until the *phalanx* had been formed and the men had recovered their breath.

Even when these objects had been attained, he could not immediately see how he was to act. He knew from past experience that the horses would not charge the elephants; and it appeared hazardous in the extreme to form the *phalanx* into detached columns, and lead them through the intervals between the elephants, against the enemy's infantry; for if these maintained their ground for ever so short a period, the elephants, by a transverse motion, might break the continuity of the columns and throw them into irreparable confusion.

But the 11,000 commanded by Alexander were soldiers, to a man, long accustomed to victory, and full of confidence in themselves, in each other, and in their leader. They knew that, as long as they kept together in their chivalry, it was of little consequence whether the enemy was on their flank, in their rear, or in front. They had not heard of the strange doctrines, propagated by the military pedants of modern days, that men might be fairly beaten on the field of battle, and yet, from ignorance of this vital fact, most unfairly persevere in fighting, and thus wrest the victory from their conquerors. Such an army, in Alexander's hands, was a weapon which he could wield at will, and which as truly obeyed the orders communicated in words as the spear did the impulse of the hand.

The infantry were ordered to remain where they were, and not to move before they saw the success of the cavalry. The latter were formed into two divisions, of unequal force. The larger, commanded by Alexander himself, advanced in an oblique direction, in order to turn the left wing of the enemy and attack him in the flank. Coenus, with the smaller division, was detached to perform the same manoeuvre on the right of the Indian Army.

Porus disregarded the movement of Coenus, but being alarmed by the appearance of the powerful body of cavalry with which Alexander was threatening to attack his left wing, instantly ordered his own cavalry of the right to move up by the rear to the support of his left; at the same time, he attempted to change his front so as to place the advancing Macedonians between him and the river.

Alexander, first sending out the mounted archers—to attack the front of the left wing, and cover his movements—by the discharge of missiles, turned it himself, and prepared to attack it in the flank before it could change its front. Coenus in the meantime had not only turned the enemy's right wing, but had resolutely pursued the cavalry originally posted there, until it had joined the left. The Indian cavalry were thus compelled to oppose a double front, one to Alexander, the other to Coenus; and while they were in the act of doing so, the king charged.

The Indians, instead of receiving this manfully, took refuge among the elephants, which by the change of front were now brought to face the Macedonian cavalry; but the *phalanx* under Seleucus, who had been attentively waiting for an opportunity, advanced and saved the cavalry from the charge of the elephants. Then occurred a contest to which the Macedonians had hitherto witnessed nothing similar. The elephants boldly advanced against the masses of infantry, and where they made an impression caused great confusion. The archers and the Agrians on the other hand, directed their missiles not so much against the animals as against their guides; for an elephant deprived of his guide was as dangerous to one party as to the other.

While this novel contest was going on, the Indian cavalry recovered their courage and order, and sallied forth to support the elephants, but they were again met and driven back by Alexander and his horse, who both in personal strength and skill surpassed the Indians. Coenus had already broken through, and the whole Macedonian cavalry were thus united. At the head of these Alexander made repeated and desperate charges upon the Indian infantry, and where he charged entirely broke their ranks.

The scattered troops universally took refuge among the elephants, which by the activity of the Macedonian infantry were gradually driven upon each other; many, therefore, irritated by their wounds, and deprived of their guides, became furious, and attacked friends and foes indiscriminately; but their assailants gave them no respite;— giving way whenever a furious animal rushed from the crowd, they pressed forwards upon the others.

At last, the elephants wearied out ceased to charge, and began to retire, trumpeting loudly with their uplifted trunks, a sure sign that they had become unmanageable. Arrian compares their retreat to the motion of the ancient war-galley, retiring in presence of an enemy with the stern foremost and the beak to the foe.

Alexander then stationed his cavalry at intervals round the confused mass; and the *phalanx* in closest order, with shield linked to shield, and pikes projecting, advanced and bore down all opposition.

At this moment Craterus brought up his troops, and pursued the enemy, who were flying in all directions through the intervals between the Macedonian cavalry. According to Arrian, twenty thousand of the Indian infantry, and three thousand of their cavalry, fell in this bloody battle; the chariots and surviving elephants were all captured.

Porus himself, inferior to his antagonist in military skill and talents, but not in valour, fought as long as he could keep any of his troops together. His height exceeded the common stature of man, and he rode an elephant of proportionate size. He was completely cased in armour with the exception of his right arm, which was bared for the combat. His *cuirass* was of great strength and beautiful workmanship, and when afterwards examined excited the admiration of the Macedonians; it was probably scale armour.

Alexander had long witnessed the gallant bearing of the Indian king, and the perseverance with which he maintained the combat, for the battle lasted till two o'clock in the afternoon. Anxious to save the life of so brave an opponent, especially as he could see that a wound in the shoulder had in some degree disabled his right arm, the king desired Taxiles to ride up and persuade him to surrender. Taxiles, however, was an ancient foe of Porus; and this gallant prince no sooner discovered him approaching, than he turned his elephant against him, and would have slain him, had not the speed of his horse quickly borne him beyond the reach of his weapons.

Alexander, probably more amused than displeased with this result, sent other messengers in succession, and finally Meroes, an Indian, who, as he found, was an old friend of the king. Porus listened to him, and being overpowered by thirst caused by loss of blood, the pain of the wound, and the noon-tide heat, descended from his elephant; he then drank and cooled himself, and was conducted by Meroes to Alexander, who, attended by a few friends, rode forward to meet the first potentate whom he had captured on the field of battle. He admired not only the size and handsome person of the prisoner, but the total absence of servility that characterized his bearing. He approached with all the confidence with which one brave man should always approach another, and with a consciousness that he had not impaired his claims to respect, by gallantly defending his native kingdom against invaders.

Alexander was the first to speak, and asked if he had any request to make?

"Only to be treated like a king, O Alexander," was the short and expressive answer.

"That shall be done (said the victor) on my own account; but ask any particular favour—and it shall be granted for your own sake."

"I have nothing further to ask," said Porus, "for everything is comprehended in my first request."

This was an enemy according to Alexander's own heart; he treated him with marked honour, gave him his freedom on the spot, restored his kingdom, and afterwards added largely to its extent. He was not disappointed in the estimate he had made of the Indian's character, and found him ever after an attached friend and a faithful subject.

The Macedonians who fell in the battle were buried with public honours. Then thanksgiving sacrifices were offered to the gods, and the usual games and festivities closed the ceremony.

Craterus was ordered to superintend the building of two new cities, one on each bank of the Hydaspes. The object was to secure the passage in future. The one on the left bank was named Nicæa, the other Bucephala, in honour of the favourite Bucephalus which died in the battle without a wound, being worn out by age, heat, and over-exertion. He was then thirty years old, and had been presented to Alexander in early life by Demaratus the Corinthian. He was a large, powerful, and spirited horse, and would allow no one but Alexander to mount him. From a mark of a bull's head imprinted on him he had his name Bucephalus, though some say that he was so called because being a black horse he had on his forehead a white mark resembling a bull's head.

Once this famous charger, whose duties were restricted to the field of battle, was intercepted and fell into the hands of the Uxians. Alexander caused a proclamation to be made, that, if Bucephalus were not restored, he would wage a war of extirpation against the whole nation. The restoration of the animal instantly followed the receipt of the notification. So great was Alexander's regard for his horse, and so great the terror of his name among the barbarians.

Arrian writes:

Thus far let Bucephalus be honoured by me for the sake of his master.

The whole country between the Hydaspes and the Acesines was reduced, and placed under the government of Porus.

The population was great and wealthy, for Alexander received the submission of thirty-five cities, not one of which contained fewer than five thousand inhabitants. The Acesines (the modern Chun-ab) was then crossed without much difficulty, for the natives offered no opposition;—but the channel, as described by Ptolemy, the son of Lagus, was nearly a mile broad. The principal chief between the Acesines and the Hydraotes was another Porus, surnamed *the Coward* by the Macedonians. Previously he had sent ambassadors and submitted himself to Alexander's authority, but, on hearing that his enemy the brave Porus was in high honour with his victor, he lost confidence and fled with all his warriors beyond the Hydraotes.

Alexander sent Hephæstion to take possession of his dominions and deliver them to his rival. A second embassy also arrived from Abissares, bringing large sums of money, forty elephants, and promises of unconditional submission. But Alexander, who had discovered that previous to the battle this prince had been on the point of joining Porus, sent back a peremptory order for him to appear in person or expect a hostile visit. He then led his army across the Hydraotes, (the modern Iravati or Ravee,) and heard that a warlike nation called Cathaians had roused two other independent tribes to arms, and were preparing to receive him under the walls of a strong city called Sangala. This nation, both from its name and for other reasons, appears to have been Tatar, and not to have been long established in the country. Porus and Abissares had lately united arms and invaded their settlements, but had been driven back with loss.

The Macedonians arrived before Sangala on the evening of the third day after crossing the Hydraotes; and found the Cathaian troops encamped on a rising ground close to the city. Their camp was surrounded with a triple line of waggons—which with the absence of elephants—amounts almost to conclusive proof of their Scythian origin. Alexander attempted to charge the waggons with his cavalry, but the Cathaian missiles easily repulsed him. The infantry of the *phalanx* was then brought up, and carried the first line without much difficulty; but the second was not forced without considerable loss, as they could not advance in order until they had withdrawn all the waggons of the first line. They succeeded at last in bursting the triple barrier and driving its defenders into the town.

This was enclosed with a brick wall, and had a shallow lake on one side. The inhabitants had no confidence in their fortifications, and repeatedly attempted to break out and escape. But the Macedonians had already thrown up a double rampart round the whole city except on the lake side. The besieged, therefore, determined to ford this in the night and march away. Intimation of their plan reached Alexander, who commissioned Ptolemy to prevent its execution. This officer in haste gathered all the waggons which had formed the triple barrier, and drew them up in a single line round the edge of the lake. The Cathaians sallied out at midnight, crossed the lake, but failed to force the hastily erected barrier, and retired again to the city.

By this time the engines had battered down the walls:—the army entered the breach and carried the place by storm. Seventeen thousand of the Cathaians were slain, and seventy thousand taken prisoners. A hundred Macedonians fell, twelve hundred were wounded—Lysimachus and several other leaders being among the latter. The great disproportion between the wounded and the slain proves that the Cathaian weapons were principally arrows and hand-missiles, which seldom proved fatal to men well furnished with defensive armour.

Eumenes, the secretary, (now mentioned for the first time,) was sent with three hundred cavalry to the two other tribes, who had made common cause with the Cathaians. His orders were to promise an amnesty for past proceedings and protection for the future, provided they would submit; but they had already heard of the capture of Sangala, and moved away in a body. Alexander pursued eagerly, but could not overtake them, and in all probability, they did not halt until they had gained the mountains, whence the Hydraotes descends. The territories of the three tribes was given to Indians who in ancient days had been independent, and who in the present instance had willingly submitted to the Macedonians. It appears more than probable that they had been deprived of them by the intrusive Cathaians.

Here Alexander received information, that India beyond the Hyphasis—the modern Bezah, or perhaps the united streams of the Bezah and Sutlege—was very fertile, inhabited by warlike nations skilled in agriculture, and wisely governed. He might also have heard of the magnificent Palibothra, the Indian Babylon, superior in wealth and power to the Assyrian, the seat of the great monarch whose authority extended over all the Indian peninsula, and who could lead into the field six hundred thousand infantry, thirty thousand cavalry, and nine thousand elephants. He heard also, that these animals in the vale of the Ganges were far larger and bolder than those of northern India. These reports excited the spirit of Alexander, and he prepared to cross the Hyphasis, and follow the great road that would conduct him to Palibothra, situated, according to Arrian, at the junction of the Erannoboas and the Ganges.

But the Macedonians were worn out with wounds, fatigue, and disease. During this campaign they had been constantly drenched with the rains, from which they suffered more than from all their other perils and labours. Besides this they had been disappointed in their Indian expedition in every way. To use Arrian's words:

> They discovered that the Indians had no gold, and that they were by no means luxurious in their mode of living, that they were large of size, exceeding the common stature of Asiatics, and by far the most warlike of the then inhabitants of Asia.

Frequent meetings therefore took place in the camp, and the formation of circles round individual speakers proved that the minds of the men were deeply agitated. In these meetings the more quiet characters only lamented their lot, while others vehemently encouraged their comrades to stand firm to each other, and to refuse to cross the Hyphasis even if Alexander led the way.

The king soon discovered the symptoms of approaching mutiny, and that the disinclination to march farther south had extended from the privates to the officers. Before, therefore, this feeling should assume any more offensive form, he called a council of war, to which all the officers of superior rank were summoned. And as the speeches reported by Arrian bear strong internal marks of being copied from the original historians, I here introduce them.

Alexander said:

> Macedonians and Allies, seeing that you do not follow me into dangers with your usual alacrity, I have summoned you to this assembly, that either I may persuade you to go further, or you persuade me to turn back. If you have reason to complain of our previous labours, or of me your leader, I have no more to say; but if by these labours we have acquired Ionia, the Hellespont, with Phrygia, Cappadocia, Paphlagonia, Lydia, Caria, Lycia, Pamphylia, Phoenicia, Egypt, Cyrenaica, part of Arabia, Colo-Syria, Mesopotamia, Babylon, Susiana, Persia, Media, and all the provinces governed by the Medes and Persians, and others never subject to them;—If we have subdued the regions beyond the Caspian Gates and Mount Caucasus, Hyrcania, Bactria, and the countries between Caucasus, the River Tanais, and the Hyrcanian sea;—If we have driven the Scythians back into their deserts, and the Indus, the Hydaspes, the Acesines flow within our empire, why do you hesitate to pass the Hy-

phasis also, and add the nations beyond it to the Macedonian conquests? Or do you fear the successful resistance of any of these barbarians, of whom, some willingly submit, others are overtaken in their flight, others escape, and leave their territories to be distributed by us among our Allies?

For my own part, I recognise no limits to the labours of a high-spirited man, but the failure of adequate objects; yet if any one among you wishes to know the limits of our present warfare, let him learn that we are not far from the River Ganges and the Eastern Ocean. This, I venture to assert, is connected with the Hyrcanian Sea, for the great ocean flows round the whole earth; and I shall prove to the Macedonians and their Allies, that the Indian Gulf flows into the Persian, and the Hyrcanian into the Indian. From the Persian Gulf our fleet shall carry our arms round Africa, until it reach the pillars of Hercules, and Africa within the pillars be entirely subject to us.

Thus, the boundaries of our empire will be the same as those with which the deity has encircled the earth. But if we now turn back, many warlike nations between the Hyphasis and the Eastern Ocean, many in a northern direction between these and the Hyrcanian Sea, and the Scythian tribes in the latter vicinity, will remain unsubdued. And there is cause to fear lest the conquered nations, as yet wavering in their fidelity, be excited to revolt by their independent neighbours, and the fruits of our numerous labours be thus entirely lost, or secured only by a repetition of the same labours and dangers.

But persevere, O Macedonians and Allies—glorious deeds are the fruits of labour and danger. Life distinguished by deeds of valour is delightful, and so is death when we leave behind us an immortal name.

Know ye not that our ancestor did not, by remaining at Tirinthus, Argos, or even in the Peloponnesus and Thebes, attain that glorious fame which elevated him to the real or imaginary rank of a god? Nor were the labours of Dionysus, a more venerable deity than Hercules, trifling. But we have advanced beyond Nysa; and the rock Aornos, impregnable to Hercules, is in our possession. Add therefore the remainder of Asia to our present acquisitions, the smaller portion to the greater; for we ourselves could never have achieved any great and memorable deeds had we lingered in Macedonia, and been content without exertion to preserve our homes and repulse the neighbouring Thracians, Illyrians, Triballi, or those Greeks who might prove hostile to us. If I, your leader, exposed you to labours and dangers from which I shrunk myself, there would be cause for your faint-heartedness, seeing that you endured the toils, and others enjoyed the rewards; but our labours are in common; I, equally with you, share in the dangers, and the rewards become the public property. For the conquered country belongs to you; you are its *satraps*; and among you the greater part of its treasures has already been distributed. And when all Asia is subdued, I promise, and I call Jupiter to witness, not only to satisfy, but exceed the wishes of every individual;—either in person to lead, or safely to send into Macedonia, all who wish to return home;—and to render those who may remain in Asia objects of envy to their returning friends.

This speech was succeeded by a deep silence. They could not approve, yet no one wished to be the first to oppose. Alexander repeatedly called on some individual to express his sentiments, even if unfavourable to his proposal; yet all still remained silent. At length Coenus, the son of Polemocrates, the oldest of the generals, took courage and thus spoke—

Since you, O King, are unwilling to lead the Macedonians further by the mere exercise of your authority, but propose to do so only in case you succeed in persuading them, and by no means to have recourse to compulsion, I rise to speak, not on behalf of myself and the great officers now present—who, as we have been honoured especially, and have most of us already received the reward of our labours, and exercise authority over others, are zealous to serve you in all things—but in behalf of the great body of the soldiers. Nor will I advance what is calculated to gain their favour alone, but what I judge most advantageous to you for the present, and safest for the future.

And my age, the high authority delegated to me by yourself, and the unhesitating boldness which I have hitherto manifested in all dangerous enterprises, give me the privilege of stating what appears to me the best.

The number and magnitude of the exploits achieved under your command by us, who originally accompanied you from Macedonia, are in my opinion so many arguments for placing a limit to our labours and dangers; for you see how few of the Greeks and Macedonians, who originally commenced the expedition, are now in the army. When you saw the Thessalians no longer encountering dangers with alacrity, you acted wisely and sent them home from Bactra. Of the other Greeks, some have been settled in the cities founded by you, where all are not willing residents; some still share in our toils and perils. They and the Macedonians have lost some of their numbers on the field of battle; others have been disabled by wounds; others left behind in various parts of Asia; but the majority have perished by disease.

A few out of many now survive. Nor do they possess the same bodily strength as before, while their spirits are still more depressed. Those whose parents are still living, long to revisit them. All long to behold once more their wives, their children, and the homes of their native land. This natural desire is pardonable in men who, by your munificence, will return powerful and wealthy—not, as before, poor and without influence. Do not, therefore, wish to lead us contrary to our inclinations. For men whose heart is not in the service, can never prove equally useful in the hour of danger. And, if agreeable, do you also return home with us, see your mother once more, arrange the affairs of Greece, and place in your father's house the trophies of our great and numerous victories.

When you have performed these duties, form a fresh expedition against these same eastern Indians, if such be your wish, or to the shores of the Euxine Sea, or against Carthage, and the parts of Africa beyond Carthage. You may select your object, and other Macedonians and other Greeks will follow you—men young and vigorous, not like us old and exhausted. They, from inexperience, will despise the immediate danger, and eagerly anticipate the rich rewards of war. They will also naturally follow you with the greater alacrity, for having seen the companions of your former dangers and toils return to their homes in safety, wealthy instead of poor, and from obscurity raised to great distinction. Besides, O King, moderation in prosperity is above all things honourable, and although you, at the head of your brave army, have nothing to dread from mortal foes, yet the visitations of the divinity are not to be foreseen, and men therefore cannot guard against them.

At the close of the speech, the officers present expressed their sympathy with the sentiments of Coenus by a general murmur of approbation, and the tears which rolled down the cheeks of many veterans showed how earnestly they longed to turn their faces homewards. But the disappointment was greater than the ardent feelings of Alexander could well bear. Equally displeased with the remonstrance of Coenus, and with the hesitation of the others, the king broke up the council abruptly. Next day he again summoned it, and angrily declared that it was his intention to advance, but not to enforce the attendance of any Macedonian—that he would retain only those who were willing to follow their sovereign-that the rest might return home, and tell their families that they had deserted Alexander in the midst of his enemies. When he had hastily spoken these few words, he retired to his tent. There he secluded himself for three days, refusing admission to his most intimate friends, and evidently expecting some favourable change in the minds of the soldiers.

But when a deep silence continued to pervade the camp, and the troops manifested great sorrow at the king's displeasure, but no inclination to change their resolution, he yielded to necessity, and took the course best adapted to maintain his own dignity. He sacrificed, and found, as might be expected, the omens decidedly adverse to the passage of the Hyphasis.

He then called together the oldest officers and his own most intimate friends, and through them announced to the army the unfavourable state of the auspices, and his consequent intention to return. The announcement was welcomed with shouts of joy; most of the soldiers wept aloud, and, crowding round the king's tent, implored countless blessings upon his head, who, invincible to others, had allowed himself to be overcome by them.

On the banks of the Hyphasis he erected twelve towers in the shape of altars; monuments of the extent of his career, and testimonies of his gratitude to the gods. On these gigantic altars he offered sacrifices with all due solemnity, and horse races and gymnastic contests closed the festivities.

We must all sympathize with the feelings of the Macedonian veterans, so simply and yet eloquently described by Coenus, and while we respect the firmness of their resolution, admire their calm and tranquil manner of expressing it. But would it had been otherwise! The great barriers that protect Hindostan had been forced, and the road to Palibothra was open. According to the *Sandracottus*, (or great Indian sovereign,) with whom Seleucus formed a treaty of friendship and alliance, his immediate predecessor was a usurper and a tyrant, and consequently odious to his subjects. Since the defeat of Porus on the Hydaspes, Alexander had met no serious resistance, except from the Cathaians; nor does it appear, from good authority, that any nations to the east of the Hyphasis had combined for the purpose of mutual defence.

It is certain that there were no troops on the left bank of the Hyphasis. According to Curtius, the country between the Hyphasis and the Ganges was a desert, for the space of eleven day's journey. On the Ganges, the Gandarides and the Prasians were the two predominant nations.

****

Plutarch, with the most culpable negligence, unless indeed a more serious charge may justly be brought against him, boldly conducts Alexander to the Ganges, and lines its opposite banks with innumerable foes.

****

Had the Macedonians persevered, and made themselves masters of the peninsula, we might have derived most valuable information on points concerning which we must now remain ignorant: for hitherto the literary remains of the ancient Hindoos have not presented any distinct notices that can be referred to the era of Alexander. All is enveloped in the clouds of mythology and allegory, where nothing clear and definite can be discerned.

Perhaps these opinions are liable to be condemned; but according to my views much false logic and fictitious humanity have been expended upon the conquests of Alexander: for I see not how the progress of a civilized and enlightened conqueror among barbarous nations can be regarded otherwise than beneficial. An Alexander in Africa would be the greatest blessing that could visit that great continent. Since history has recorded the annals of nations, colonization and conquests have been the two main instruments of civilization.

Nor do I see why Ashantees, Caffres, or any other dominant tribes should be supposed to have a prescriptive right to murder and enslave their fellow Africans, and to renew their atrocities three or four times in a century, much less why a Christian sovereign should be blamed, were he effectually to subjugate the barbarians, and put an end to all such enormities in future.

Alexander returned from the Hyphasis, recrossed the Hydraotes and Acesines, and arrived on the banks of the Hydaspes. In building the new cities of Nicæa and Bucephala, sufficient allowance had not been made for the rise of the river. The waters had therefore seriously damaged them. The towns were now repaired, and the mistake corrected. Here a third embassy from Abissares waited upon Alexander, and among other presents brought thirty more elephants. A severe illness was alleged to be the sole cause of the king's absence; and as, upon inquiry, the allegation appeared true, the apology was accepted, and the future amount of tribute determined.

During the whole summer, part of the troops had been engaged in ship-building, on the banks of the Hydaspes. The timber was found in the mountain forests through which the river descended into the plain, and consisted, according to Strabo, of firs, pines, cedars, and other trees well adapted for the purpose. The men employed in felling the timber disturbed a great multitude of monkeys and baboons. These, flocking to the crown of a hill, whence they could view the destruction of their ancient sanctuaries, presented to the workmen the appearance of disciplined troops, and they were hastily preparing to arm themselves and march against their supposed foes, when they were undeceived by their native comrades.

It is a melancholy consideration that hitherto on this globe a high degree of civilization has first destroyed national feelings or patriotism, then national independence, as the inevitable consequence, and, finally, national existence. The Chaldæan and Assyrian have been swept from the face of the earth; the descendants of the Medes and Persians are outcasts from their country; a few Copts represent the ancient Egyptians; the Greek is the barbarian slave of a barbarian tyrant; and Italy, with her double wreath, with her two eras of light and liberty, is partly enslaved and partly barbarized.

Thus, also the Hindoos have, for centuries, been the prey of more warlike tribes, who have fought and bled for the sovereignty of that great peninsula, while the inhabitants have remained passive spectators of the contest, as if a change of masters was to them a matter of indifference. China alone has escaped the common fate, not so much from its admirable constitution, as from its great population and exclusion from the rest of the world—two circumstances that have enabled it twice to absorb its bandit conquerors without any material change in the nature of the institutions and of the people.

It must not be supposed that the inhabitants of Southern Greece, the descendants of the heroes of Marathon, Salamis and Platæa, partook largely in the glorious deeds of the Macedonians. We have already seen the paltry quota which originally joined Alexander from the confederated states. These had been gradually falling away, and few of any consideration had reached India. Alexander, in order to obtain an effective fleet, had appointed most of his great officers to be temporary *trierarchs*. These of course would be required, after the manner of the Athenians, to equip and man their own gallies in the most gallant style. And as Arrian, in his abridgement of the *Voyage of Nearchus*, has given a list of their names, I transcribe it here, as useful to show who the master-spirits were who worked the great revolution in the eastern world.

Trierarchs.

Hephæstion ...	son of	Amyntor....	
Leonnatus	——	Eunus......	
Lysimachus ...	——	Agathocles..	
Asclepiodorus..	——	Timander ...	
Archon .:.....	——	Cleinias	Pellæans.
Demonicus....	——	Athenæus ...	
Archias	——	Anaxidotus..	
Ophellas	——	Seilenus	
Timanthes	——	Pantiades ...	
Nearchus	——	Androtimus ..	
Laomedon	——	Larichus....	Amphipolitans.
Androsthenes..	——	Callistrates ..	
Craterus......	——	Alexander...	Orestians.
Perdiccas	——	Orontes	
Ptolemy	——	Lagus.......	Eordæans.
Aristonous	——	Peisæus	
Metron	——	Epicharmus .	from Pydna.
Nicarchides ...	——	Simus......	
Attalus	——	Andromenes .. a Stymphæan,	
Peucestas	——	Alexander .. a Miezian.	
Peithon	——	Crateas ..... from Alcomenè.	
Leonnatus	——	Antipater .. from Ægæ.	
Pantarchus....	——	Nicolaus ... —— Alorus,	
Mylleas	——	Zoïlus ..... —— Berœa.	

The above were all Macedonians. The following were Greeks:

Medius	son of	Oxynthemis .. from Larissa.	
Eumenes......	——	Hieronymus .. —— Cardia.	
Critobulus	——	Plato........ —— Cos.	
Thoas	——	Menodorus ..	Magnesia
Mæandrius....	——	Mandrogenes.	
Andron.......	——	Cabelus...... —— Teos.	
Nicocles......	——	Pasicrates ...	Cyprus.
Nithadon	——	Prytagoras ...	

And one Persian,

Bagoas ...... son of ...... Pharnuches.

This list, which, with the exception of Seleucus, embraces every

189

man of note in the army, does not contain the name of a single citizen of any of the southern republics. Had there been an Athenian even of minor consideration present, he would no doubt have held a distinguished situation in a naval armament. But the republicans of Greece had no part or portion in the glory of the war. Hence arose that jealousy of the Macedonian fame, that bitter hostility to Alexander, who had so dimmed and obscured their exploits by the splendour of his renown, and, as the literature of Greece was in their hands, that systematic attempt to depress his fame and blacken his character.

It is also curious, that in the above list we do not find a single native of Lyncestis, although it was the largest province of Macedonia. Either the Lyncestians, with the true feelings of a mountain clan, had retired from the service when their chief was slain, or Alexander, after that event, did not feel that he could trust them in confidential situations.

While all were busily engaged in preparing for the voyage, the veteran Coenus fell ill and died. He had taken a distinguished part in all the great battles; was an officer in whom Alexander had placed implicit confidence; and he was buried with all the magnificence and honours which circumstances would admit. Curtius imputes a brutal observation to Alexander on the occasion, "that Coenus had made a long speech for the sake of a few days' life." But the general did not make a long speech. The historian composed, indeed, a long one for him; and if any one wishes to see the difference between ambitious declamation and the simple eloquence of a soldier, let him compare the speech recorded by Arrian with the one invented by Curtius.

An assembly of the general officers and of the deputies from various nations was then held, in which Porus was proclaimed king of seven Indian nations that comprised within their limits two thousand cities. The three hundred horsemen were sent back to the city of Dionysus, and Philip appointed *satrap* of the country immediately to the west of the Indus. The army was then separated into three divisions: Hephæstion led one, including the elephants, amounting to two hundred, down the left, and Craterus another division down the right bank. The third embarked with Alexander on board the fleet, consisting of eighty *triaconters*, and of more than two thousand river craft of every description, partly built and partly collected. The *triaconters* were thirty-oared gallies, constructed on the plan of the ancient ships of war. Nearchus was appointed admiral, and Onesicritus, a Greek islander, chief pilot or master of the whole fleet. The crews consisted of Phoenicians, Cyprians, Carians and Egyptians, who had followed the expedition.

When all the preparations had been completed, sacrifices were offered to Neptune, Amphitritè, the Naïades, and other gods. A public feast with the usual games followed. The army then embarked with the dawn; and Alexander, standing on the prow of his own ship, poured from a golden cup a libation into the stream of the Hydaspes. He then invoked the river god of the Acesines, of which the Hydaspes was a tributary, and the still more powerful deity of the Indus, into which the united waters of both discharged themselves. Great as were the honours paid by the Greeks to their streams, they fell infinitely short of the veneration in which these are to this day held by the Hindoos. The trumpet then gave the signal for casting off, and the whole forest of vessels moved majestically down the river.

The strokes of the innumerable oars, the voices of the officers who regulated the motions, and the loud cries of the rowers as they simultaneously struck the waters, produced sounds singularly pleasing and harmonious. The banks, in many places loftier than the vessels, and the ravines that retired from either side, served to swell, re-echo, and prolong the notes. The appearance also of the gallant soldiers on the decks, and especially of the war horses—seen through the latticework of the sides of the strong vessels, purposely built for their conveyance—struck the gazing barbarians with astonishment and admiration.

Even Hercules and Dionysus were sure passed, for neither tradition nor fable had ascribed a naval armament to them. The Indians of Nicæa and Bucephala, whence the fleet departed, accompanied its motions to a great distance, and the dense population on both sides, attracted by the sounds, rushed down to the edge of the river, and expressed their admiration in wild chaunts and dances. Arrian writes:

For the Indians are lovers of the song and the dance ever since Dionysus and his Bacchanalians revelled through their land.

In eight days, the fleet arrived near the confluence of the Hydaspes and the Acesines. The channel of their united streams is contracted immediately below the point of junction. The current is consequently sharp and rapid, and strong eddies are formed by the struggling waters that swell in waves and encounter each other, so that the roar of the conflict is audible from a great distance. Alexander and the crews had been forewarned by the natives of these narrows, probably the remains of a worn-down cataract. Yet as they approached the conflu-

191

ence, the sailors were so alarmed by the loud roar of the waters, that they simultaneously suspended the action of their oars, and even the regulators became mute, and listened in silence to the harsh greetings of the sister streams.

On nearing the upper edge of the narrows, the pilots ordered the rowers to ply their oars with their utmost activity, and thus rapidly impel the vessels over the boiling surge. The rounder and shorter vessels passed through in safety; but the gallies, the extreme length of which rendered the exposure of their broadsides to the current particularly dangerous, were not so fortunate. Several were damaged, some had the blades of their oars snapped asunder, and two fell aboard of each other, and sunk with the greater part of their crews. A small promontory on the right side offered shelter and protection, and here Alexander moored his partly disabled fleet.

The Indians on each side had hitherto submitted, or if refractory, had been easily subdued; but Alexander here received information that the Malli and Oxydracæ, two powerful and free states, compared by Arrian for their military skill and valour to the Cathæians, were preparing to give him a hostile reception, and dispute the passage through their territories. The Malli occupied the country between the lower part of the courses of the Hydraotes and the Acesines, and also the district beyond the Hydraotes in the same line. The plan agreed upon by the two nations was, for the Malli to send their warriors lower down into the country of the Oxydracæ, and to make it the scene of warfare. The Malli looked upon themselves as sufficiently protected from any lateral attack by a considerable desert that intervened between their upper settlements and the banks of the Acesines.

Craterus and Hephæstion had already arrived at the confluence. The elephants were ferried across and placed under the care of Craterus, who was to continue his route along the right bank of the Acesines. Nearchus was ordered to conduct the fleet to the junction of the Hydraotes and Acesines. The remaining troops were divided into three parts. Hephæstion with one division commenced his march five days before Alexander, and Ptolemy was ordered to remain with another for three days after Alexander had departed. The intention of this distribution was to distract the enemy's attention, and that those who fled to the front should be intercepted by Hephæstion, those who fled to the rear by Ptolemy. The different bodies were told to meet again at the confluence of the Hydraotes and Acesines.

Alexander selected for his own division the guards, the bowmen, the Agrians, the brigade of Companion infantry, all the mounted archers, and one half of the Companion cavalry. With these he marched laterally from the left bank of the Acesines, and encamped by the side of a small stream which skirted the western edge of the desert, that intervened between him and the upper settlements of the Malli upon the Hydraotes.

Here he allowed the men to take a short repose, after which they were ordered to fill all their vessels with water. He then marched during the remainder of the day and all night, and with the dawn arrived before a Mallian city, the inhabitants of which had no fears of being attacked thus suddenly from the side of the desert. Many, according to the early habits of their country, were already in the fields. When these had been slain or captured, Alexander placed detachments of cavalry round the town, until the arrival of the infantry. Their march across the desert had exceeded twenty-five miles, nevertheless, as soon as they had come up, they carried by storm first the city and then the citadel, although the Malli fought boldly and resolutely.

But Alexander's march across the desert had taken them by surprise, and entirely deranged the plans of their leaders, who had conducted their warriors down the river. The cities therefore, even the most important, were evacuated on the king's approach, and their inhabitants either fled beyond the Hydraotes or took refuge in the dense jungles that lined the banks of that river.

The capture of the first city was the morning's work; the afternoon was given to repose. At six in the evening the march was resumed, and continued through the night; and with the break of day the army reached the Hydraotes—where they overtook some of the fugitive Malli, in the act of crossing the river. All who refused to surrender were put to the sword: the main body escaped into a city strongly walled and situated. Against these Peithon was detached, who stormed the place and captured the garrison.

Alexander then crossed to the left bank of the Hydraotes, and arrived at a Brachman town. It is impossible to say whether all the inhabitants were Brachmans or Brahmins, or whether the city was merely the property of that dominant caste. They, as was their bounden duty, had been active in exciting their countrymen against the invaders, and were not backwards in giving them a brave example. When the walls had been undermined and breaches made, the Brachmans retired to the citadel, which was gallantly defended. Alexander himself was the first to scale the walls, and remained for a time the sole captor of the fortress. Five thousand Indians were slain, as no quarter could be given either to the warriors, who fought while life remained, or to the inhabitants, who closed their doors and set fire to their houses with their own hands.

The army then reposed for one day, after which Peithon and Demetrius, a cavalry officer, were sent to scour the jungles on the left bank of the Hydraotes. Their orders were to put all who resisted to the sword. It was in these jungles probably that Peithon killed the largest snake which the Macedonians saw in India. It was twenty-four feet long; and although this is but a small size for a boa-constrictor, it was a monster to which the Greeks had seen nothing similar, as the marshes of Lerna and the borders of the Lake Copaïs had, since the heroic ages, ceased to teem with these enormous reptiles.

But the Indians assured them that serpents of a far greater magnitude were to be seen. According to Onesicritus, the ambassadors of Abissares mentioned in Alexander's court, that their sovereign possessed two, of which the smaller was eighty, the larger one hundred and forty cubits long. It is curious that the Macedonians did not see a Royal Bengal Tiger, although in modern days his ravages are very destructive between Guzerat and the lower Indus. They saw his skin, and heard exaggerated tales respecting his size, strength, and ferocity. Is it a fair inference from his nonappearance in the vales of the Indus and its tributaries--that the natives of those regions were, at the period of the Macedonian invasion, more powerful, populous, and warlike, than in our days?

Alexander himself marched against the principal city of the Malli; but it, like many others on the left bank of the Hydraotes, was found evacuated:—the inhabitants having crossed to the right bank, where the whole warlike force of the nation was now united. Their numbers amounted to 50,000, and their intention was to dispute the passage of the Hydraotes and prevent him from recrossing that stream. Thither, therefore, without delay he directed his course, and as soon as he saw the enemy on the opposite bank, dashed into the river at the head of his cavalry. The Ravee or Hydraotes is in July more than five hundred yards broad, and twelve feet deep. In the dry season the breadth remains nearly the same, but the depth does not exceed four feet. The autumn being far advanced at the time that Alexander crossed, the waters were probably at their lowest point of depression.

We may well be astonished at the extraordinary boldness, not to say rashness, with which the king, unsupported by infantry, prepared to ford a river of this magnitude, in the face of more than 50,000 enemies. But during these operations he was evidently acting under morbid excitement. He was angry with his soldiers, who, while they loved and adored him, had yet thwarted his schemes of universal conquest, and checked him in the full career of victory. He, therefore, expended his wrath and soothed his irritation by courting dangers, setting his life at nought, and like the heroes of old, achieving victory with his own right hand and trusty sword. His energy was terrific, and the Indians were paralyzed by the reckless daring that characterized every action.

On the present occasion, as soon as they saw that he had gained the middle of the stream, they retired, but in good order, from the bank. He pursued, but when the Malli perceived that he was not supported by infantry, they awaited his approach and vigorously repelled the charges of the cavalry. Alexander then adopted the Parthian tactics, wheeled round their flanks, made false attacks, and thus impeded their retreat, without bringing his cavalry in contact with their dense mass of infantry. But the light troops, the formidable Agrians, and the archers, soon came up, and were instantly led on by himself, while at the same time the *phalanx*, bristling with pikes, was seen advancing over the plain.

The Indians, panic-struck, broke their ranks and fled into the strongest city in the neighbourhood. Alexander, pursued with the cavalry, slew many in their flight, and when he had driven the survivors into the city, surrounded it with detachments of cavalry, until the arrival of the infantry. It was now late in the day, and the soldiers were wearied with the length of the march, the horses fatigued with the sharpness of the pursuit, and with the toilsome passage of the river. The following night was therefore given to repose.

Next day the army was formed into two divisions; Perdiccas led one, and Alexander the other. The assault was given; and the king's division soon broke open a postern gate and rushed into the city. The defenders immediately quitted the walls, and hurried into the citadel. The desertion of the walls was regarded by Perdiccas as a proof of the capture of the city. He, therefore, suspended the attack from his side. Alexander had closely followed the retreating enemy, and was now preparing to storm the citadel, of which the defenders were numerous and resolute.

Some were ordered to undermine, and others to scale the walls. But the motions of those who were bringing up the ladders seemed slow to his impatient mind. He, therefore, seized a scaling-ladder from the foremost bearer, placed it against the wall, and ascended under the protection of his shield. He had captured one fortress already, and seemed determined to owe the possession of another to his own personal prowess. Close behind the king ascended Peucestas, bearing the sacred buckler, taken from the temple of the Ilian Minerva. He was followed by Leonnatus, the son of Eunus, a commander of the body guard. Abreas, a soldier of the class to whom, for superior merit, double pay and allowances were assigned, was ascending by another ladder.

The Indian wall had no battlements nor embrasures. Alexander, therefore, placing the lowest rim of his shield on the coping, partly with it thrust back his immediate opponents, and partly swept them off with his sword. He then mounted and stood alone on the wall. At this moment, the guards alarmed beyond measure by the dangerous position of the king, crowded the ladders, which broke under their weight.

The Indians easily recognised Alexander, both by the splendour of his arms, and by his uncalculating boldness. At him, therefore, was aimed every missile, both from the neighbouring bastions, and from the body of the place, whence, as the wall on the inside was low, he could be struck almost with the hand; but no one came near him. He felt that while he remained thus exposed, the peril was great, and active exertion impossible. He scorned to leap back into the arms of his beseeching guards; but were he to spring into the citadel, the very boldness of the deed might appal the barbarians and ensure his safety. Even should the event prove fatal, the feelings of Alexander were in unison with those of the Homeric Hector:

At least let me not perish ingloriously without exertion, but in the performance of some great deed of which posterity shall hear.

Animated by this principle, he sprung from the wall into the fortress, and the gleamings of his armour flashed like lightning in the eyes of the barbarians; for the moment they retired—but were immediately rallied by the governor, who himself led them to the attack. Alexander had, for greater safety, placed his back against the wall. In this position he slew his first assailant, the governor, with the sword—checked the advance of second, and of a third with large stones, favourite weapons with the Homeric heroes—and again with his sword slew the fourth, who had closed with him. The barbarians, daunted by the fate of their comrades, no longer drew near, but formed themselves into a semicircle, and showered missiles of every description upon him.

196

At this critical moment Peucestas, Leonnatus, and Abreas, who, when the ladders broke, had clung to the walls, and finally made their footing good, leaped down and fought in front of the king, Abreas soon fell, being pierced in the forehead by an arrow. The ancients wore no vizors, and trusted to the shield and eye for the protection of the face. But a vizor would not have availed Abreas in the present case, for the Indian arrow, as described by Arrian, was irresistible, he says:

> The bow is six feet long, the archer places the lower end on the ground, then steps forward with his left foot, draws the string far back, and discharges an arrow nearly three cubits long. No armour can resist it, when shot by a skilful Indian archer, nor shield, nor breastplate, nor any other defence.

This Alexander himself was doomed to experience, for one of these formidable archers, taking his station at a proper distance, took deliberate aim, and struck him on the breast, above the pap. The arrow pierced through his *cuirass*, formed as it was of steel of proof, and remained deeply fixed in the bone. Severe as the wound was it did not immediately disable him for further exertion, or as Homer would say, "relax his limbs," and while the blood was warm, he continued to defend himself. But in a short time, the loss of blood and the extreme pain necessarily attendant on every motion, brought on a dizziness and faintness, and he sunk down behind his shield and dropped his head on its uppermost rim. The very position indicates great self-possession, for helpless as he was, he presented no vulnerable part to the enemy.

Peucestas and Leonnatus performed their duty gallantly and affectionately; they neglected their own persons, and held both their shields in front of their bleeding sovereign. While thus engaged they were both wounded with arrows, and Alexander was on the point of fainting.

But the Macedonians were scaling the wall in various ways:—some drove pegs into it and thus climbed up, others mounted on their comrades' shoulders, and everyone, as he gained the summit, threw himself headlong into the citadel. There, when they saw Alexander fallen, for he had swooned at last for want of blood, they uttered loud lamentations, and hurried to place themselves between him and his assailants. Some broke the bar of a postern gate and admitted their companions.

But as the narrow entrance did not allow many to pass through at the same time, the excluded troops, who now heard that the king was slain, became furious, smote down the wall on each side of the gate, and rushed in through the breach. Alexander was placed on his shield, the bier of the ancient warrior, and was borne out by his friends, who knew not whether he was alive or dead. The soldiers then gave the reins to their angry passions, and every man, woman, and child, within the walls, were put to the sword.

This perilous adventure of the conqueror Asia was variously described by his numerous historians, some of whom were far more anxious to study effect than to ascertain the truth. Arrian says:

> According to some, Critodemus of Cos, a physician of the race of Æsculapius, enlarged the wound and extracted the arrow; according to others Perdiccas, by Alexander's own desire, as no surgeon was present, cut open the wound with his sword, and thus extricated the arrow. The operation was accompanied with great loss of blood; Alexander again fainted, and further effusion was thus stayed . . . . . According to Ptolemy the breath, together with the blood, rushed through the orifice . . . . . Many fictions also have been recorded by historians concerning this accident, and Fame, receiving them from the original inventors, preserves them to this day.
>
> Nor will she cease to hand down such falsehoods to posterity except they be crushed by this history. The common belief is, that this accident befell Alexander among the Oxydracæ; but it occurred among the Malli, an independent Indian nation. The city was Mallian, the archer who wounded Alexander was a Mallian. They had certainly agreed to join the Oxydracæ, and give battle to Alexander, but the suddenness and rapidity of his march across the desert had prevented either of these peoples from giving any aid to the other.

Before the king's wound would allow him to be moved, the various divisions of the Grand Army had arrived at the confluence of the Hydraotes and Acesines. The first account that reached the camp, was that Alexander had been killed, and loud were the lamentations of all as the mournful tidings spread from man to man; then succeeded feelings of despondency and doubt, and the appointment of a commander-in-chief seemed likely to be attended with difficulties and danger. Many Macedonians appeared to possess equal claims; some from high birth and seniority, others from greater talents and popularity—and no one since Parmenio's death had been regarded by all as the second in command.

Alexander led 120,000 men into India, an army composed of the boldest and most adventurous spirits of the different regions which he had traversed. It was not likely, that when the master spirit, the guiding mind, the only centre of union, was lost, this great mass of discordant materials would continue to act on common principles. Many *satraps*, who hated the Macedonian supremacy, were personally attached to Alexander; when the only link was broken, their revolt would necessarily follow. The conquered nations, also, no longer paralyzed by the magic of a name, would rise and assert their national independence; finally, the numerous and warlike tribes, hitherto unsubdued, would beset their homeward path, and treat them more as broken fugitives than returning conquerors.

Depressed by these considerations, the Macedonians felt that, deprived of their king, they had innumerable dangers and difficulties to encounter.

When the report of his death was contradicted, they could not believe his recovery possible, and still regarded his death as inevitable; even when letters from himself, announcing his speedy arrival at the camp, were received, the soldiers remained incredulous–suspecting them to be forgeries of the commanders of the guard, and the other generals. Alexander, therefore, anxious to obviate any commotions, was conveyed as soon as he could be moved with safety, to the banks of the Hydraotes; there he was placed on board a vessel and sailed down the river.

When he drew near to the camp, he ordered the awning which overhung the couch on which he was reclining, to be removed; but the troops, who crowded the banks, imagined they saw the dead body of their king. When, however, the vessel drew nearer, Alexander raised his arm and stretched his hand out to the multitude; this signal proof of life and consciousness was welcomed with loud cheers, and the whole body of soldiers lifted up their hands to heaven, or stretched them towards the king, while tears involuntarily gushed from many eyes.

He was carried from the vessel; but borrowing new strength from his enthusiastic reception, refused the litter which was offered by the guards, and called for a horse. He mounted, and rode slowly through the crowd. This additional proof of his convalescence was hailed with redoubled cheers and applause: on approaching the royal tent he dismounted and walked. Then the soldiers crowded around him; some touched his hands, some his knees, some the hem of his garments, some, satisfied with a nearer view, implored blessings on him and withdrew, and others covered him with garlands and the flowers of the clime and season.

The friends who supported his steps were harsh in their reproofs of his reckless conduct, and blamed him in no measured terms for endangering his life without an adequate object, and performing the duties of a soldier and not of a commander-in-chief. A Boeotian veteran had tact enough to observe, from the king's countenance, that these remonstrances were far from agreeable, and certainly not the more so as they were founded in truth; he, therefore, approached, and in his native dialect said, "O Alexander, actions characterise the hero;" and then repeated an Iambic line expressive of this sentiment:

He who strikes must also bleed.

Alexander was pleased with the readiness and aptness of the quotation, and the wit of the veteran, Boeotian as he was, procured him present applause and future patronage.

The friends on whom Alexander leaned after dismounting were most probably Hephæstion and Craterus, the two chief commanders in the stationary camp. The former, mild and gentle, cannot be suspected of treating his indulgent sovereign with asperity; but Craterus, who was accused by Alexander himself of "loving the king more than Alexander," might justly remonstrate with the hero for rashly endangering the invaluable life of the prince.

The Malli and Oxydracæ sent embassies to the naval station. The deputies were commissioned to present the submission of both nations; the Malli soliciting pardon for their resistance, the Oxydracæ, for their tardy surrender. According to their declarations, they had enjoyed national independence since the conquest of India by Dionysus, but understanding that Alexander, also, was of the race of the gods, they were willing to obey his *satrap* and pay a stipulated tribute.

The punishment inflicted upon the Malli, was, in Alexander's estimation, sufficient to ensure their future obedience; but from the Oxydracæ he exacted 1,000 hostages, the bravest and noblest of the nation. Not only were these immediately sent, but 500 war-chariots, with their equipments, were added. The king, pleased with this magnificent proof of goodwill and sincerity, accepted the gift and returned the hostages.

These Malli and Oxydracæ are represented, probably in name, certainly in situation, by the modern inhabitants of Moultan and Outch; the former is on the left of the Acesines, with the cognate city of Mulkan between the Hydraotes and Hyphasis; Outch is lower down, not far from the confluence of the Hyphasis and Acesines. Both nations were added to the *satrapy* of Philip.

While the wound was healing and Alexander recovering his strength, the army were employed in building additional ships. Near the confluence was a large banyan tree, below which, according to Aristobulus, fifty horsemen could at the same time be shaded from the sun. It might be worth ascertaining, as connected with the age of this species of tree, whether there be one of great size and apparent antiquity in this vicinity. Onesicritus, as quoted by Strabo, has so accurately described the mode in which one of these natural phenomena increases to a forest, that it is evident he had seen one of the greatest magnitude, perhaps equal to give refuge under its branches to 10,000 men.

On some part of the river, between Nicæa and the stationary camp, Alexander had visited a prince by name Sopeithes, who voluntarily submitted to the invader; his dominions were celebrated for a race of fierce dogs, equal, according to the accounts of both Curtius and Strabo, to the English bulldog.

CHAPTER 14

Tenth Campaign, B.C. 325

Alexander, with an increased fleet, fell down the Acesines into the Indus; here he was joined by more vessels, which had been built in various places on the latter river. He ordered a town to be built, and naval docks constructed, at the confluence, as in his estimation it was a spot well calculated to become the site of a powerful city. A strong body of men was left there, including the Thracians of the army, and all were placed under the superintendence of Philip. His father-in-law, Oxyartes, visited him here, and was appointed *satrap* of the Paropamisan districts.

Thence he sailed down the Indus to the Royal Palace of the Sogdi, deriving their name most probably, like their northern namesakes, from the great vale occupied by them. The elephants, under Craterus, had been repeatedly ferried across, as the nature of the country favoured their movements on either side. They were now transferred to the right bank for the last time, and advanced through the country

201

of the Arachosii and Drangæ, of whom Arrian makes the Indus the eastern limit.

He himself sailed down the river into the dominions of Musicanus, said to have possessed the wealthiest and most productive regions in that part of India. This description suits well with the rich and well-watered plains between the lower course of the Aral, (the Arabis of Ptolemy,) and the Indus. . . . *Musicanus* and *Oxycanus* (the appellation of a neighbouring chief) point, probably, the names of the territories, governed by these princes;—as the word *khawn* is constantly found, even to this day, on the lower Indus; such are *chack-khawn*, *khawn-gur*, and *gui-khawn*, and other similar compounds. . . Musicanus, (who perhaps might be properly described, in the modern English fashion, as the Rajah of Moosh, and Oxycanus, as the Rajah of Ouche,) had sent no ambassadors to make peace, offer presents, or request favours; nor taken any step which a wise governor ought to have done, on learning the approach of the extraordinary conqueror, whom the current of the Indus was certain to bear into the heart of his dominions.

He took the alarm, however, when Alexander had reached the upper confines of his realms, and came to meet him with presents, with all his elephants, and what was more likely to procure favour, with an apology for his previous neglect. He was restored to his government, but Alexander admiring the advantageous site of his principal town, built within it a citadel, well calculated in his opinion to keep the neighbouring tribes in awe. We have seen before, that even in the case of Taxiles, he made no exception, but placed a garrison in his capital. His plan was, to treat friendly chiefs with great kindness, but to put it out of their power to revolt.

Oxycanus attempted resistance, but Alexander captured his two principal cities, and himself in one of them, with his cavalry and light troops alone; for, as Arrian strongly expresses it, the minds of all the Indians were struck with servile terror by Alexander and his success.

He then entered the dominions of Sabbas or Sambus, who formerly had been appointed *satrap* of these regions by Alexander, but who, like the cowardly Porus, no sooner heard that Musicanus, his enemy, had been well treated by the king, than he fled into the desert.

On approaching his capital, Sindo-mana, of which the very name proves its situation on the Indus, called by the natives, both in ancient and modern times, the Sinde, the Macedonians found the gates open, and the public officers ready to deliver up the treasures, and the elephants—as, according to them, Sabbas had fled, not from disaffection to Alexander, but from fear of Musicanus. The capital of Sabbas could not have been very far from the modern Sehwaun, or Sebaun. It appears that the Brachmans had instigated the partial revolt of Sabbas; Alexander, therefore, attacked and captured a city belonging to that influential caste, and put to death the most guilty.

While he was thus occupied, the revolt or rather rebellion of Musicanus, was announced to him. He, also, was induced by the Brachmans to take this rash step. Alexander instantly returned, took and garrisoned most of his towns, and sent Peithon against Musicanus himself. Peithon captured him and the leading Brachmans, and brought them to Alexander. Probably the insurrection had been characterized by atrocious deeds, for Alexander ordered the whole party to be conducted to the capital, and there hanged.

He was now approaching the upper end of the delta of the Indus, where the river divides into two streams of unequal size, that enter into the sea, more than 100 miles distant from each other. The enclosed space was named Pattalenè by the Greeks, from the city of Pattala, situated within the delta, below the point of division, probably at no great distance from the modern Hydrabad; they may be the same cities, as some Hyder might easily have imposed his own name on the ancient Pattala. The governor of Pattalenè withdrew into the desert with most of his people; but the latter, on being pursued and informed that no injuries were to be inflicted upon them, returned to their homes. Hephæstion was ordered to build a citadel, and construct docks and a harbour at Pattala, while Alexander himself sailed down the right branch into the ocean.

Dr. Vincent writes:

That Alexander had conceived a plan of the commerce which was afterwards carried on from Alexandreia in Egypt to the Indian ocean, I think capable of demonstration by his conduct after his arrival at Pattala. In his passage down the Indus, he had evidently marked that river as the eastern frontier of his empire; he had built three cities and fortified two others on this line, and he was now preparing for the establishment of Pattala at the point of division of the river, and planning other posts at its eastern and western mouths.

He had selected the best sailing and largest vessels for his voyage into the ocean, but his progress immediately after leaving Pattala was at first slow, from want of pilots; this difficulty was increased by the regular monsoon, which blew up the river with great violence. Alexander's light craft were seriously injured by the rough contest between the winds and the currents, and some even of the *triaconters* went to pieces. The damage was repaired, and the land force that was accompanying the motions of the fleet, was ordered to bring in prisoners, from whom persons capable of steering the vessels were selected.

On reaching the estuary, which was more than twelve miles broad, they encountered a brisk gale, which compelled them to seek protection in a small creek; here they moored for the night. Next day they were astonished to find that the waters had retired, and that the vessels were aground. This astonishment was redoubled, when they witnessed the furious return of the waters at the regular hour. The tides in the great Indian rivers, called bores, are of the most formidable description; they instantaneously raise the level of the rivers, from six to twelve feet, and rush up the stream with inconceivable force and velocity. For this phenomenon, the sailors of the Mediterranean, and especially of the Ægean, where the tides are scarcely perceptible, were by no means prepared.

From this place, two light boats were sent to examine the passages, and returned with the information, that they had discovered an island well furnished with harbours, and otherwise adapted for the objects in view. The small fleet re-commenced its voyage, and reached the island in safety. The natives called it Killuta. Alexander landed, and offered a sacrifice to those gods, whom, according to his own declaration, the oracle of Ammon had indicated. This fact, is worthy of being recorded, as proving that as early as his Egyptian voyage, he had contemplated his visit to the shores of the eastern ocean, and his wish to open a communication between it, and his western dominions.

About twelve miles lower down, he found a smaller island, whence an unimpeded view of the ocean was commanded. He landed here also, and sacrificed to the same gods. Next day he entered the ocean, and spread his sails on waves before unvisited, or, if visited, undescribed by Europeans. The bull, the favourite victim at the altar of Neptune, was sacrificed, and precipitated into the sea: and not only libations were duly poured into the "wineless waves" but the golden bowls and *pateræ* were likewise consigned to the bosom of the deep. These were thanksgiving offerings for past success. The future was not overlooked, for the king bound himself by fresh vows, for the return of his fleet in safety, from the estuary of the Indus, to the mouths of the Tigris and Euphrates.

Then he returned to Pattala, where the citadel was already completed. Hephæstion was ordered to proceed with the formation of the
docks and harbours, while he himself sailed down the left branch. This
brought him to a spacious lake, on one side of which, finding a place
well adapted for a naval station, he ordered another harbour to be
formed. Native pilots guided the fleet through the lake, and eventually
into the ocean;—but the king was satisfied that the western branch
was better calculated for navigation than the eastern. He marched
for three days along the shore of the ocean between the two great
mouths, and sunk wells at regular intervals, for the purpose of furnish-
ing his future navy with fresh water. He then returned to the ships and
sailed back once more to Pattala.

The king now began to prepare in earnest for the homeward
march; Craterus already with the elephants, the heavy baggage, the
feeble, the old, and the wounded, and with three brigades of the *phalanx*, had marched to the right from the dominions of Musicanus, in
order to conduct his division by easy roads and through the fertile
territories of the Drangæ and Arachosians, to the capital of Carmania.
A considerable portion of the fleet was ordered to remain at Pattala,
for the purpose of commanding the navigation of the Indus, and the
communication between the different settlements. Nearchus with the
largest and the most sea-worthy ships, was ordered to wait for the
commencement of the trade wind from the north-east, which usually
sets in about the beginning of November.

Alexander himself left Pattala in the beginning of September, B.C.
325, and began his march to the westward. Hephæstion conducted
one detachment along a more inland route, while the king at the
head of his most active troops turned to the left, and followed the
sea shore. His great object was the safety of his fleet; and he had no
hopes that in strange seas and on rocky shores, where the inhabitants
were described as barbarous in the extreme, and water and provisions
scarce, Nearchus could ever accomplish his purpose without the co-
operation of the land forces. His determination therefore was at all
risks to advance along the sea-coast, and prepare provisions and sink
wells for the use of the fleet.

Between the lower course of the Indus and the Arabis of Arrian the
king found, and subdued, a tribe of savages, called from the river, Ara-
bitæ. To the west of these lived an Indian nation named Oreitæ—who
probably occupied the vales of the modern Pooralee, and its tributaries. They also, after some brief demonstrations of resistance, submitted.

Alexander ordered a town to be built at a place called Rambacia, in their territory; appointed Apollophanes *satrap* of the Oreitæ; and left Leonnatus, latterly one of his favourite officers, with a strong force, to preside over the establishment of the new city, to accustom the Oreitæ to obey their *satrap*, but above all to collect provisions, and wait on the coast until the fleet under Nearchus had arrived, and past the shore of that province in safety.

Here the king was joined by Hephæstion; and the united force, principally composed of picked men, ventured into the desert of Gedrosia, the modern Macran. During sixty days spent in traversing this waste from the edge of Oreitia to Pura, they had to struggle against difficulties greater than were ever before or after surmounted by a regular army. The ancients knew nothing of this extensive desert, more than was communicated by the survivors of this desperate experiment. We in modern times know as little of it beyond its extreme edges, where some miserable tribes of Balooches contrive to support a wretched existence. Edrisi, the Nubian geographer, to whom the sandy wastes of Africa were well known, gives the following more formidable character of the desert of Makran:—

> To the east of Persia and Carmania, lies that immense desert, to which no other in the world can be compared. There are many villages and a few cities on its extreme skirts. . . . . That great desert is bordered by the provinces of Kirman, Fars, (Persis,) Moultan, and Segestan. But few houses are to be seen in it. Men on horseback cannot cross it without great difficulty. Unloaded camels traverse a few paths, which (with God's assistance) I proceed to describe.

But all the lines indicated by Edrisi are through the northern parts, and throw no light on the route followed by Alexander. I shall therefore restrict myself to Arrian's narrative, and merely add a few circumstances from Strabo.

The commencement of their march in the desert was over a region covered with myrrh-bearing shrubs, and the plant whence spikenard was extracted. The Phoenician merchants who accompanied the army recognised these aromatics, and loaded beasts of burden with them. The trampling of the long columns crushed the fragrant stems, and diffused a grateful perfume through the still atmosphere. But the sandy desert is the native soil of aromatics, and the Macedonians soon found that the balmy gales and precious odours were no compensation for the want of the more substantial necessaries of food and water. They were compelled to make long marches by night, and at a considerable distance from the sea, although Alexander was particularly anxious to keep near the shore; for the maritime part was one series of naked rocks.

Thoas, the son of Mandrodorus, was sent to examine if there were harbours, anchoring grounds, fresh water, and other such facilities for the progress of the fleet, to be found on the coast; on his return he announced that he had discovered only a few starving fishermen, who dwelt in stifling hovels, the walls of which were formed of shells, and their roofs of the backs and ribs of large fish, and who procured a scanty supply of brackish water by scraping holes in the sandy beach.

Alarmed by this representation, as soon as he had reached a district in the desert where provisions were more plentiful, or probably a magazine had been formed, he loaded some beasts of burden with all that he could secure, sealed the packages with his own signet, and sent them to the coast for the use of the navy; but the escort lost their way among the barren sands; their own allowances failed; and regardless of the king's displeasure, the men broke open the packages and devoured the contents. Nor did this conduct meet with any animadversion—as it was proved to have been the result of extreme hunger.

By his own exertions he collected another supply, which was safely conveyed to the sea side by an officer named Cretheus. He also proclaimed large rewards for all such inhabitants of the more inland regions, as should drive down their flocks and herds, and carry flour and meal to the naval forces. Hitherto his care and fears were principally on their account; but he was now entering the heart of the desert, where the safety of his accompanying land force became a doubtful question.

All the companions of Alexander, who had followed him from Macedonia to the Hyphasis, agreed that the other labours and dangers in their Asiatic expedition, were not to be compared with the fatigues and privations of the march through Gedrosia. The burning heat and the scarcity of water proved fatal to a great portion of the men, and to almost all the beasts of burden. For the desert was like an ocean of moving sand, and assumed all the fantastic shapes of driven snow.

The men sunk deep into these banks or wreaths, and the progress of all the wheeled vehicles was soon stopped. The length of some of their marches exhausted them to the last degree, for these were regulated not by the strength of the men, but by the discovery of water. If after a night's march they reached wells or rivulets in the morning, there was not much suffering. But if the march was prolonged till the sun was high in the heavens, and darted his noontide rays upon their heads, their thirst became intolerable and even unquenchable.

The destruction of the beasts of burden was principally the work of the men, who in their hunger killed and devoured not only the oxen but horses and mules. For this purpose, they would linger behind, and allege on coming up, that the animals had perished of thirst or fatigue. In the general relaxation of discipline, which invariably accompanies similar struggles for life, few officers were curious in marking what was done amiss. Even Alexander could only preserve the form of authority, by an apparent ignorance of disorders which could not be remedied, and by conniving at offences which severity could not have checked.

But the destruction of the beasts of carriage was the death-warrant of the sick and exhausted, who were left behind without conductors and without consolers. For eagerness to advance became the general characteristic, and the miseries of others were overlooked by men who anticipated their own doom. At such moments the mind would naturally recur to the old traditions-that of the innumerable host led by Semiramis to India, only twenty survived the return through this desert; and that the great Cyrus was still more unfortunate, arriving in Persis with only seven followers—while the bones of the rest of his soldiers were left to bleach in the deserts of Gedrosia—amidst such appalling recollections the strong man could not sympathize deeply with his feebler comrade, but husbanded his own strength for the eventual struggle.

As most of the marches were performed by night, many were overpowered by sleep and sunk on the road side. Few of these ever rejoined the army; they rose and attempted to pursue the track, but a consciousness of their desolation and the want of food, for famine in all its horrors was in the rear of such an army, soon paralyzed all exertion, and after floundering for a short period among the hillocks of yielding sand, they would lay themselves down and die.

Another and most dissimilar misfortune overtook them. They had encamped one evening in the bed of a torrent, from the cavities in which they had scantily supplied themselves with water, when late at night, in consequence of a fall of rain among the mountains, the waters suddenly descended with the force and depth of an impetuous river, and swept everything before them.

Many helpless women and children, whom the love and natural

affection of their protectors had hitherto preserved, perished in the flood; which also carried away the royal equipage, and most of the remaining beasts of burden. A similar misfortune had indeed befallen them in India; but they had then encamped too near the brink of the magnificent Acesines; and were not prepared to fear a like disaster from the sudden swell of a paltry torrent in Gedrosia.

Many perished from drinking immoderate draughts of water. For as soon as it became known that the head of the column had arrived at wells, streams, or tanks, the soldiers, eager to allay their burning thirst, broke their ranks, rushed to the spot, and drank at their own discretion; the most impatient even plunged into the water, as if anxious to imbibe the cooling moisture at every pore. This intemperance proved equally fatal to man and beast. Alexander therefore, taught by experience, made the troops halt at the distance of a mile, or a mile and a half, from the watering places, and employed steady men in conveying and distributing the water among the soldiers.

One day, the army was thus toiling along through the yielding sand, parched by thirst, and under the scorching rays of a midday sun. The march had continued longer than usual, and the water was still far in front, when a few of the light troops, who had wandered from the main body, found at the bottom of a ravine a scanty portion of brackish water. Had it been thickened with the golden sands of the Pactolus, it could not have been more highly estimated, nor collected with more scrupulous care. A helmet served for a cup, and with the precious nectar treasured in this, they hurried to the king. The great officers had long ceased to use their horses; every general, for the sake of example, shared the marching a-foot at the head of his own brigade.

Alexander himself, who never imposed a duty on others, from which he shrunk in person, was now on foot, leading forwards the *phalanx* with labour and difficulty, and oppressed with thirst. He took the helmet from the hands of the light trooper, thanked him and his comrades for their kind exertions, and then deliberately, in sight of all, poured the water into the thankless sands of the desert. The action, as Arrian justly observes, marks not only the great man, able to control the cravings of nature, but the great general. For every soldier who witnessed the libation, and the self-denial of his king, received as strong a stimulus to his fainting faculties, as if he had partaken of the refreshing draught.

At one period, the guides confessed that they knew not where they were, nor in what direction they were moving. A gale of wind had swept the surface of the desert, and obliterated every trace in the sands; there were no landmarks by which they could ascertain their position, no trees varied the eternal sameness of the scene, while the sandy knolls shifted their ground, and changed their figures with every fresh storm. The inhabitants of these deserts had not, like the Libyans and Arabs, learned to shape their course by the sun and stars;—the army therefore was in the greatest danger of perishing in the pathless wild.

Alexander, thus thrown upon his own resources, took with him a few horsemen, and turning to the left, hastened by what he deemed the shortest cut to the sea shore. His escort dropped off by degrees, and five alone remained when he was fortunate enough to reach the coast. On digging into the sandy beach, these had the inexpressible pleasure of seeing pure and sweet water oozing into the cavities. Notice of the discovery was instantly communicated to the main body, and all were brought down to the shore.

Along this they marched for seven days, and were supplied with water from these temporary wells. Then the guides recognised their way, and all again directing their course inland, arrived at Pura, the capital of Gedrosia, where, after a desert march of sixty days' continuance, their severe sufferings terminated.

Such is Arrian's account. Strabo adds:

Many sunk down on the road side, exhausted by fatigue, heat and thirst. These were seized with tremors, accompanied by convulsive motions of the hands and feet, and died like men overpowered by rigors and shivering fits. . . . . There was a tree, not unlike the laurel, which proved poisonous to the beasts of burden. These, after browsing it, lost the use of their limbs, foamed at the mouth, and died. There was also a prickly plant, the fruit of which crept, like a cucumber, along the ground. This, when trodden upon, spurted a milky juice, and if any drops of it struck the eyes of man or beast, instant blindness followed. There was danger also from venomous serpents, that lurked under some shrubs which grew on the sea shore. Their bite was instant death.

It is said that the Oreitæ anointed their arrow-points, made of fire-hardened wood, with a deadly poison; and that Ptolemy, the son of Lagus, was at the point of death from such a wound, but that Alexander, in his sleep, saw a person who showed him a root peculiar to that country, and ordered him to crush it and apply it to the wound; that on awaking he recollected his dream, and by searching soon found the root, which abounded in the neighbourhood, and applied it with success: and that the barbarians, perceiving that a remedy had been discovered, made their submissions. . . . .

Most probably some person acquainted with the secret gave Alexander the information, and the fabulous part was the addition of flatterers.

Pura, the capital of Gedrosia, is either the modern Bunpore itself, or must have been situated in its immediate vicinity. For, with the exception of the Bunpore River, there is no stream within the prescribed limits capable of fertilizing a district large enough to support a metropolis, and to recruit the famished army of Alexander. Arrian's Pura may still lurk in the last syllable of Bunpore, especially as the numerous Pores of India have no connection with the names of cities in Makran. Ptolemy calls the capital of Gedrosia Easis, probably a misprint for Oasis, the general appellation for isolated and fertile spots surrounded by deserts. The *satrap* of Gedrosia, Apollophanes, had shamefully neglected his duty, and left undone all that he had been ordered to do. On him therefore fell the blame of the soldiers' sufferings, and he was degraded from his office, and succeeded by Thoas, the son of Mandrodorus. But he soon died, and Sibyrtius was appointed to the united *satrapies* of Arachosia and Gedrosia.

As the king was marching from Pura to the capital of Carmania, the modern Kirman, he received intelligence that Philip, whom he had left in command of all the country to the west of the upper Indus, had been slain, in a mutiny, by the Greek mercenaries under his command, but that the mutiny had been quelled, and the assassins put to death, by the Macedonian troops. Alexander did not immediately appoint a successor,

but sent a commission, empowering Eudemus, a Greek, and the Indian Taxiles, to superintend the *satrapy* for a short time.

At Kirman Alexander was joined by Craterus. It does not appear that he had had to encounter any great difficulties. His course must have been up the Aral and down into the vale of the Heermund. This great river would conduct him through the rich territories of the Euergetæ and lower Drangiana, till its waters terminate in the swampy lake of Zurrah. From the western edge of the lake to Kirman, there is a regular caravan road, which, with common precautions, can be traversed by armies.

Here also arrived Nearchus, the admiral of the fleet, who had conducted his charge in safety from the mouth of the Indus to Harmozia, on the coast of Carmania. The city and its name were in later ages transferred from the continent to the island which, under the style of Ormus, became, for a time, the most celebrated mart in the Indian seas. But its glory has past away, and the "throne of Ormus" is now a barren rock.

Of all the voyages distinctly recorded by the ancients, this was the boldest, most adventurous and successful. Its able conductor was one of the earliest friends and favourites of Alexander, and was one of the five exiled from Macedonia for their attachment to the prince. Nearchus, by birth a Cretan, was, by admission, a citizen of Amphipolis on the Strymon, whence he called himself a Macedonian. Many of the ancients suspected his credibility as an author, and for this two good reasons might be assigned: first, he was a Cretan, and that for a popular argument was sufficient—for, according to the well-known axiom,

All Cretans are liars.

Secondly, Onesicritus, his master of the fleet, wrote an account of the same voyage; nor did he scruple to introduce into it the most improbable fictions and romances; so that Strabo calls him the arch-pilot not only of the fleet, but of falsehood. The ancients had no means of deciding between the conflicting testimonies of the admiral and the master, and, as a natural inference, doubted the credibility of both. Arrian alone, with his keen perception of the difference between truth and falsehood, after attentive examinations, ascertained the value of the narrative, and pronounced Nearchus to be an "approved writer."

But still, implicit confidence cannot be placed in the admiral's statements. One feels that he does not tell "*the whole truth and nothing but the truth.*" He was evidently a vain man; and probably was not, after Alexander's death, treated by the great Macedonian officers with all the deference to which he thought himself entitled. He therefore dwelt rather offensively on every proof of Alexander's friendship and affection for him, as if labouring to show that the king made no difference between him and Macedonians by birth. If we make allowance for this feeling, and for one or two extraordinary statements, we may confidently rely upon the general facts of the narrative.

There arrived also, at Kirman, Stasanor, *satrap* of Areia and Zaranga, and the son of the *satrap* of Parthia and Hyrcania. These officers had anticipated the result of the march through Gedrosia, and brought with them horses, mules and camels, for the use of the army. The troops left in Media were also conducted thither by their generals, Cleander, Sitalces and Heracon. These great officers were publicly accused, both by the natives and their own soldiers, of sacrilege, in plundering temples and ransacking the tombs of the dead, and of tyranny, in perpetrating various acts of extortion and outrage on the property and persons of the living.

When the charges had been fully substantiated, they were condemned and executed, as a warning to all other *satraps* of the certain fate that awaited such malefactors under the administration of Alexander. It was the knowledge of his inflexibility upon this point, and of his determination to protect the subject from the extortion and tyranny of the *satraps*, that preserved tranquillity in the numerous provinces of his extensive empire.

With the exception of the Bactrian and Sogdian insurrection, caused by the artifices of Spitamenes, there does not appear to have occurred one single rebellion of the people, from the shores of the Hellespont to the banks of the Indus, from the borders of Scythia to the deserts of Æthiopia. Several *satraps* attempted to wear the *cidaris* upright, or, in the language of scripture, to exalt their horn, but were easily put down, without even the cost of a battle.

CHAPTER 15

Transactions of the Tenth Year in Asia, B.C. 324

The fable-loving historians of Alexander's life are more than usually luxuriant in their descriptions of the Bacchanalian processions, and wanton revelry of the march from Carmania to Persis. According to Curtius, all the roads were strewed with flowers; all the villages were hung with garlands; before every door were placed capacious wine vessels, whence the soldiers drank at their own discretion, while long tents, supported on waggons joined together, and furnished with delicacies of every kind, conveyed along the Bacchanalian route. For seven whole days the army drank, feasted, and advanced—advanced, feasted, and drank, in a state of riotous intoxication. That very clever writer, but most ignorant man, affirms with an oath, that a thousand sober barbarians could have easily massacred the whole army of helpless drunkards.

According to Plutarch, who is no less absurd, for seven days Alexander marched through Carmania with Bacchanalian pomp. Upon a magnificent chariot, drawn by eight horses, was placed a lofty platform, where he and his chief friends revelled day and night. The carriage was followed by many others, some covered with rich tapestry and purple hangings, and others shaded with branches of trees, fresh gathered and flourishing. In these were the rest of the king's friends and generals, crowned with flowers and heated with wine. In this whole company there was not to be seen a shield, helmet, or spear, but instead cups, flagons and bowls.

These the soldiers dipped in large vessels of wine, and drank to each other, some as they marched along, and others seated at tables, which were placed at proper distances on the way. The whole country resounded with flutes, clarionets and songs, and with the dances and riotous frolicking of the women. This disorderly and dissolute march was attended with all the licentious ribaldry of the Bacchanalians, as if Bacchus himself had been present to carry on the debauch.

Arrian writes:

> Not a word of this procession is mentioned by Ptolemy the son of Lagus, Aristobulus, or any other author entitled to belief on the subject, and this alone is sufficient to induce me to reject the whole account as unworthy of credit.

But there are other reasons for rejecting it. The season was the very depth of winter. There could not, therefore, be any flowers, any burning sun, any leafy boughs, or want of them. The whole fiction was probably grounded on the fact recorded by Aristobulus, that Alexander in Carmania offered a thanksgiving sacrifice for his Indian victories and safe return, and that the religious ceremonies were terminated by gymnastic games and theatrical representations. As the latter had been intermitted for the last six years, their revival would naturally be celebrated with due honours and sacrifices to Dionysus, to whom all dramatic entertainments were sacred.

From Kirman, Hephæstion conducted the main body of the army, the baggage, and the elephants to the sea, as the road to Susiana along the coast was better supplied with provisions, and the climate warmer. Alexander himself, with the Companion cavalry, and a select force of infantry, marched to Pasargada.

According to Aristobulus, Alexander early expressed an anxious desire, if ever he subdued Persia, to examine the tomb of Cyrus the Great. Herodotus and Xenophon had given very contradictory accounts of his death:—the former asserting that he had been defeated, slain, and decapitated by the Scythian queen Tomyris;—while, according to the latter, he had attained length of days, and been gathered to his fathers in peace. It is impossible to impute this intention of Alexander to any other cause than the desire to decide between these two conflicting testimonies; and an examination of the body would enable him conclusively to determine the question.

During his hostile visit to Persis, he had found means to examine the tomb, and Aristobulus, who recorded the particulars, was the officer employed upon the occasion. It occupied the centre of the royal park at Pasargada, and was embosomed in a shady grove. The surrounding lawn was irrigated by various streamlets from the River Cyrus, and clothed with deep and luxuriant herbage. The tomb itself was a square building of hewn stone. The basement, of solid masonry, supported on one side a range of steps, that led to a small door in the face of the upper story. The entrance was so narrow, that it was difficult for a man, below the usual size, to force his way in.

Aristobulus, however, succeeded in gaining entrance, and carefully examined the whole. The chamber was roofed with stone. In the centre stood a couch, or bed, supported on golden feet, and covered with purple cushions. On the couch was placed a golden coffin, containing the embalmed body of Cyrus. Over all was spread a coverlet of the richest Babylonian tapestry. There were robes and tunics and drawers of the finest texture, and of every variety of colour.

On the table were placed ornaments of various kinds, gold cups, scimitars, chains, bracelets, earrings, set in gold, and gemmed with precious stones. On the wall was engraved the following inscription in the Persian language:—

O man, I am Cyrus, son of Cambyses, who acquired the empire for the Persians, and reigned over Asia. Do not, therefore, grudge me this tomb.

At the foot of the range of steps which led to the door in the chamber, was built small residence for the *Magi*, to whose care the sepulchre was entrusted.

A sheep, and a corresponding quantity of wine and corn, were allowed for their daily subsistence, and a horse every month to be sacrificed to the manes of Cyrus.

But although Aristobulus might have satisfied Alexander, no information has reached us respecting the state in which the body was found; whether it corresponded with Xenophon's description, or attested the superior judgment of Herodotus, who, among various Persian reports, had preferred that which recorded his defeat by Tomyris, and the separation of the head from the body.

Many reasons might be alleged why Alexander should be loath to confirm the truth of the defeat of the great conqueror of Asia by the still formidable Scythians, but not a single one for suppressing its contradiction, had the body been found unmutilated. Moreover, the positive manner in which both Strabo and Arrian speak of the misfortune of Cyrus, proves, almost to a demonstration, that Herodotus, as to this matter, had been the historian, and Xenophon the novelist.

Alexander, in the language of Greece, was a Philo-Cyrus, and admired and venerated the founder of the Persian monarchy. He was, therefore, deeply shocked to find on his return to Pasargada, that the tomb which had been so religiously preserved and honoured for more than two centuries, had, during his absence in the east, been sacrilegiously profaned and plundered; for, on a second visit, nothing was found but the body, couch, and coffin. The lid was stolen, the corpse dragged out and shamefully mangled, and the coffin itself bore marks of violent attempts to break it to pieces, and, by crushing together the sides, to make it portable.

It is worthy of remark, that the body of Alexander himself, a greater conqueror than Cyrus, was, for the sake of the golden coffin, treated in a similar manner by Cocces, and Ptolemy, surnamed the Intruder. The great, if they wish their ashes to repose undisturbed, should leave their wealth on this side of the grave; any superfluous decoration of the tomb but serves to tempt the hand of the spoiler.

Alexander, with pious care, commissioned Aristobulus to restore everything to its prior state, and when that was accomplished, to build up the door with solid mason work. The *Magi*, suspected of having connived at the sacrilege, or at least criminally neglected their duty, were put to the torture; but they persisted to affirm their innocence and their ignorance of the offenders, and were dismissed. As Strabo properly observes, the failure to carry away the golden coffin, is a convincing proof that the attempt had been made in haste by some band of prowling robbers, and not under the sanction of any constituted authorities.

The Pasargadæ, according to Herodotus, were the leading Persian clan or tribe. To it belonged the royal family of the Achæmenidæ, who, since the days of Cyrus, had possessed the empire of Asia. Pasargada, apparently named from his own tribe, was built by Cyrus on the spot where he had gained his final victory over the Medes. Men of great learning and judgment have fallen into error, from confounding Pasargada with Parsagarda, the oriental name of Persepolis. The mistake is as old as Stephanus Byzantius. Were the site of Pasargada discovered, we might still hope to find the basement of the tomb of Cyrus.

From Pasargada Alexander went to Persepolis, or Parsagarda, where, as Arrian says, he repented of his deed as he viewed the melancholy ruins of the royal palace.

Phrasaortes, the *satrap* of Persis, had died, but Orxines, a Persian nobleman, had, without waiting for Alexander's nomination, usurped the office. Nor had this bold deed, when first communicated to Alexander, excited his displeasure, as it seemed to originate in conscious worth. But when he had arrived in Persis, so many acts of violence and oppression were laid to the self-elected *satrap's* charge, and supported by Persian evidence, that the king, who had not spared his own officers, condemned Orxines to death.

Peucestas, who already for his faithful services in the Mallian citadel, had been appointed one of the commanders of the body guard, was further rewarded with the *satrapy* of Persis. Immediately on being appointed, he adopted the Persian dress, applied himself to the study of the language, and in other points conformed to the Oriental habits. This conduct proved offensive to many Macedonians, but was applauded by Alexander, and rewarded by the warm attachment of the Persians.

The attention of Alexander during the intervals of his Indian campaigns, had been considerably attracted to those religious devotees, whom the Greeks complimented with the name of *Gymnosophists*, or naked philosophers. At Taxila he understood that a college of these devotees resided in a grove near the suburbs, under the care and instruction of Dardanis. Onesicritus, who was himself a disciple of "the dog," was sent to summon Dardanis to the royal presence.

But he refused to obey—and would not allow any of his hearers to visit the king. He said that he was as much the son of Jupiter as Alexander, that he wanted nothing which Alexander could bestow, nor feared anything which he could inflict; that the fruits of the earth in their due season sufficed him while living, and that death would only free his soul from the incumbrance of the body, at the best but a troublesome companion. Alexander respected the independent spirit of the savage, and gave him no further molestation; but he persuaded another *Gymnosophist*, by name Calanus, to abjure his ascetic habits and follow him. His fellow religionists loudly accused him of having forsaken the only road to happiness for the sake of the forbidden enjoyments of Alexander's table; but Calanus persevered, and accompanied his patron into Persis.

Here his health began to decline, and he therefore announced his resolution to burn himself alive before any greater evils overtook him. Alexander having in vain attempted to dissuade him, ordered Ptolemy, the son of Lagus, to prepare a magnificent pile, and to see that all was conducted with, order and propriety. He himself, from feelings which we must respect, refused to witness the horrid ceremony, although the Macedonians in general crowded to the sight. Calanus rode to the pile at the head of a long procession, ascended and took his place calmly, and while the fire was consuming his flesh, never moved a limb. The trumpets sounded a charge, the soldiers raised the regular war shout, and, according to some authors, even the elephants raised their trunks, and loudly trumpeted their approbation of their heroic countryman.

Not many years after, the Macedonians, at the same place, witnessed the *suttee* of the widow of an Indian warrior. The description given by Diodorus Siculus, is applicable to the same abomination as practised in our own days; but it would be worthwhile to inquire why self-immolation has ceased to be practised by men, and why women, whose will is not so independent, should now be the sole victims. For if the one custom has either been suppressed by authority, or fallen into desuetude from other causes, it may be fairly inferred that no absolutely insuperable difficulties oppose the abolition of the other.

From Persepolis, Alexander marched into Susiana. At the bridge across the Pasitigris or Caroon, in the vicinity of the modern Shuster, he had the pleasure to find Nearchus and the fleet, who had circumnavigated in safety from Harmozia into the bosom of the Susian province. The admiral joined the land army in its westward march to Susa.

Here also the *satrap* Abulites had abused his authority, and with his son, Oxathres, was accused by the Susians of tyranny and oppression. They were both found guilty and put to death. Many *satraps* had acted thus on the supposition that there would be no future account, no day of reckoning. Most men either hoped or feared that Alexander would never return with life. They took into consideration the sword, the climate, the elephants, the wild beasts, the rivers, the desert, and the other perils to which he recklessly exposed himself, and thought they might calculate, without much risk, on final impunity.

Among the most notorious offenders was the wretched Harpalus, who had been left to superintend the treasury at Ecbatana. On hearing of the fate of Cleander, Sitalces, and Heracon, the associates of his crimes, he hastily took 5,000 *talents* from the treasury, hired the services of 6,000 mercenaries, and, under their escort, safely arrived with his stolen wealth at Mount Tænarus in Laconia. He attempted to excite the Athenians to take up arms, but the assembly for the time had the wisdom to reject his persuasions and his bribes. Thence he wandered to Crete, where soon after he was put to death by Thimbron, the chief officer of his own mercenaries.

Alexander was so shocked by this double villainy of Harpalus, that he could not for some time be brought to believe it. He even threw into prison the first person who brought information of his robbery and flight. His temper was not improved by this event, and it was observed, that thenceforward, he was more inclined to listen to accusation, and less ready to pardon offences. Experience was doing its natural work, and impressing him with the stern necessity of preferring justice to mercy, and of not allowing petty offenders to swell, by long impunity, to the full proportion of state criminals.

He had no doubt discovered by this time, that the Medes and Persians, for it is difficult to draw a distinction between them, were the finest and most trust-worthy race in Asia. He had long ceased to regard them with feelings peculiarly hostile, and now prepared to draw closer the union between them and the Macedonians. At Susa he collected all the nobles of the empire, and celebrated the most magnificent nuptials recorded in history. He married Barcinè, or Stateira, the daughter of the late king, and thus, in the eyes of his Persian subjects, confirmed his title to the throne.

His father, Philip, was a polygamist in practice, although it would be very difficult to prove that the Macedonians in general were allowed a plurality of wives; but Alexander was now the King of Kings, and is more likely to have been guided by Persian than Grecian opinions upon the subject. Eighty of his principal officers followed the example, and were united to the daughters of the chief nobility of Persia. To Hephæstion was given the second daughter of Darius—Alexander being anxious that his own and Hephæstion's children should be as closely connected by blood as their fathers by friendship.

To Craterus, next in favour to Hephæstion, superior to all in authority, was given Amastrinè, the daughter of Oxyartes, the brother of Darius. These three princesses, distinguished as they were by this selection, were all destined to early widowhood and a life of sorrow. Amastrinè alone was equal to the struggle. After the death of Craterus she married Dionysius, despot of the Bithynian Heracleia, and gave her name to the town Amastris founded by herself on that coast. Her influence was so great in that country as to induce King Lysimachus to become her husband.

To Perdiccas was given the daughter of Atropates, the *satrap* of Media: she also was soon a widow, but her father, after the assassination of his son-in-law, declared himself independent and founded the last Median kingdom, called from him Atropatenè, by the Orientals Adherbijan.

To Ptolemy and Eumenes were given Artacana and Artonis, the daughters of Artabazus. The brothers-in-law took different sides in the succeeding dissensions;—Eumenes fell; but Ptolemy became the father of a long line of kings.

To Nearchus was given a daughter of the Rhodian Mentor, by Barcinè, a Persian lady.

To Seleucus was given Apama, the daughter of the brave and patriotic Spitamenes. This was the happiest union:—from it sprung the Seleucidæ, who for three centuries ruled the destinies of Western Asia; and the numerous cities honoured with the name of Apameia proved the love of her husband and the filial affection of her son.

The marriages, in compliment to the brides, were celebrated after the Persian fashion, and during the vernal equinox. For at no other period, by the ancient laws of Persia, could nuptials be legally celebrated. Such an institution is redolent of the poetry and freshness of the new world, and of an attention to the voice of nature, and the analogies of physical life. The young couple would marry in time to sow their field, to reap the harvest, and gather their stores, before the season of cold and scarcity overtook them. It is difficult to say how far this custom prevailed among primitive nations, but it can scarcely be doubted that we still retain lingering traces of it in the harmless amusements of St. Valentine's Day,

On the wedding-day Alexander feasted the eighty bridegrooms in a magnificent hall prepared for the purpose. Eighty separate couches were placed for the guests, and on each a magnificent wedding-robe for every individual. At the conclusion of the banquet, and while the wine and the desert were on the table, the eighty brides were introduced; Alexander first rose, received the princess, took her by the hand, kissed her, and placed her on the couch close to himself. This example was followed by all, till every lady was seated by her betrothed. This formed the whole of the Persian ceremony—the salute being regarded as the seal of appropriation.

The Macedonian form was still more simple and symbolical. The bridegroom, dividing a small loaf with his sword, presented one half to the bride; wine was then poured as a libation on both portions, and the contracting parties tasted of the bread. Cake and wine, as nuptial refreshments, may thus claim a venerable antiquity. In due time the bridegrooms conducted their respective brides to chambers prepared for them within the precincts of the royal palace.

The festivities continued for five days, and all the amusements of the age were put into requisition for the entertainment of the company. Athenæus has quoted from Chares, a list of the chief performers, which I transcribe more for the sake of the performances and of the states where these lighter arts were brought to the greatest perfection, than of the names, which are now unmeaning sounds. Scymnus from Tarentum, Philistides from Syracuse, and Heracleitus from Mitylenè, were the great jugglers, or as the intimates, the wonder-workers of the day. προσκυνησις,

After them, Alexis, the Tarentine, displayed his excellence as a rhapsodist, or repeater, to appropriate music, of the soul-stirring poetry of Homer. Cratinus the Methymnæan, Aristonymus the Athenian, Athenodorus the Teian, played on the harp—without being accompanied by the voice. On the contrary, Heracleitus the Tarentine and Aristocrates the Theban, accompanied their harps with lyric songs. The performers on wind instruments were divided on a similar, although it could not be on the same principle. Dionysius from Heracleia, and Hyperbolus from Cyzicum, sang to the flute, or some such instrument; while Timotheus, Phrynichus, Scaphisius, Diophantus, and Evius, the Chalcidian, first performed the Pythian overture, and then, accompanied by choruses, displayed the full power of wind instruments in masterly hands.

There was also a peculiar class called eulogists of Bacchus; these acquitted themselves so well on this occasion, applying to Alexander those praises which in their extemporaneous effusions had hitherto been confined to the god, that they acquired the name of Eulogists of Alexander. Nor did their reward fail them. The stage, of course, was not without its representatives:—Thessalus, Athenodorus, Aristocritus, in tragedy—Lycon, Phormion, and Ariston, in comedy—exerted their utmost skill, and contended for the prize of superior excellence. Phasimelus, the dancer, was also present.

It is yet undecided whether the Persians admitted their matrons to their public banquets and private parties;—but if we can believe the positive testimony of Herodotus, such was the case; and the summons of Vashti to the annual festival, and the admission of Haman to the queen's table, are facts which support the affirmation of that historian. The doubts upon the subject appear to have arisen from confounding the manners of Assyrians, Medes, and Parthians, with those of the more Scythian tribes of Persis.

We read in *Xenophon* that the Persian women were so well made and beautiful, that their attractions might easily have seduced the affections of the Ten Thousand, and have caused them, like the lotus-eating companions of Ulysses, to forget their native land. Some little hints as to the mode in which their beauty was enhanced and their persons decorated, may be expected in the *Life of Alexander*, who, victorious over their fathers and brothers, yet submitted to their charms.

The Persian ladies wore the tiara or turban, richly adorned with jewels. They wore their hair long, and both plaited and curled it; nor, if the natural failed, did they scruple to use false locks. They pencilled the eyebrows, and tinged the eyelid, with a dye that was supposed to add a peculiar brilliancy to the eyes. They were fond of perfumes, and their delightful *ottar* was the principal favourite. Their tunic and drawers were of fine linen, the robe or gown of silk—the train of this was long, and on state occasions required a supporter. Round the waist they wore a broad zone or cincture, flounced on both edges, and embroidered and jewelled in the centre. They also wore stockings and gloves, but history has not recorded their materials.

They used no sandals; a light and ornamented shoe was worn in the house; and for walking they had a kind of coarse half boot. They used shawls and wrappers for the person, and veils for the head; the veil was large and square, and when thrown over the head descended low on all sides. They were fond of glowing colours, especially of purple, scarlet, and light-blue dresses. Their favourite ornaments were pearls; they wreathed these in their hair, wore them as necklaces, ear-drops, armlets, bracelets, anklets, and worked them into conspicuous parts of their dresses. Of the precious stones they preferred emeralds, rubies, and turquoises, which were set in gold and worn like the pearls.

Alexander did not limit his liberality to the wedding festivities, but presented every bride with a handsome marriage portion. He also ordered the names of all the soldiers who had married Asiatic wives to be registered; their number exceeded 10,000; and each received a handsome present, under the name of marriage gift.

The Macedonian Army did not differ in principle from other armies. The conquerors of Asia were not all rich; great plunder and sudden gain are in general lavishly spent. Many were in difficulties, and deeply indebted to the hoard of usurers, plunder-merchants, and credit-givers, that in all ages have been the devouring curse of European as well as of Asiatic armies. Alexander, aware of this, determined to signalise the season of rejoicing by a general payment of all his soldiers' debts. He therefore, by a public order, announced this generous intention, and ordered all bonds, contracts, and other securities, to be brought by the debtor and creditor to the officers of the treasury, who were to register the debtor's names and pay all debts legally due.

Few were bold enough to accept this princely offer, as most suspected it to be a test to enable the king to distinguish the frugal and the prudent from the extravagant and dissolute. Alexander was displeased with this distrust, as, according to him, "kings should not dissemble with their subjects, nor subjects with their kings." He then ordered tables covered with gold to be placed in various parts of the camp, and nothing more was required than for the debtor and creditor to present themselves, receive the money, and cancel the securities before the officers. Twenty thousand *talents* were thus disbursed; and the soldiers felt more grateful for the delicacy of the manner than the substantial nature of the relief. Political economists will exclaim against the measure—moralists will blame it as a direct premium for the production of false documents;—it is useless to argue the question, for there is no apparent danger that the example will ever be imitated.

Separate rewards were assigned to every man who had distinguished himself, either by superior conduct or brilliant actions, during the late campaign. Peucestas and Leonnatus received crowns of gold for their good service in the Mallian citadel;—the latter had also enhanced his claim by gaining a decisive victory over the Oreitæ. Nearchus and Onesicritus were honoured in the same manner, for the skill and success with which they had conducted the fleet from the Indus to the Persian Gulf.

The 30,000 boys who had been selected in the upper provinces were now full grown, and were conducted by their respective officers to Susa, to be reviewed by the king. They had been fully instructed in the Greek language and the Macedonian discipline, and received from Alexander the honourable name of Epigoni. Such was the appellation given to Diomed and his six companions, who had taken Thebes, besieged in vain by their fathers. By giving this name to the young warriors, Alexander clearly intimated his intention to achieve by their aid the conquests which the Macedonian veterans had left unfinished. The name was preserved, and, in the history of the Asiatic Greeks, belongs to the successors of those great generals who, after Alexander's death, became the founders of so many new dynasties. The first race of warrior kings were called the Diadochi.

The sight of the 30,000 Epigoni, in the spring of life, armed and disciplined after the Macedonian fashion, gave deep offence to the veterans. The Median dress of Alexander, the intermarriages, and their celebration according to oriental forms, the Persian robes and language of Peucestas, and the king's approbation of his conduct, served to feed discontent;—but all these were trifles when compared with the steps taken to enable the king to dispense with the services of the Macedonians. For the innovations were not confined to infantry; the Companion cavalry had been largely recruited from the bravest and most skilful horsemen of Bactria, Sogdiana, Arachosia, Zarangia, Areia, Parthia, and Persis. Even a fifth brigade was raised, principally consisting of barbarians.

It was commanded by Hydaspes, a Bactrian; under him served the sons of the highest nobility of the empire, and among them Itanes, the brother of the Queen Roxana. The Macedonian lance replaced the more inefficient javelin, and a heavy sword the light and curved scimitar. The purpose of these measures was obvious; the Macedonians saw with indignation that their king was determined to be emancipated from military thraldom, and to place himself beyond the control of their wayward disposition. They had mutinied on the banks of the Hyphasis, because they were wearied with wars, marches, and conquests, and now they were ready to mutiny on the banks of the Choaspes, because their indulgent king had complied with all their wishes.

As a body they were unable to conceive any system of rational conquest, and, far from sympathizing with the forecast of their own enlightened prince, wished rather to imitate the career of the Scythians, who, nearly 300 years before, had subdued all Western Asia, and pitched their camp in its fairest provinces. For eight-and-twenty years their sole occupation was to destroy, to ravish, to plunder, to revel;—

then arrived the period of reaction, and of unsparing retribution: the chiefs were massacred at a drunken feast, and all the men were cut to pieces.—These, nevertheless, were the victors whose example had most charms for the private Macedonians.

Alexander next undertook to explore the rivers of Susiana, and to view the sea-coast at the upper end of the Persian Gulf. He therefore, with his guards and a small detachment of the Companion cavalry, marched to the Karoon or Pasi-Tigris and embarked on board the fleet. Hephæstion conducted the rest of the army by land.

The fleet fell down the Pasi-Tigris, a magnificent stream, not inferior after its junction with the Coprates, the modern Ab-Zal, to the Tigris or Euphrates.

★★★★★★★★★★

Strabo informs us that the name Pasi-Tigris, which according to oriental etymologists signifies *the eastern Tigris*, was applied by some Greeks to the Shat-ul-Arab, on the supposition that it was a Greek name, and signified the united waters of all the rivers connected with the Tigris.

★★★★★★★★★★

When Alexander sailed on its bosom the country on both sides was highly cultivated, and abounded with an active population. The climate of Susiana is hotter than in the neighbouring provinces—its southern aspect, and hollow site below Mount Lagnos, adding power to the sun and sultriness to the air. Its fertility, under a judicious system of irrigation, is equalled by Babylonia alone. In ancient times the return of wheat and barley crops was a hundred and sometimes two hundred fold. In our days a few straggling Arabs pasture their flocks on the banks of the great streams, and loosely traverse what they do not occupy.

Alexander with the best sailing-vessels entered the Persian Gulf by the main channel of the Karoon, and then coasted to the right until he arrived at the mouth of the great estuary, now called the Shat-ul-Arab, into which the waters of the Euphrates and Tigris, the Gyndes, and the Choaspes are discharged. The heavier and more disabled vessels did not venture into the gulf, but passed from the Karoon into the Shat-ul-Arab, along a canal now called the Hafar. The whole fleet joined at the western mouth of the Hafar Cut, and sailed up the estuary to the place where Hephæstion and the rest of the army were encamped. From the camp the fleet sailed upwards, and entered the separate channel of the Tigris. Here it had to encounter the numerous *bunds*, dykes, or cataracts, with which the Assyrian kings had curbed and intersected the stream.

Ancient Assyria was not like Egypt benefitted by river inundation. For the earthy particles, borne down by the floods of the Tigris and Euphrates, are deeply impregnated with the salts of the desert, and, instead of nourishing plants, prove destructive to vegetation. The same waters when low, and after the noxious particles have subsided, possess the most fertilizing qualities, and, wheresoever they are carefully admitted and gradually diffused, will change the barren desert into a smiling garden.

The Assyrian kings, anxious to guard against the evil and to secure the good, had constructed immense works for two contrary purposes. The first were mounds, of great height and solidity, raised to confine the rivers within their banks, and prevent the noxious floods from spreading over the plains. Many of these were carried across the isthmus between the two rivers—so that, if the floods burst the embankments on any one point, the evil might be partial. The second were the dykes or *bunds* by which, in the season of low water, the level of the river was raised so as to enter the numerous canals, and diffuse the fertilizing streams over the greatest possible surface of ground. These were sometimes formed of stone, and many still remain—lasting monuments of the skill and industry of the ancient Assyrians. The rivers were divided by these works into a succession of steps, each terminated by a fall, greater or less, according to the elevation of the *bund*. The Greeks therefore called them cataracts or waterfalls.

The Macedonians imagined that, as the Persians were not a naval power, these obstructions were intended to impede the entrance of hostile fleets into the bosom of the country. Alexander could hardly have been ignorant of their real use, but his views were not confined to agriculture. An enlarged commerce, and the creation of a powerful fleet on these streams, were among his favourite objects. He therefore destroyed all the *bunds* between the mouth of the Tigris and the city Opis, and reduced the river to its natural level. On the supposition that they were defences he is said to have declared, "that such devices were not for conquerors."

The city Opis was not far from the mouth of the River Gyndes; at this period it was a city of some importance, but the foundation of Seleuceia higher up the river proved its ruin. Alexander either landed here and marched with all the army along the royal road to Susa, or, as stated by Pliny, sailed from the estuary into the Eulæus or Choaspes, the modern Kerah, and ascended by that stream to Susa.

There he summoned the Macedonians to a general assembly, and announced his intention to grant a discharge to all who were invalid from age, wounds, or disease, and to have them conducted in safety to their several homes. He promised "to render the condition of those who were to remain still more enviable, and thus to excite other Macedonians to share their labours and dangers."

Alexander had a right to expect that this announcement would be hailed with gratitude and applause. It comprehended every request made by Coenus in behalf of the veterans, nor could they for a moment doubt the liberality of the provision intended for them on their retirement. But the Macedonians had long been ripe for mutiny. The barbarians among the Companion cavalry, the formidable array of the Epigoni, their Macedonian arms and discipline, were grievances that could be no longer borne, especially as they proved their king's intention to act and speak in future without consulting the pleasure of the military assembly.

The whole body, therefore, broke out into loud and mutinous cries, called upon him to discharge them all, and to "take his new father Ammon for his associate in future campaigns." But Alexander was too well prepared to be intimidated by this violent explosion; he rushed from the tribunal, and being supported by his great officers, entered the crowd, and ordered the guards to seize the ringleaders. He pointed out the most guilty with his own hand, and when thirteen had been thus apprehended, he ordered them all to be led to instant execution. When by this act of vigour, he had terrified the assembly into a state of sullen silence, he reascended the tribunal and thus spoke:—

I have no intention, Macedonians, to dissuade you from returning home; you have my full leave to go your own way; but I wish to remind you of the change in your circumstances, of your obligations to my family, and of the manner in which you now propose to repay them. I begin, as in duty bound, with my father Philip. At his accession you were poverty-stricken wanderers, mostly clad in skins, herding your scanty flocks on the bare hills, and fighting rudely in their defence against the Illyrians, Triballi, and Thracians. Under him you exchanged your garbs of skin for cloaks of cloth. He led you from the hills to the plains, taught you to withstand the barbarians on equal ground, and to rely for safety on personal valour, not on mountain fastnesses.

He assembled you in cities, and civilized you by useful laws and institutions. He raised you from a state of slavery and dependence, to be the masters of the barbarians, by whom you had so long been despoiled and plundered. He added Thrace to your empire, occupied the most advantageous situations on the sea-shore—thus securing the blessings of commerce and enabling you to convert the produce of the mines to the best advantage. Under him you became the leaders of the Thessalians, of whom previously you entertained a deadly terror. By the humiliation of the Phocians, he opened a broad and easy entrance into Greece, which before could be entered only by one narrow and difficult pass.

By the victory at Chæroneia, where, young as I was, I shared in the danger, he humbled the Athenians and Thebans, the eternal plotters against the peace of Macedonia, and converted you from being the tributaries of Athens and the vassals of Thebes, to be the lord-protectors of both states. He then entered the Peloponnesus, arranged its affairs, and was declared captain general of all Greece against Persia. This appointment was no less honourable to himself in particular, than to the Macedonians in general. These are my father's works—great, if estimated intrinsically—trifling, if compared with the benefits conferred by me.

At my accession I inherited a few gold and silver cups, and sixty *talents* in the treasury, while my father's debts exceeded five hundred. I made myself answerable for these, and borrowed eight hundred more in my own name; then leaving Macedonia, which furnished you with only a scanty subsistence, I immediately opened the passage of the Hellespont, although the Persians were then masters of the sea. With my cavalry alone I conquered the *satraps* of Darius, and added to your empire Ionia, Æolia, the Phrygias and Lydia. I besieged and took Miletus, and as the other provinces gave in their submission, appointed you to draw the revenues. You derive the advantages accruing from Ægypt and Cyrenè, acquired by me without a blow. You possess Colo-Syria, Palestine, Mesopotamia, Babylon, Bactra, and Susa. To you belong the wealth of Lydia, the treasures of Persia, the luxuries of India and of the eastern ocean.

You are *satraps*, generals, and colonels. What do I retain from the fruits of all my labours but this purple robe and *diadem?* Individually I have nothing. Nobody can show treasures of mine which are not yours, or preserved for your use, for I have no temptation to reserve anything for myself. Your meals differ not from mine, nor do I indulge in longer slumbers; the luxurious among you fare, perhaps, more delicately than their king, and I know that he often watches that you may sleep in safety.

Nor can it be objected that you have acquired all by your toils and dangers, while I, the leader, have encountered neither risks nor labours. Is there a man among you who is conscious of having toiled more for me than I for him? Nay more, let him among you who has wounds to show, strip and display the scars, and I will show mine, for no part of my person in front has escaped unwounded, nor is there a hand-weapon or missile of which I bear not the mark on my body. I have been struck hand to hand with the sword, by javelins, arrows and darts discharged from engines. It is under showers of stones and steel-shod missiles that I have led you to victory, glory and wealth, by sea and land, over mountains, rivers, and desert places.

I have married from the same class as yourselves, and my children and the children of many among you will be blood-relations. Without inquiring into the manner in which they were contracted, I have paid all your debts, although your pay is great, and the booty from captured cities has been immense. Most of you possess crowns of gold, lasting monuments of your own valour and my approbation. Those who have fallen have finished their course with glory, (for under my auspices no Macedonian ever perished in flight) and have been honoured with splendid funerals; statues of bronze preserve the memory of most of them in their native country; their parents receive particular honours, and are free from all public duties and imposts. It was my intention to have sent home all the invalids, and to have made their condition enviable among their fellow citizens; but since it is your wish to depart altogether, depart all of you, and on your return home, announce, that after Alexander, your king, had conquered the Medes, Bactrians, and Sacæ; had subdued the Uxians, Arachosians, and Drangians; had added to the empire Parthia, Chorasmia, and Hyrcania, and the shores of the Caspian sea; had led you over Mount Caucasus and through the Caspian gates, beyond the Oxus and Tanais, and the Indus, pre-

viously crossed by Dionysus alone, and the Hydaspes, the Acesines, and the Hydraotes; and had your hearts not failed, would
have led you beyond the Hyphasis also; after he had entered
the ocean by both mouths of the Indus, had passed through the
Gedrosian desert, never before traversed by an army, and had
conquered Carmania and Oreitia during the march—when his
fleet had circumnavigated from India into the Persian Gulf—
and all had arrived at Susa—you there deserted him and turned
him over to the care of the conquered barbarians. These facts,
faithfully reported, cannot fail to gain you the applause of men
and the favour of the gods. Depart.

With these words he descended hastily from the tribunal and entered the palace. There he remained secluded from public view for
two days, but as the Macedonians showed no signs of submission, he
took more decisive measures. Had he yielded on the present occasion,
his real authority must have ceased, and a mutiny would have become
the natural resource whenever the army judged itself aggrieved. On
the third day, therefore, he summoned the Persian nobility to the palace; with their assistance he formed a barbarian force, modelled on
the same principle and armed in the same manner as the Macedonian
Army. The Epigoni furnished abundant materials, and the whole soon
assumed the names and divisions of its prototype.

The barbarian *phalanx* had its select brigade called Agema. A division of the barbarian companion cavalry received the same distinguished name. Persian guards were also embodied to represent the
favoured Hypaspists or Argyraspides, (silver shields,) who had been Alexander's constant attendants on all dangerous services. These arrange-
ments were galling enough, but the revival of the Persian bodyguard,
called the Royal Kinsmen, who alone had the privilege of saluting the
king of kings, alarmed the Macedonians beyond measure, and proved
that nothing but instant submission could save them from being all
discharged and dispersed.

For two days they had remained under arms on the ground where
the assembly had been held— expecting probably that the third day
would, as before, produce a change in their favour. But when the
result proved so contrary to their hopes, they hurried in a body to
the gates of the palace, and piled their arms to show the nature of
their application. They here loudly implored the king to come forth;
declaring their willingness to give up the surviving ringleaders, and

their determination not to quit the spot by night or day before they received pardon and mercy,

When this change was reported to Alexander, he hastened forth; nor on witnessing their humble behaviour and expressions of sorrow, could he refrain from tears. He remained thus for some time—wishing to speak, but unable to express his feelings, while they still persevered in their supplications.

At last, Callines, a commander of the Companion cavalry, whose age and rank gave him superior privileges, spoke in behalf of all:

The Macedonians are principally grieved because you have made Persians your relations, and Persians are called the kinsmen of Alexander, and thus allowed to kiss you, while no Macedonian enjoys that privilege.

The king immediately answered:

But you are all my kinsmen, and shall henceforwards bear that name and enjoy the distinction annexed to it.

Upon this Callines approached and kissed him, and his example was followed by others. Thus, the reconciliation was sealed, and the soldiers resumed their arms, and returned to the camp with loud *pæans* and acclamations.

Thus terminated a mutiny that broke out without any specific cause, and was quelled without concessions. The king's victory was complete, and the establishment of a Persian force under separate officers enabled him to hold the balance between his old and new subjects. In order to celebrate the happy reconciliation, a public banquet was provided, to which all of rank and distinction—Greeks and Asiatics—were invited. The guests were nine thousand in number. The Grecian priests and the oriental *Magi* prefaced the libation with the usual prayers, and implored the gods to confirm and perpetuate the concord and union of the Macedonians and Persians.

At the close of this prayer every individual poured the libation, and the *pæan* or thanksgiving hymn was chaunted by nine thousand voices. As some readers may find it difficult to conceive how nine thousand guests could be accommodated at the same banquet, I add for the sake of illustration a description of a similar feast from Diodorus Siculus.

When the troops arrived at Persepolis, Peucestas, the *satrap*, offered magnificent sacrifices to the gods and to Philip and Alexander. Victims and all other requisites for a banquet had been collected from all parts of Persis, and at the conclusion of the sacrifices the whole army sat down to the feast. The troops were formed into four concentric circles. The circumference of the outermost circle was ten *stadia*. This was composed of the Allies and mercenaries. The circumference of the second circle was eight *stadia*; it was composed of the Argyraspides and the other troops, who had served under Alexander.

The third circle was four *stadia* in circumference, and included the cavalry, the officers of inferior rank, and the friends of the generals, both civil and military. The centre was two *stadia* in circumference, and the space within was occupied by the tents of the generals, of the chief officers of the cavalry, and of the noblest Persians. In the very middle were the altars of the gods and of Alexander and Philip. The tents were shaded with green boughs, and furnished with carpets and tapestry hangings—as Persis furnishes in abundance all materials for luxury and enjoyment. The circles were formed so judiciously, that although there was no thronging nor crowding on each other, the banquet was within the reach of all.

Peucestas had arranged his guests after the model furnished by Alexander. For at the reconciliation dinner (if I may venture upon the word), immediately round the king the Macedonians were seated- next to them the Persians—and beyond the Persians the individuals of other nations, according to their rank and dignity. Nor, perhaps, would we be wrong in supposing the whole order to have been Persian and not Grecian. For the great king used to give public banquets at periodical seasons, not only to his courtiers and guards, but to the deputies from his numerous *satrapies*.

On such occasions, we learn from the *Book of Esther*, the king occupied the chief place of honour, while immediately in front of him were the representatives of the seven great families of Persia, with the other guests behind them, according to their rank. We are informed by Herodotus that the Persians regarded themselves as the centre of the created world, and the noblest tribe on the face of it; and that other nations partook of honour and nobility in proportion to their propinquity to the influence-spreading centre. Had therefore the original etiquette of the Persian court been enforced, the Macedonians must have been placed in the rear of their own Thracian dependants.

A scrutiny now took place, and a selection was made of all the Macedonians whom age, wounds, or other accident had incapacitated for active service. Their number exceeded ten thousand. Alexander allowed them full pay until they reached their several homes, and presented every invalid with a *talent* more than was due to him. As many had children by Asiatic women, he took the maintenance and education of all these upon himself, that they might not give rise to jealousies and domestic disturbances between their fathers and their connections in Macedonia. He promised to educate them like Macedonian soldiers, and in due time to conduct them home and present them to their veteran fathers.

But what the invalids regarded as the highest compliment, was the appointment of Craterus take the charge of them. The health of this amiable man and great officer, had declined of late, and a return to his native air was judged advisable for its re-establishment. He was to conduct the veterans home, and to succeed Antipater in the regency of Macedonia, and the management of Greece. Antipater had discharged his duties with great judgement, prudence, and success: nor does Alexander's confidence in him appear ever to have been shaken. But the continued complaints of Olympias, a restless and, as she afterwards proved herself, a blood-thirsty woman, had of late grown more violent; and Antipater also had been compelled to represent in more severe terms, the turbulence and ferocity of her conduct. Olympias received from her son everything that he could give, but political power; while nothing but the possession of this, could satisfy her imperious temper. She was loud in her accusations of Antipater, who, according to her, had forgotten the hand that raised him, and exercised his authority as if inherent in himself.

Alexander, therefore, anxious to prevent any act of violence, in which the increasing animosities of the two parties appeared every instant liable to explode, sent Craterus, whom in Arrian's words, he loved as his life, to act on this delicate occasion; and ordered Antipater to lead a new levy of Macedonians into Asia.

The parting between the veterans and Alexander was most touching. Every soldier was permitted to take personal leave. All were in tears, nor was the king an exception; it was not possible for him whose heart was so warm, and his affections so strong, to take leave without deep emotions, of the rugged veterans whose foster-child he had been in earlier years, and with whom in youth and manhood he had fought, bled, and achieved victories of unparalleled importance. The late quarrel and reconciliation were calculated to increase the feelings of mutual good-will; for a commander is never so kind as when his authority is established beyond dispute;—nor the attachment of soldiers so strong, as when tempered with the conviction that they cannot offend with impunity.

Autumn was now approaching, and Alexander marched from Susa to Ecbatana. His hurried advance through Media, had not allowed him time to examine that rich province, and its splendid capital. He therefore devoted the short season of repose, to the inspection and improvement of his chief cities. From Susa, he marched to the Pasi-Tigris, and encamped in the villages of Caræ, probably the site of the modern Shuster. Thence he advanced to Sitta or Sambana, where he rested seven days; at the next stage he found the Celona, a Boeotian tribe, carried into captivity by Xerxes, and placed among these mountains. They still retained traces of Grecian manners, and language, but were rapidly barbarising.

Their situation was about midway between Shuster and Ispahan. Near them was Bagistanè, a delightful spot, abounding with streams, rocks, springs, groves, and all that can render oriental scenery picturesque and pleasing. A park and palace ascribed to Semiramis, furnished accommodations for the court, and Alexander lingered for thirty days amidst beauties of nature, better adapted, according to Diodorus, for the enjoyment of gods, than of mortals.

During this stay, he interfered between his two friends, Hephæstion and Eumenes, who had long been at variance with each other. The cause did not originate with the secretary, nor had he any wish to entertain a feud with the favourite of his sovereign. But the commander of the Companion cavalry scorned the advances of the Cardian, the former *amanuensis* of Philip, and threatened him with future vengeance. Unfortunately we have only the termination of the quarrel, as reported by Arrian, who writes:

Hephæstion dreading this speech was reconciled reluctantly to Eumenes.

The substance of the king's speech as given by Plutarch, was a remonstrance with Hephæstion, who, without the king's favour, would be a person of no weight; while Eumenes, on the contrary, was a man whose talents would render him conspicuous and formidable in any situation.

Alexander thus showed not only his ability to estimate duly the talents of his officers, which perhaps is no uncommon power—but, what is far more rare, firm determination to support the useful, against the arts and influence of the agreeable character, and to patronise merit, even if obnoxious to favourites.

In this vicinity, were the famous pastures, wherein the royal broodmares reared their numerous foals. Before the war, one hundred and fifty thousand horses of all kinds and ages, were said to have grazed in these pastures, but when Alexander visited them, the number did not exceed fifty thousand. The rest had been stolen during the troubles. Arrian, from inattention, confounded two accounts given by Herodotus, and affirmed the identity of these herds, with the Nysæan steeds. But the Nysæan plain, as distinctly mentioned by Strabo, was close to the Caspian gates; and the number of Nysæan horses, so far from being countable by thousands, was very limited. No more than seventeen of these highly-prized animals formed part of the procession in the advance of the Persian Army under Xerxes, and even one was regarded as a fit present for a king. Their description suits well the cream-coloured horses of the royal Hanoverian stud.

It is in these rural retreats that some writers place the interview between Alexander and the Amazons; others again in Hyrcania. According to the former, Atropates, the *satrap* of Media, presented Alexander with a hundred Amazons, armed, mounted, and equipped; but the silence of Ptolemy and Aristobulus outweighs the assertion of others. If, however, a hundred young maidens, in the Amazonian dress, with the right bosom bare, armed with the bow, the quiver, and the *pelta*, and taught to manage their chargers with ease and elegance, were really presented to Alexander by Atropates, it is easy to account for their masquerading dress.

Atropates was the governor of the very countries where the Amazons were supposed to have resided, and a wish expressed by Alexander to see some of the race, if still existing, was enough to recall them from the dead. Without some such supposition, it is difficult to account for the belief, universal among inferior writers, of the Amazonian visit. Ptolemy and Aristobulus, aware of the facts of the case, might easily have left the device of Atropates unnoticed. The writers who describe the appearance of the fair warriors, add, that Alexander sent a gallant message to their queen, and ordered the young ladies to be immediately escorted beyond the precincts of the encampment, before the younger officers undertook to put the valour and gallantry of the maiden chivalry to proof in arms.

When Alexander reached Ecbatana, he offered a splendid sacrifice in gratitude for his continued prosperity. This was followed by the contests of the *palæstra*, and theatrical representations. During the festivities, Alexander repeatedly entertained his friends, and the wine was not spared. The Medes and Persians, as I before remarked, were deep drinkers; but the following passage from Ælian is curious, as it infers that such was not the custom among the Greeks of his day:

> When Aspasia was first introduced to the younger Cyrus, he had just finished his dinner, and was preparing to drink after the Persian fashion; for the Persians, after they have satisfied their appetite with food, sit long over their wine, pledge each other in copious draughts, and gird themselves to grapple with the bottle as with an antagonist.

Heracleides of Cuma, as quoted by Athenæus, goes still further, and writes, that:

> Those guests of the king of kings who were admitted to share the royal compotations, never quitted the presence in the possession of their senses.

A fever, which attacked Hephæstion at this time, might, therefore, have been produced by hard drinking, as asserted by some writers; but the hardships which he had lately undergone, and the continual change of climate, are of themselves sufficient causes. It was the seventh day of his illness, Alexander was presiding at the games, and the stadium was full of spectators, when a messenger brought information that Hephæstion was alarmingly ill: Alexander hurried away, but his friend was dead before he arrived.

Arrian says:

> Various writers, have given various accounts of Alexander's sorrow on this occasion. All agree that it was excessive, but his actions are differently described, as the writers were biased by affection or hostility to Hephæstion, or even to Alexander. Some, who have described his conduct as frantic and outrageous, regard all his extravagant deeds and words on the loss of his dearest friend, as honourable to his feelings, while others deem them degrading and unworthy of a king and of Alexander. Some write, that for the remainder of that day he lay lamenting upon the body of his friend, which he would not quit until he was torn away by his companions; others, that he remained

there for a day and a night. Others write, that he hanged the physician Glaucias;—because, according to one statement, he gave him wrong medicine; according to another, because he stood by and allowed his patient to fill himself with wine.

I think it probable that he cut off his hair in memory of the dead, both for other reasons and from emulation of Achilles, whom from his childhood he had chosen for his model. But those who write that Alexander drove the hearse which conveyed the body, state what is incredible. Nor are they more entitled to belief who say that he destroyed the temple of Æsculapius at Ecbatana, the deed of a barbarian, and inconsistent with the character of Alexander, but more in unison with Xerxes' wanton outrages against the divinities, and with the fetters dropped by him into the waves, in order, forsooth, to punish the Hellespont.—

The following anecdote does not appear to me altogether improbable. Many embassies from Greece, and among others, deputies from Epidaurus, met him on the road between Ecbatana and Babylon. Alexander granted the petition of the Epidaurians, and presented them with a valuable ornament for the temple of Æsculapius; adding, however, 'Although Æsculapius has used me unkindly, in not saving the friend who was as dear to me as my own life.—'

Almost all agree, that he ordered Hephæstion to be honoured with the minor religious ceremonies due to deified heroes. Some say that he consulted Ammon, whether he might not sacrifice to Hephæstion as to a god, and that the answer forbad him. All agree in the following facts, that for three days he tasted no food, nor permitted any attention to his person, but lay down, either lamenting or mournfully silent; that he ordered a funeral pile to be constructed at an expense of 10,000 *talents*; (some say more,) that all his barbarian subjects were ordered to go into mourning; and that several of the king's companions, in order to pay their court, dedicated themselves and their arms to the deceased.

Thus Arrian: The passage has been introduced partly for the curious information contained in it, and partly for the sake of enabling the modern reader to see from what a mass of contradictory matter the historian had to select his facts.

From Ecbatana, Alexander returned to Babylon. The royal road, connecting the capitals of Media and Assyria passed through the territories of the Cossæi, a mountain tribe who occupied the valleys and high ground between the upper part of the courses of the modern Abzal and Caroon. These bandits used to receive a tribute, under the name of presents, from the king of kings, as often as he travelled between Babylon and Ecbatana. It may be inferred that, like the Uxians, they had not failed to demand the same from Alexander; but he, although the winter was far advanced, made war upon them and pursued them into their mountain fastnesses.

In Arrian's words:

> Neither the winter nor the ruggedness of the country were any hindrances to Alexander and Ptolemy the son of Lagus, who commanded a division of the army.

It is in the winter season alone that the robbers who inhabit the high mountains of Asia, can be successfully invaded; if assailed in summer, they move from hill to hill, sink one while into the abysses of their ravines, and at another time ascend to the loftiest peaks. Their flocks, partly concealed in retired vales, partly accompanying their movements, furnish them with provisions; but if the principal villages, where they keep their stores, flocks, and herds, be captured during the winter season, the inhabitants must either perish or come to terms. It was when the snow was knee-deep on the ground, that Timour at last conquered the Curds of Mount Zagrus, a race cognate with the Cossæi.

After Alexander had compelled these to surrender, he built towns and fortresses in the most commanding positions, in order to restrain their depredations in future; but the cure was only temporary; they soon relapsed into their ancient habits, and when Antigonus had to pass through the vale of the Abzal, to the vicinity of Ecbatana, in his expedition against Eumenes, his army narrowly escaped destruction from these Cossæi, to whom he had refused the customary gratuity.

As Alexander was advancing towards Babylon, he met numerous embassies—sent from various nations to congratulate him on his final success, and the acquisition of the empire of Asia. Here presented themselves ambassadors from Libya—from the Bruttii, Lucanians, and Tuscans of Italy—from Carthage—from the Æthiopians—from the Scythians in Europe—from the Celtæ and the Iberi, whose dress was then first seen, and their names heard by the Greeks and Macedonians. Some of these sought the king's friendship and alliance; some protection from more powerful neighbours; others submitted their common disputes to his arbitration. This universal homage was regarded, both by Alexander and his friends, as a recognition of his sovereignty over the known world. His fame had made a deep impression on the nations of the west.

The Greeks of Italy and Sicily extolled the glory of the captain-general of the Greeks, and threatened the barbarians who harassed them with his vengeance. The fall of Tyre was an event calculated to give a shock to the nations from the Phoenician coast to the British Isles. The lamentations of Carthage for her mother city, and her known fears of a similar fate, were sufficient to spread the terrors of Alexander's name from coast to coast, and to indicate him as the vanquisher of the proud and the refuge of the distrest. The Spanish Iberi would have ample cause to complain of the encroachments of the Carthaginians on their shores; while the embassies of the Tuscans and Lucanians could hardly have any other object than to represent the power, the ambition, and the king-detesting tyranny of Rome.

Aristus and Asclepiades, two historians not distinguished for their credulity, wrote that Roman ambassadors visited Alexander, who, after giving them audience, foretold their future greatness, from witnessing the steadiness, the enterprise, and free spirit of the men, and from hearing an accurate account of their political constitution. Arrian says:

> I have mentioned this not as certain, nor yet as altogether to be disbelieved.

Strabo writes that Alexander sent an embassy to Rome, to remonstrate against the piracies of the Tuscans under the supposed protection of the Romans.

Livy is very eloquent in his attempt to prove that, if Alexander had invaded Italy, he would have been assuredly defeated and vanquished by the Romans. But partiality must either have blinded his judgment, or induced him to suppress his honest convictions. It required more than ordinary hardihood to assert the superiority of Papirius Cursor over the conqueror of the East. Had Alexander entered Italy, it would have been at the head of an irresistible force by land and sea. The Greeks, Lucanians, and Samnites, would have hailed him as a deliverer, and their bravest warriors would have fought under his banners. The Samnites alone, three years after Alexander's death, were strong enough to gain the famous victory at the defile of Caudium, and the Tuscans were successfully struggling against the despotism of Rome.

Alexander had found eight hundred thousand *talents* in the different treasuries of the empire. His resources, therefore, were inexhaustible; and these, applied with the extraordinary activity and perseverance which characterized all his operations, would not have left the Romans one hope of finally saving themselves. If, in later years, Pyrrhus, the needy prince of the small kingdom of Epirus, with his confined means, shook Rome to her foundations, it is idle to suppose that, in a far feebler state, she could for a moment have withstood the whirlwind shock of Alexander's chivalry. He did not trust for victory to the activity of the *phalanx*, but maintained it as a tower of strength, as a fortress in reserve, round which the broken part of his forces might always rally.

For attack he trusted to his cavalry, mixed with infantry—to his mounted archers and dartmen—to his bowmen—and especially to his Agrians, a species of light-armed regular infantry. If with these he made an impression upon the enemy's thronged ranks, broke their lines, or confounded their order, he then brought up the *phalanx* with its serried front of iron pikes, and swept them off the field.

The Romans would probably have fought bravely, but they had neither the skill nor the strength to contend with Alexander. In his days their arms and discipline were very deficient; nor was their resolution, as proved by the surrender at Caudium, of that stern cast which knows no alternative between death and victory.

Although they may in the history of the world be regarded as the political heirs of Alexander, yet a long period elapsed before they entered on their inheritance. They never took possession of the extensive empire between the Euphrates, the Indus, and the Jaxartes; and the Macedonian had been dead for nearly three hundred years, before the kingdom of the son of Lagus was added to the dominion of Rome.

Chapter 16

Last Year of Alexander's Life, B.C. 323

Alexander had crossed the Tigris on his road to Babylon, when a deputation of Chaldæan priests waited upon him, and besought him not to enter the city, as their god Belus had communicated to them, that a visit to Babylon at that time would not be to the king's advantage. Alexander, startled at the warning not to enter the city which he intended for the capital of his empire, repeated to his friends a line from Euripides, the sceptical poet of Greece, expressing that:

A fair guesser is the best prophet,

—and signified his determination to proceed. It appears that he suspected the motives of these Chaldæan diviners. The work of re-building the great temple of Belus had proceeded but slowly, and Al-exander, displeased at this, had announced his intention to employ the whole army in its completion. This announcement was by no means agreeable to the Chaldæans, to whom Alexander had restored the broad lands with which the Assyrian kings had endowed the temple; for as long as the edifice remained unfinished, the priests enjoyed its ample revenues without deductions, but these, as soon as it was com-pleted, would be principally expended on the victims, lights, incense, and numerous servants whom the pomp and ceremony of Assyrian worship rendered necessary.

Of the extent of this expenditure, and of the magnificence of the worship, some idea may be formed from a fact stated by Herodotus, that during the festival of Belus one thousand *talents* of frankincense were consumed on one altar. Alexander was, therefore, led to believe that the warning voice proceeded from the self-interest of the priests, and not from the provident care of their god.

The Chaldæans, thus unexpectedly baffled, and probably conscious that the monarch was likely to be as safe within as without the walls of Babylon, now took up a new position; and said the danger might be averted were the king and the army to make a circuit, and enter the city by the western in place of the eastern gate. Alexander attempted to comply with this advice, but as the marshes and lakes above the town rendered its execution difficult, he gave up the endeavour, and entered by the fatal portal.

It is the fashion of our days to suppose that there can be no com-munications between the material and the spiritual world, and that man from the hour of his birth has to struggle forwards under the sole guidance of laws immutably connected with his organisation; but this is an idle supposition, which never amounts to belief in the mind of the most degraded disciple of the stye. In all cases of overpowering alarm or affliction the Epicurean belies his principles, calls for divine aid, and attempts by loud supplications to rouse his God from his death-like tranquillity.

The great body of mankind, impressed with a belief of their de-pendence upon the spiritual world, have in all ages been more inclined to run into the opposite extreme, and to welcome the doctrine, according to which our thoughts, words, and actions are not under our own control, but mere modes of the divine will, of which the human being is the passive instrument. But as the divine will is eternal and immutable, so must everything connected with man and his destiny, the day of his birth, his character in life and the hour of his death, be eternally and immutably fixed.

Thus, the Moiræ of the Greeks and the Fata of the Latins left man no choice but to advance along the path which had been marked out for him before his birth—to lengthen or shorten which was not given either to Man or to God. The believers in this doctrine were anxious to discover the moment pre-destined to terminate their own lives, and the lives of those in whose fate they were deeply interested. An immutable truth placed beyond the reach of contingency was not supposed beyond the reach of human knowledge. Nature herself was believed to intimate, by various signs, that the appointed hour of every individual was drawing nigh—that the thread of his existence was gradually winding up, and would soon be snapt asunder.

But as the human mind could not rest satisfied with the supposed discovery of a truth which could not be avoided, the believers in Fate soon admitted a doctrine utterly subversive of their own original principles;—namely, that when signs or omens of impending evil were given, the evil itself might be averted by certain ceremonies and expiatory sacrifices. On this admission was founded the whole fabric of heathen superstition, and the science of augury, divination, and propitiation. The diviners, with admirable inconsistency, held at one time that the impending evil had been averted by their exertions, and at another, that destiny could not be controlled nor the fates changed.

The signs and warnings were supposed to be more distinct and frequent, when the fate of the mighty on the earth was trembling in the balance. Accordingly omens, which could not be mistaken, are said to have preceded the deaths of all the great men whose lives have been particularly recorded by ancient writers. As part, therefore, of the history of the opinions and feelings of the day, those which were supposed to have indicated the approaching death of Alexander, deserve attention.

Aristobulus writes that Apollodorus of Amphipolis, one of the Companions, had been left behind to command the military force under Mazæus, the *satrap* of Babylon. On Alexander's return from India, he had been summoned to the camp, and had witnessed the punishment of various *satraps*. Alarmed by their fate, he sent to consult his brother Peithagoras, a diviner, who, by inspecting the entrails of victims, could foretell future events.—Peithagoras sent back to inquire whom he most dreaded, and heard from his brother that it was the king himself and Hephæstion. The diviner then consulted the victims with respect to Hephæstion; and, on finding the liver imperfect, informed his brother by a sealed letter that he need not be afraid of Hephæstion, who would soon be out of the way. Apollodorus received this letter at Ecbatana the day before Hephæstion's death.

Peithagoras then sacrificed concerning Alexander, found the same imperfection in the liver, and transmitted the information to his brother. He to prove his loyalty, showed the letter to Alexander, who commended his openness, and on arriving at Babylon, asked Peithagoras what the inauspicious omen was. The diviner replied that it was the absence of the head of the liver. The king then asked what this foreboded, and was honestly answered, 'some great misfortune.' Alexander, so far from being angry with Peithagoras, treated him with greater consideration, because he had honestly told him the truth. Aristobulus writes that he received this account from Peithagoras himself.—

It is easy to remember prophetical sayings after the event has taken place, and many Macedonians recalled to mind that Calanus took leave of all his friends but the king, whom he said he was soon to see at Babylon. Such reports lose nothing by transmission; we ought not therefore to be surprised that Cicero, in his work on divination, asserts as a well-known fact that Calanus distinctly foretold the impending death of Alexander.

Numerous embassies from Grecian states waited the king's arrival at Babylon; they were all complimentary, and received due honours. To them was entrusted the care of the trophies which Xerxes had carried away from Greece, and which the king ordered to be reconveyed to the several cities whence they had been removed. Athenæus has quoted a passage from Phylarchus descriptive of the appearance of Alexander's court on public days, which, in the absence of better authority, I introduce here:

The golden plane trees, the vine of pure gold loaded with clusters of emeralds, Indian carbuncles, and other invaluable gems, under which the kings of Persia used to sit and give audience, were not equal in value to the sum of Alexander's expenses for one day. His tent contained a hundred couches, and was supported by eight columns of solid gold. Overhead was stretched cloth of gold wrought with various devices, and expanded so as to cover the whole ceiling. Within, in a semi-circle, stood five hundred Persians, bearing lances adorned with pomegranates. Their dress was purple and orange. Next to these were drawn up a thousand archers, partly clothed in flame-coloured and partly in scarlet dresses. Many of these wore azure-coloured sashes.

In front of these were arranged five hundred Macedonian Argyraspides. In the middle of the tent was placed a golden throne, on which Alexander sat and gave audience, while the great officers of the guard stood behind and on either side of him. The tent on the outside was encircled by the elephants drawn up in order, and by a thousand Macedonians in their native dress. Beyond these were arranged the Persian guard of ten thousand men, and the five hundred courtiers allowed to wear purple robes. But out of this crowd of friends and attendants, no one dared to approach near to Alexander, so great was the majesty with which he was surrounded.

But neither the homage of suppliant nations nor the pomp and magnificence of his court, could divert the active mind of Alexander from useful projects. He sent Argæus with a band of shipwrights to the shores of the Caspian Sea with orders to cut timber in the Hyrcanian forests, and to build ships on the plan of the Grecian war vessels. For he was anxious to discover with what sea the Caspian communicated. The Greek philosophers reasoning from analogy, had not given credit to Herodotus concerning its alleged isolation. Nor was their scepticism blameable. Herodotus wrote only from report; and as his account of the rivers that flow into that sea is grossly erroneous, his accuracy respecting the sea itself can be regarded only as casual.

The narrow outlets that connect the Mæotic with the Propontis, the Propontis with the Euxine, the Euxine with the Mediterranean, and the Mediterranean with the Atlantic, had prepared them to expect a similar outlet in the Caspian. They would not, therefore, without a careful investigation of every creek on its coast, allow the anomaly of an inland sea that did not communicate with the circumambient ocean. Alexander did not live to hear of the success of his plans, but Seleucus carried them into execution, and a fleet under his admiral, Patrocles, was employed to survey carefully the shores of the Caspian.

The dangers attendant on the navigation of that rude and boisterous bason seem, however, to have been too great for the courage of Patrocles. His pretended discoveries of the mouths of the Oxus and Jaxartes, and of a south-east passage into the Indian Ocean, are proofs that he never in reality fulfilled his commission, nor examined the shores. Had Alexander himself lived, the veil of darkness that enveloped those regions for thirteen centuries longer would probably have been removed.

The Indian fleet, under Nearchus, had sailed from the great estuary, up the Euphrates to Babylon.

Alexander, on his return to Ecbatana, found it there, as well as two *quinqueremes*, four *quadriremes*, twelve *triremes*, and thirty *triaconters*, which had arrived from the Mediterranean. The vessels had been taken to pieces on the Phoenician coast, carried by land to Thapsacus, re-constructed there, and navigated down the Euphrates to Babylon. There he ordered a harbour large enough to accommodate a thousand ships of war, to be excavated on the banks of the Euphrates, and covered docks in proportion to be constructed. Sailors from all parts of the Mediterranean hurried to man his fleet; among these the fishermen of the murex or purple-fish, on the Phoenician coast, are particularly mentioned. Agents were sent to engage the most skilful seamen, and to purchase the ablest rowers for his service. In a word, it was his intention to form on the Susian and Babylonian coast, a second Phoenicia—equal in wealth and population to the Syrian.

He had fixed upon Babylon for the seat of empire, as the central spot between Egypt and the Mediterranean on one side, and the Indus and Eastern Ocean on the other. The fertility of Assyria was boundless, and its revenues, in the time of Herodotus, formed a third of the annual receipts of the Persian kings. But these had neglected the interests of Assyria, and the ruined cities on the banks of the Tigris, described by Xenophon, attest the extent of desolation. It was Alexander's policy to heal the wounds inflicted by them and to restore Assyria to her ancient supremacy. But before this could be done effectually, and an unrestrained communication opened between the provinces of the south-western empire, it was necessary to reduce the Arabs to subjection.

Their position to the west of Babylonia made incursions into the province easy, and their command of the course of the Euphrates enabled them to exact ruinous sums from the merchants navigating that river. His plan for their subjugation was for the fleet to circumnavigate the Arabian Peninsula, and its motions to be attended by a land force. Thirty oared gallies were sent successively to examine the southern shores of the Persian Gulf, and to report the state of the Arabian coast. Hiero, a sea captain from Soli, ventured furthest. His orders had been to sail round into the Red Sea, until he arrived in the vicinity of the Egyptian Heröopolis. But when he had coasted along the whole extent of the shore within the gulf, and doubled the formidable cape now called Ras Musendoon, his heart also failed him, and he ventured to announce to Alexander the greatness of the undertaking.

But difficulties only stimulated him, and the preparations for the departure of the great expedition were carried on without any cessation. Had it set out under the command of the king, the probability is that it would have proved successful. The Arabs were not formidable in the field; and an active land force, supported by a large fleet, might, without enduring much hardship or opposition, have made the circuit of the peninsula. The fertile spots between Muscat and Mocha, and Mocha and Mecca, are numerous enough to furnish ample provision for an invading army; and from Mecca he could easily have transferred his troops to the Egyptian shore, where the resources of the valley of the Nile were at his command.

Ælius Gallus, who invaded Arabia under the auspices of Augustus, found no resistance from the natives, and during an eight months' campaign lost only seven soldiers by the enemy's weapons. Nor is the boasted invincibility of the Arabs founded in truth. Sha-Poor, or Sapor, one of the greatest monarchs of the Persian dynasty of Sassan, marched victoriously from Hira, on the western frontier of Babylonia, to Gathreb or Medina, on the Arabian Gulf; and the great Nushirwan completed the conquest of Arabia, and compelled every *sheik* and *saladin* within the peninsula to acknowledge him as their head.

It cannot therefore be supposed that Alexander's activity, forethought and prudence, in proportioning the means to the end, could in the common course of calculation have failed. Probably also, as the expedition was to partake of the character of a voyage of discovery as well as of conquest, the *sheiks* would have soon discovered that resistance would only irritate, and cause the conqueror to delay his course and exterminate, while a ready submission would save the inhabitants from all molestation, save the transmission through their territories of the travelling force.

While the preparations were still continued, the king turned his attention to the canals and irrigation of Assyria. To the west or south-west of Babylon was a long succession of large cavities or depressions in the soil, into which the superfluous waters of the Euphrates could be turned in the season of the floods. These cavities were supposed to have been the works of former Assyrian kings, and were equal in extent to an inland sea. The canal, which connected the Euphrates with these reservoirs, was called the Pallacopas; its upper end being in the right bank of the great river, about thirty-six miles above Babylon. The entrance into the Pallacopas was opened during the floods, in order to relieve the banks near and below Babylon from part of the pressure of the waters; but when the floods subsided, it was necessary again to obstruct the entrance, and to prevent the water in its fertilising state from escaping into the lakes.

It was easy to cut the bank, and admit the flood waters into the Pallacopas, and thence into the great basons; but it was a Herculean task to repair the breach, and compel the Euphrates to resume its ordinary channel. The *satrap* of Assyria had every year to employ 10,000 men, for three months, in the work of obstruction. Alexander sailed up the Euphrates, and examining the mouth of the Pallacopas, found it impossible to remedy the evil at the point where the cut was annually made, as the whole soil in the vicinity was gravelly and alluvial, and almost defied the task of obstruction; but on examining the bank higher up the stream, he found, about four miles from the ancient place, a spot where the bank below the surface was rocky. Here he ordered a new channel to be excavated, which might, with comparative ease, be obstructed in the proper season.

As the spring floods had already commenced, he sailed down the Pallacopas into the lakes. On arriving at the foot of the hills, below which in after ages the Arabs built Cufa, he fixed on the site of the last Alexandreia founded by him. It is supposed to have been the Hira of a later period.

Thence he sailed back towards Babylon, pleased that he had thus escaped the misfortune foretold by the Chaldæan Seers. The lakes on which he was sailing were studded with small islands, many of which were crowned with the sepulchres of the ancient kings of Assyria. As he was steering his own vessel between those islets, the broad-brimmed hat, which he wore as a protection against the heat, and round which the royal *diadem* or band was wreathed, was blown over-board by a violent gust of wind. The hat fell into the water, but the *diadem* being lighter was carried by the wind into some tall reeds, that grew around one of the royal tombs.

A sailor swam ashore, recovered the *diadem*, and, in order to pre-serve it dry while he was swimming back, placed it on his head. For this presumption, according to Aristobulus, the man, who was a Phoe-nician sailor, received a flogging; according to others, who were more anxious for an antithetical sentence than for the truth, he received a *talent* for his good service and death for his presumption. According to a third account, the recoverer of the *diadem* was Seleucus, whose future greatness, as the most powerful of the successors of Alexander, was thus indicated. These various accounts prove that the incident at the time was looked upon as a trifle, and that, after Alexander's death, the superstitious narrated it according to their own fancies.

At Babylon Alexander found Peucestas, who had brought 20,000 Persian recruits and a considerable force of Tapeiri and Cossæi, whom the Persians represented as their most warlike neighbours. These were not incorporated with the already existing Persian force, but formed into a separate body. The lowest division of this new *phalanx* was called a *decad*, although it contained sixteen individuals, of whom twelve were Persians. The front and rear men were Macedonians, with an increased pay; as were the two officers answering to the modern sergeants, whose duty it was to drill and discipline the division. The superior officers of this new corps were all Macedonians, so that its establishment must have caused an immense promotion among them. It is curious that, while the four Macedonians bore the arms of the Greek heavy-armed infantry, the twelve Persians were partly armed with bows and partly with darts. This new force appears to have been admirably adapted for the service which the army had to expect in its march round Arabia.

The naval preparations were carried on without intermission. Cy-press trees, the only ship-timber on the banks of the Euphrates, were cut down, and new ships constructed. The rowers and pilots were exercised daily, and prizes awarded for superior activity and skill in the management of the vessels.

Ambassadors from southern Greece now came to present Alex-ander with golden crowns; and these, on advancing to his presence, appeared in the sacred garlands, which were never worn by deputies, except when commissioned to consult oracles, or to carry gifts to the shrines of distant deities. But while these servile republicans hailed him with divine honours—while the bravest and best disciplined army on the face of the earth loved him as their leader and revered him as their king—while his newly-created fleet was furrowing with unwonted keels the bosom of the Euphrates, and preparing to spread its sails on seas unknown—while he was anticipating the fulfilment of his early dreams of becoming the master of the gold, the aromatics, the myrrh, and the frankincense of the hitherto untouched Sabæa, and of compelling the sons of the desert to add a third god to their scanty Pantheon—while he was preparing to forge the last link of the golden chain which was to bind together his subjects on the Indus, the Tigris, and the Nile, by the strong ties of mutual advantages—the scene was suddenly changed, and he was cut down in the prime of life, in the height of his glory; and in the middle of his vast projects.

Arrian says:

> And perhaps it was better thus to depart, to the extreme regret of all men, while his glory was unstained, and before he was overtaken by those calamities to which mortals are exposed, and on account of which Solon advised Croesus to consider the end of life, and to pronounce no man happy on this side of the grave.

A few days before his last illness, he was busily employed in super-intending the formation of his new corps.

The tent, which was his favourite residence, was erected on the plain; and in front was placed the throne, whence he could inspect the proceedings. In the course of the day, he retired to quench his thirst, and was attended by all the great officers, who left the throne under the sole care of the *eunuchs* of the palace. An obscure Greek, who was on the field, seeing the throne and the seats on both sides empty, with the *eunuchs* standing in rows behind, walked up, and deliberately seated himself upon the throne. The *eunuchs*, it appears, were prevented by the etiquette of the Persian court from disturbing the intruder, but they raised a loud cry of lamentation, tore their garments, beat their breasts and foreheads, and showed other signs of grief, as if some great misfortune had befallen them.

The event was judged to be highly important, and the intruder was put to the torture in order to discover whether he had accomplices or not in this overt act of treason—for such it was considered to be by all the Persians of the court. But the only answer which they could extract from the unhappy man was, that he had acted most unintentionally, and without any ulterior views. This confession, in the opinion of the diviners, gave a more fatal complexion to the omen. Without a knowledge of eastern customs, it would have been impossible to discover why so much importance was paid to a trifling occurrence; but the following passage from the Emperor Baber's autobiography will illustrate this and other obscure points of eastern history.

> It is a singular custom in the history of Bengal that there is little of hereditary descent in succession to the sovereignty. There is a throne allotted for the king, there is in like manner a seat or station assigned for each of the *amîrs*, *vazîrs*, and *sobdars*. It is that throne and these stations alone which engage the reverence of the people of Bengal. A set of dependants, servants, and attendants are annexed to each of these situations; when the king wishes to dismiss or appoint any person, whosoever is placed in the seat of the one dismissed is immediately attended and obeyed by the whole establishment of dependants, servants, and retainers annexed to the seat which he occupies; nay, even this rule obtains even as to the royal throne itself; whoever kills the king and succeeds in placing himself on that throne is immediately acknowledged as king. All the *amîrs, vazîrs*, soldiers, and peasants, instantly obey and submit to him, and consider him as much their sovereign as they did their former prince, and obey his orders as implicitly. The people of Bengal say, 'We are faithful to the throne; whoever fills the throne we are obedient and true to it.'

To this passage the editor of Baber adds the following note:

> Strange as this custom may seem, a similar one prevailed down to a very late period in Malabar. There was a jubilee every twelve years in the Samorin's country, and anyone who succeeded in forcing his way through the Samorin's guards and slew him reigned in his stead. The attempt was made in 1695, and again a few years ago, but without success.

The Persians and Medes were not Hindoos, but seem to have adopted many ceremonies from the Assyrians, who were a cognate people with the Egyptians and Indians. This doctrine of obedience to *the throne* had been established for the safety of the great body of the nation during civil contests. It furnished a valid excuse for obeying the king *de facto,* without inquiring into his title *de jure.* But the very principle adopted to ensure the national tranquillity became one great cause of civil wars. For when any bold adventurer succeeded in gathering a sufficient number of marauders, bandits, and outcasts not troubled with any conscientious scruples on the subject of passive obedience, he boldly claimed the throne, and success formed the best of titles.

The chance of battle might prove fatal to the reigning monarch, and thus at once convert the loyal troops into a band of rebels. The Persians under Cyrus the Younger did not salute him as king, until they had witnessed the defeat of the Royal Army; although Cyrus had long before claimed the crown, because he was a better man than his brother.

The assassination of Darius by Bessus and his accomplices must be referred to the same principle. By the murder of his sovereign, Bessus transferred his rights to himself. But had Darius fallen alive into the hands of Alexander, they would have devolved upon the captor. Many battles in the east have been lost in consequence of this feeling. Mahmoud of Ghisni gained the battle which opened India to his army, because the elephant of his victorious opponent became unruly and bore the *rajah* off the field. And Dara, a descendant of the same Baber from whom we derive the knowledge of this feeling, lost the throne of Delhi, because in the battle which secured the crown to his brother Aurungzebe he happened to dismount from his elephant in the heat of the contest.

From this digression we may form some opinion of the reasons which induced the Persians to treat with such severity the chance-occupant of the royal seat of Alexander.

Previous to setting out on the Arabian expedition, the king, according to his usual practice, offered a splendid sacrifice for its success; wine and victims were distributed among the divisions and subdivisions of the army, and the great officers were entertained magnificently by the monarch himself. The wine circulated freely until the night was far spent; the king then rose and was retiring to his tent, when Medius, the Thessalian, who, since the death of Hephæstion and the departure of Craterus, had most personal influence with him, besought him to visit his lodgings, where he would find a pleasant party assembled. For what followed Arrian has copied the *Royal Diary,* in which the movements and health of the king were made known to the public. It forms the most ancient series of bulletins on record, and is here presented to the reader, reduced from the indirect to the direct form:

The king banqueted and drank wine with Medius; he then rose from table, bathed and slept.

He again dined with Medius, and drank till late at night; on rising from the table he bathed, and after bathing, ate a little, and slept there, for he was now in a fever.

He was carried on a couch to the place of sacrifice, and sacrificed according to his daily custom. After finishing the service, he lay down in the public room until it was dark. During the day he gave orders to the leaders concerning the march and voyage; the land forces were told to be ready to commence their march on the fourth, and the fleet, which he proposed to accompany, to sail on the fifth day. He was then conveyed in a litter to the riverside, where he was placed on board a vessel and ferried across into the park. There he again bathed and went to rest.

Next day he bathed and offered the usual sacrifices; he then returned to his chamber, where he lay down and conversed with Medius. Orders were given to the generals to attend him next morning. After this he dined sparingly, and was carried back to his chamber. During the whole of this night, for the first time, there was no intermission of fever.

Next day he bathed and sacrificed, then gave orders to Nearchus and the other leaders to be ready to sail on the third day.

Next day he bathed again, offered the appointed sacrifices, and finished the service; and although there was no remission in the violence of the fever, he yet called in the leaders and ordered them to have everything in readiness for the departure of the fleet. In the evening he bathed, and after bathing was very ill.

Next day he was removed to the house close to the great swimming-bath, where he offered the appointed sacrifices. Ill as he was, he called in the principal officers, and gave orders about the expedition.

On the following day it was not without difficulty that he was carried to the altar and offered the sacrifice; he would nevertheless give further orders to the great officers concerning the voyage.

Next day, although extremely ill, he offered the appointed sacrifices, and ordered the generals to remain assembled in the court, and the *chiliarchs* and the *pentacosiarchs* in front of the gates. Being now dangerously ill, he was carried from the park into the palace; when the generals entered, he knew them, but said nothing, as he was speechless. The fever was very violent during the night.

And the following day and night.

And the following day."

This was the account written in the *Royal Diary:*

> Upon this (continues Arrian) the soldiers became eager to see him; some to see him once more alive, others because it was reported that he was already dead, and a suspicion had arisen that his death was concealed by the chief officers of the guard—but the majority, as I think, from sorrow and anxiety for their king; they therefore forced their way into his chamber. As the men past his couch in succession, he, although speechless, greeted them individually, by raising his head with difficulty and by the expression of his eyes.

According to the *Royal Diary:*

> Moreover, Peithon, Attalus, Demophon, Peucestas, Cleomenes, Menidas, and Seleucus, slept in the temple of Serapis, and asked the god if it would be desirable and better for Alexander to be conveyed to the temple, and to supplicate the god and be healed by him; but the answer from the god forbad his removal, declaring that it would be better for him to remain where he was. The companions reported this answer, and Alexander not long after expired, as if, under all circumstances, that were the better fate.

The account given by Ptolemy and Aristobulus does not essentially differ from this. According to some writers, his friends asked him to whom he bequeathed the empire, and he answered "to the strongest;" according to others he added, "that he foresaw a bloody competition at his funeral games."

These extracts from Arrian contain all that can be regarded as authentic respecting the last illness and death of Alexander; for Plutarch, who has given a version of the *Royal Diaries*, agreeing most points with the above, has most unfairly suppressed every notice of the impending expedition, in order to make his readers believe that the great man, whose life he was recording, had latterly lost all vigour of mind and energy of character, and become the abject slave of intemperance and superstition.

The fever to which he fell a victim, was probably contracted in his visit to the marshes; and the thirst which compelled him on a public day to quit his military duties, proves that it was raging in his veins before it absolutely overcame him. The exertions at the public banquet, and the protracted drinking at the house of Medius, must have seriously increased the disease. Strong men, like Alexander, have often warded off attacks of illness by increased excitement, but if this fail to produce the desired effect, the reaction is terrible. It is curious that no physician is mentioned. The king seems to have trusted to two simple remedies, abstinence and bathing.

His removal to the summer house, close to the large cold bath, shows how much he confided in the latter remedy. But the extraordinary fatigues which he had undergone, the exposure within the last three years to the rains of the Punjab, the marshes of the Indus, the burning sands of Gedrosia, the hot vapours of Susiana, the frost and snow of Mount Zagrus, and the marsh miasma of the Babylonian lakes, proved too much even for his iron constitution. The numerous wounds by which his body had been perforated, and especially the serious injury to the lungs from the Mallian arrow, must have in some degree impaired the vital functions, and enfeebled the powers of healthy reaction.

Under such disadvantages we must admire the unconquered will, the unflinching spirit with which he bore up against the ravages of the disease, his resolute performance of his religious duties, and the regular discharge of his royal and military functions. On the ninth day, when he was carried to the palace, and all the officers down to the commanders of five hundred were commanded to attend, it was evidently his intention to have taken leave and given his last orders; but nature failed, and he was unable to express his wishes when the generals were admitted. The report, therefore, of his having bequeathed the empire to the strongest is probably either an invention, or an inference from previous conversations, in which he might have foretold the natural consequences of his premature death.

The sleeping of the officers in the Temple of Serapis, is a curious fact in the history of superstition. It proves that Serapis was an Assyrian god, whom the first Ptolemy must have well known, and this utterly subverts the account preferred by Tacitus, of the introduction of the worship of Serapis into Egypt. That most felicitous painter of the darker traits of human nature, and unrivalled master in the art of hinting more than he affirms, is a gross perverter of the truth, whenever he ventures on the subject of Eastern Antiquities.

Strabo furnishes us with the best explanation of the conduct of the great officers, and of their motives for sleeping in the temple of Serapis:

> Canopus possesses the temple of Serapis, that is honoured with great reverence and distinguished for its healing powers. The most respectable characters believe this, and sleep in the temple either for themselves or for their friends. Some historians give an account of the cures, others of the oracles.

In these few words we see why the friends slept there, and why they were anxious to carry their beloved sovereign thither.

But—as many readers may be surprised to hear that Alexander died in the course of nature of a regular marsh fever, and that neither poison nor the cup of Hercules proved fatal to him—I add for their satisfaction the following paragraph from Arrian:

> I know that many other accounts have been written concerning the death of Alexander—that he died of poison sent by Antipater, and prepared by Aristotle, who since the death of Calisthenes was afraid of him; that Cassander carried this—according to some, in the hoof of a mule, (for even this absurdity has been recorded);—that Iollas, the younger brother of Cassander, administered it, as he was the royal cupbearer, and had a short time before been aggrieved by Alexander;—that Medius, the friend of Iollas, was an accomplice, and persuaded the king to join the revellers;—and that on draining the cup, he was instantly seized with sharp pangs—and quitted the party.
> One writer has even been graceless enough to affirm, that Alexander, on discovering that his illness was likely to prove fatal, rushed out with the intention of throwing himself into the Euphrates, that his disappearance might incline men to believe his divine descent and supernatural departure—that while he was quitting the palace clandestinely he was discovered by Roxana, and prevented; and that he then lamented with a sigh, 'that she had grudged him the eternal honour of being esteemed a god.' I have noticed these reports, not because they are credible, but from a wish to show that I am not ignorant of them."

Alexander (continues Arrian,) died in the hundred and fourteenth *Olympiad*, when Hegesias was *archon* at Athens, (about Midsummer, B.C. 323.) He lived, according to Aristobulus, thirty-two years and eight months, of which he reigned twelve years and eight months. In body he was most handsome, most indefatigable, most active; in mind most manly, most ambitious of glory, most enterprising, and most religious. In sensual pleasures he was most temperate, and of mental excitements insatiable of praise alone. Most sagacious in discovering the proper measures while yet enveloped in darkness, and most felicitous in inferring the probable from the apparent.

In arraying, arming, and marshalling armies most skilful. In raising the soldiers' courage, filling them with hopes of victory, and dispelling their fears by his own undaunted bearing, most chivalrous. In doubtful enterprises most daring. In wresting advantages from enemies and anticipating even their suspicions of his measures most successful. In fulfilling his own engagements most faithful, in guarding against being overreached by others most cautious. In his own personal expenses most frugal, but in munificence to others most unsparing.

If then he erred from quickness of temper and the influence of anger, and if he loved the display of barbarian pride and splendour, I regard not these as serious offences; for, in candour, we ought to take into consideration his youth, his perpetual success, and the influence of those men who court the society of kings, not for virtuous purposes, but to minister to their pleasures and to corrupt their principles. On the other hand, Alexander is the only ancient king who, from the native goodness of his heart, showed a deep repentance for his misdeeds.

Most princes, even when conscious of guilt, foolishly attempt to conceal their crimes, by defending them as rightly done. The only atonement for misdeeds is the acknowledgement of the offender, and the public display of repentance. Injuries are the less keenly felt by the sufferers, and hopes are entertained that he, who shows sorrow for the past, will not be guilty of similar offences in future. Neither do I esteem his claim to divine origin as a serious offence, as perhaps it was only a device, to ensure due respect from his subjects. Minos, Æacus, and Rhadamanthus were never accused of offensive pride, because men of old referred their origin to Jupiter: no more were Theseus and Ion, the reputed sons of Neptune and Apollo.

Yet Alexander was surely not a less illustrious king than these. I regard the Persian dress also as only a device to prevent the barbarians from regarding their king as a foreigner in all respects, and to show the Macedonians that he possessed a refuge from their military asperity and insolence. For the same reason he mixed the Persian bodyguards with the Macedonian infantry, and their nobility with his own select cavalry. Even his convivial parties, as Aristobulus writes, were not prolonged for the sake of the wine, of which he drank little, but for the sake of enjoying social converse with his friends.

Let him (concludes Arrian) who would vilify Alexander, not select a few blame-worthy acts, but sum up all his great deeds and qualities, and then consider who and what he himself is who would thus abuse the man who attained the pinnacle of human felicity—who was the undisputed monarch of both continents—and whose name has pervaded the whole of the earth. Let him consider these things—especially if he be of no consideration, a labourer in trifles, and yet unable properly to arrange even them. There did not, as I believe, in that age exist the nation, the city, nor the individual, whom the name of Alexander had not reached. My own opinion, therefore, I will profess, that not without especial purpose of the deity such a man was given to the world, to whom none has ever yet been equal.